Shelley's Satire

Shelley's Satire

Violence, Exhortation, and Authority

Steven E. Jones

NORTHERN

ILLINOIS

UNIVERSITY

PRESS

DeKalb

1994

© 1994 by Northern Illinois University Press

Published by the Northern Illinois University Press,

DeKalb, Illinois 60115

Manufactured in the United States using acid-free paper

Design by Julia Fauci

Library of Congress Cataloging-in-Publication Data

Jones, Steven E. (Steven Edward)

   Shelley's satire : violence, exhortation, and authority /
Steven E. Jones.

       p.   cm.

   Includes bibliographical references and index.

   ISBN 0-87580-186-2

   1. Shelley, Percy Bysshe, 1792–1822—Criticism and
interpretation.

   2. Verse satire, English—History and criticism.

   3. Romanticism—Great Britain.

   4. Authority in literature.   5. Violence in
literature.   I. Title.

PR5442.H62J66   1994

821'.7—dc20   93-45747

                                              CIP

To Mary Eleanor Jones

Contents

Acknowledgments

I WISH TO THANK KARL KROEBER for encouraging various stages of this project: from a master's thesis on *The Mask of Anarchy*, to a dissertation on Shelley, to drafts of the present book. Through it all, his teaching and scholarship have remained exemplary. I also owe a particular debt to Donald H. Reiman for his careful and patient responses to the manuscript, including timely reminders of facts and exhortations to further reading. I am grateful as well to a number of other readers who have offered helpful suggestions on the book (or portions of it), including Michael Neth, Carl Woodring, Michael Seidel, Mary Quinn, and, most recently, Michael Henry Scrivener. Loyola University, Chicago, provided me with the necessary leave time and support to bring the book to completion; Marian Staats and Maureen Dowd provided valuable research assistance. The Huntington Library in San Marino, California, the Bodleian Library at Oxford, Columbia University Library in New York, the Newberry Library in Chicago, and the Art Institute of Chicago—all have made available crucial materials and resources. For permission to reproduce the prints that serve as illustrations and argumentative paradigms (Figures 1–5), I wish to thank the Department of Prints and Drawings, The British Museum. Without those I have named (and others I have not), the book could not have been written. But without my family—and most of all Heidi Strawn Jones—it would not have been worth writing.

Introduction

THIS BOOK IS A STUDY OF SHELLEY'S SATIRE. Although his individual satirical poems have received praise from readers as diverse as Bertolt Brecht and F. R. Leavis, there has never been a complete study of them as a group, *as* satires.[1] One obstacle to such study has been the inchoate state of the texts themselves; some of Shelley's most interesting satiric writings exist only as rough-draft notebook fragments, until recently inaccessible to most scholars and readers (or published only in incomplete or distorted forms). More intractably, however, dominant critical preconceptions of Shelley's temperament—or the spirit of the age of Romanticism—have obscured the vital importance of these poems for Shelley's oeuvre and career.

Shelley's worldliness and political orientation are no longer in doubt, but the Victorian idea that he was somehow temperamentally squeamish has persisted. It is still often assumed that Shelley was too serious—and that Romanticism as a whole was too sincere—to indulge in satire. Such assumptions determine the canon, of course; and on this basis Shelley's satires, important documents of his effort actively to engage the social world, have been displaced, neglected, or discounted.

In fact, these ironic, public, referential, and worldly satires amount to an important countervoice within Shelley's work and within Romanticism as a whole. That voice is never simple. On the contrary, it is characterized by equivocal expressions of curse and revenge, and by a coercive rhetoric only occasionally covered with laughter. As a satirist, Shelley seeks to exhort and persuade, but through inherited forms of authority to which he is at once (artistically) attracted and (ethically) opposed. This dilemma shapes his satire and provides one of its primary topics. The satires are about rhetorical problems that they partly discover and partly generate for themselves: Shelley's curses are rooted in accursedness, his desire to legislate is based in a desperate exile, and his righteous indignation is never far from being the outcast's cry of resentment. Because he invests so much hope in the possibility of reforming his audience by changing their minds, Shelley is forced to take seriously (in a way that Byron, for example, is not) the problem of satire's double binds, its self-reflexive aggression.

The individual satires are embedded in diverse cultural contexts, within which they both exploit and attempt to resist conventions of coercion. Rhetorical strategies range from simple reversals or denials to complex medleys, combinations of satirical with more constructive or reforming modes, especially that of "oratorical" exhortation—the direct incitement to right action. In each case Shelley writes both within and against determining conventions and boundaries of the genre, while also struggling with his own increasing desire to reach an audience, fashioning an authoritative satiric persona in the midst of the competing forces of satire and society, exile and authority, violence and exhortation.

This process of self-fashioning is never fully deliberate and is never simple, much less simply progressive, but I chart at least one clear "development" in Shelley's satiric career: he grows increasingly self-conscious and increasingly troubled about linguistic aggression. His early satires often recklessly indulge in a kind of "magical" manipulation of their targets amounting to rhetorical violence. Later on, while such rhetorical effects do not disappear, they become the focus of ambivalent exploration and critique as his artistic mastery increases and the satires engage the greater complexities of collective, social violence. During Shelley's annus mirabilis of 1819–1820, his satires turn outward to face the social arena and public events of national consequence, revealing a strong desire to intervene in those events.

Even as his satires are becoming more public, however, he drafts the fragment of "A Satire upon Satire" (ca. 1820), a kind of experiment with negative results, seeming to confirm that the personal realm is inescapable when it comes to the ethics of coercion. Although this fragment has been taken as Shelley's farewell to the mode, a satiric swan song or palinode, I read it as a deeply ambivalent (and tellingly unfinished) critique of satire's potential to affect others. Its abjurations cannot simply be taken at face value: Shelley himself later said that the poem was to have contained "small knives" (which he intended to use), and although the fragment's violence is cloaked or concealed in repudiation, it is never fully relinquished.

I begin in the first chapter by addressing the problem of temperament, exposing as a red herring the issue of Shelley's "sense of humor" and his legendary moral earnestness. I argue that his diabolical indignation, the pranking, hoaxing laughter for which he is well known, is basically satiric. Moreover, all satire is as often violent as it is humorous; the hoaxer's implied aggression toward his audience is paradigmatic of the satirist's equivocal role in society. Thomas Chatterton, the famous eighteenth-century hoaxer and satirist, reconstructed for the purposes of literary history as the quintessential proto-Romantic, provides me with an example of common critical preconceptions and how they blind us to the importance of Shelley's satire.

Chapter 2 analyzes the motif of the satiric curse running throughout Shelley's work, a device at the crossroads of performative art and "magical" rhetoric. In certain of his satires Shelley's public curses come home to roost, pointing to his own status as an outcast and revealing the gulf between him and his community—as well as his strong desire to bridge that gulf. The third chapter examines another kind of "curse": the trope of damnation in *The Devil's Walk* and *Peter Bell the Third*, a powerful figure for satire's own tendency to demonize others and thus to alienate the targets of its intended reforms. Next, Chapter 4 traces a similar reciprocal violence in the fragmentary "Satire upon Satire," situating it in the social context of dueling—an elaborately encoded ritual of mutual destruction. Shelley seemed to realize that satire, like the duel, is inextricably bound up with patterns of scapegoating and coercion, and in this way the fragment is necessarily pivotal to my larger argument. The fragment ends with an unresolved question: whether satiric authority is possible at all without the menace or harm of another.

With *The Mask of Anarchy* in Chapter 5, the focus shifts from the harm of another to the harm of many others, to the public context of state and mass violence. A satiric medley combining caricature with exhortation and drawing upon a number of popular forms, this is a poem through which the satirist would play the role of representative, exhorting the people to seize the succession for themselves. In Chapter 6 I explore the problem of representation in *Oedipus Tyrannus; or, Swellfoot the Tyrant*, which along with its occasion, the Queen Caroline affair, I read in relation to the popular practices of "rough music" and urban festivals. In these activities mixed social groups act in response to the shifting authority of charisma, often under the explicit or implicit threat of violence. This reading helps me to redefine Shelley's idea of a "popular" audience, which I believe involves the projection of a multilayered group of audiences into which his poetry would intervene to spur volatile interactions and negotiations of power. But Shelley's satire is always uncomfortable with its own potential demagoguery: *Swellfoot* employs satiric social charisma in order to awaken and direct the people, but at the same time it remains deeply ambivalent about the people's readiness to inherit political power.

This ambivalence runs like a troubled stream into the diverse generic mix of "The Triumph of Life," a Dantesque dream vision with strong ties to Juvenalian satire (as I argue in the final chapter). By this point in his career (1822), Shelley no longer wishes to vent curses, but this last fragment, like the curse poems, dramatizes the dilemma of the outcast who would speak to (and for) the community. In the end, "The Triumph of Life" exposes the profound difficulties inherent in any attempt to speak with moral authority from "beside the public way." In this way, satiric authority resembles prophetic authority: both are deeply problematic in practice, which is to say, in specific social contexts. In this final chapter my arguments move beyond satire per se, to the pressing needs for authority and audience, and the sense of ethical uncertainty, out of which Shelley's satires were written in the first place.

Taken together, these satiric works tell the compelling story in one protean genre of Shelley's poetic self-fashioning—the construction of the satirist in relation to larger cultural structures.[2] Shelley's satiric persona is a subject or "self" produced in dialectical relation to the authority of genre and its conventions, among other social determinants. From this kind of "subjection" no poet can escape. His satires vividly dramatize a central problem which has continued to occupy recent historical and cultural studies: the interactions between personal agency and social determination, and how these lead to the masks and modes through which poets and the texts they produce engage, shape—and are shaped by—the world.[3]

Shelley's Satire

1 Shelley's Satires in Romantic Context

As a study of Shelley's satire, this book must address from the start two entrenched and closely related assumptions still shared by many critics: that Shelley lacked a sense of humor, and was therefore inept in the satirical mode, and that the Romantic period was essentially antisatiric; that as part of its reaction to Augustan decorum, its creation of a private lyrical sincerity, it closed itself to the possibility of public, topical satire. Both assumptions are mistaken, but they have been widespread and have functioned to prevent a full understanding of the complexities of Shelley's work and of Romanticism as a whole.

The question of Shelley's authorial temperament leads inevitably to the broader question of satire and the spirit of the Romantic age. But first, in order to understand Shelley's satire, we must get beyond the popular notion that satire is necessarily linked with humor. Much, if not most, of satire is produced less in laughter than in violence.

• • •

The idea that Shelley lacked a sense of humor goes back to the now infamous Victorian characterizations of him as angelic and otherworldly, but it persists in recent accounts.[1] Shelley himself seems to have been the first to promote this characterization; and his descendants and biographers, beginning with Mary Shelley, Thomas Jefferson Hogg, and Thomas Medwin, have been only too happy to follow and to embellish it. But from some of these same sources we also have contrary reports of Shelley's habit of shrieking with diabolical laughter (often at inopportune times— on a Scottish Sabbath or after ritually cursing his father), or indulging in waggish pranks and witty puns.[2] Clearly, anecdotes of the humorless

Shelley do not tell the whole story of his complex personality. It is significant that most accounts of Shelley's exercising his sense of humor turn on the expression of blasphemy, subversion, or absurdity, and not infrequently grow out of some conflict with authority, as a threat of rebellion or loss of control.

They also almost always include ambivalent attempts to perform for an audience, at least some portion of which is not in on the joke. In one telling anecdote, John Grove recalls that Shelley and Charles Grove went in 1811 to the British Forum, near Covent Garden:

> It was then a spouting club, in which Gale Jones and other Radicals abused all existing governments. Bysshe made so good a speech, complimenting and differing from the previous orators, that when he left the room, there was a rush to find out who he was, and to induce him to attend there again. He gave them a false name and address, not caring a farthing about the meeting, or the subjects there discussed.[3]

Even adjusting for the distortions of Grove's Victorian retrospection (it seems highly unlikely that the young radical did not care about the spouting club's subjects), this is a troubling picture of the poet as orator, apparently condescending, playing a satiric prank on the radical audience whose cause he might be presumed to share. This ambivalence—which may well have been a function of class snobbery—returns to haunt Shelley's later satirical addresses to the radical reformers, *The Mask of Anarchy* and, especially, *Oedipus Tyrannus; or, Swellfoot the Tyrant.* Any reading of Shelley's satire must keep one eye on the satirist's mixed feelings toward his audience. In spite of his real personal magnanimity and charity, Shelley's satiric sense of humor is frequently based in a deeper hostility or aggression, whose targets are sometimes unclear.

Shelley's (and his defenders') denials of a normal sense of humor almost always—by way of contrast—refer to his abnormally developed sense of moral outrage, his righteous indignation. Like the traditional satire of Juvenal, Shelley's satire is often at once moralizing and scurrilous. Two writings from his relative youth may help to focus the problem of laughter and satire. First, Shelley's own most earnest and explicit denial of humor comes in a sonnet discovered in 1976 among the Scrope Davies papers, "To Laughter."[4]

> Thy friends were never mine thou heartless fiend:
> Silence and solitude and calm and storm,

> Hope, before whose veiled shrine all spirits bend
> In worship, and the rainbow vested form
> Of conscience, that within thy hollow heart
> Can find no throne — the love of such great powers
> Which has requited mine in many hours
> Of loneliness, thou ne'er hast felt; depart!

(ll. 1–8)

Pitched as a performance of outraged sincerity, this simply declares (to the object of its anti-encomium), "Thy voice is dearest/To those who mock at Truth and Innocency" (ll. 11–12), in an earnest voice that is itself the deliberate antithesis of mockery.

But if we accept the sonnet's sincerity on its own terms, we may fail to notice a crucial fact: that the personified Laughter is demonized, made into a "heartless fiend" whose friends are thus implicitly attacked as frivolous and immoral, unable to appreciate the depths of sensibility. If we admit that "ridicule" or denigration of a target can (and often does) take such a serious tone, that it is in fact quite compatible with a certain kind of self-righteous pose, then these lines can be read as a kind of satire on the satirical, their ostentatious sincerity a rhetorical strategy for throwing into relief the mockery that is their target. The style works in effect as a rhetorical counterexample, the mirror opposite of parody (which *reproduces*, though at a critical distance, the style of the original). But this painfully earnest style can serve the same "satiric" purpose as parody.

Shelley's satire is almost always based on this kind of masked or deflected moral indignation. Even in the apparently humorous moments of his satires, (self-)righteous anger fueled by personal aggression is often just below the surface. For example, take the strange poem that Kenneth Neill Cameron has called "certainly the earliest of Shelley's poems known to be extant" — "A Cat in Distress."[5]

> You migh'n't easily guess
> All the modes of distress
> Which torture the tenants of earth
> And the various evils
> Which like many devils
> Attend the poor dogs from their birth

(ll. 7–12)

The five stanzas of the poem allude variously to inheritance, succession, tenancy, and inequality, before concluding with what sounds like a more personal, opaque, even gossipy reference:

> But this poor little Cat
> Only wanted a rat
>   To stuff out its own little maw
>   And t'were as good
> Had some people such food
> To make them hold their jaw.

(ll. 29–34)

What can literary critics profitably say about writing of this kind? The allegory and topicality are only implied ("some people"); there is very little in or outside the text upon which to build a context for explaining the poem. In this case, even that text is highly uncertain. We have extant only one copy of the poem in the hand of Elizabeth Shelley (the poet's sister), from which it was assumed by their sister Hellen (at a much later date) that Shelley had written the poem when he was about ten years old. But dating the manuscript is actually much more complicated than this would suggest.[6]

Watermarks and other evidence plausibly date the text to sometime between Shelley's seventeenth and nineteenth years. If, as seems possible, it was written around 1811 (rather than written earlier and copied later), this would place the poem in the context of Shelley's late adolescent hostility toward his father (and authority in general), perhaps during the period after his expulsion from Oxford (March 1811), a time when he was fond of hoaxes and pranks—some with aggressive or ambivalent overtones (including the radical oration at the British Forum). "A Cat in Distress" would *appear* to fit into this context, with its reference to penury and an "old fellow" who stands in the way of solvency, for example. It may have been intended as a kind of internecine family hoax. In the end, however, what this case emphasizes is how little we can know about the intentions and context of satirical texts, and yet how necessary the reconstruction of some such knowledge is to our being able to read them at all.

This problem is only more obvious and exaggerated in this case than it is in many others. It is in fact one of the central problems of satire: the very topicality of the mode makes inescapably obvious its dependence on

immanent contextual cues. There is an opacity—something of the de-
viousness and insincerity of the hoax—surrounding a great deal of satirical writing. More obviously and blatantly than some other genres, topical
satire derives its significance from something other than—outside—the
text, in fact, from the very idea of reference to a *con*text. Its signals and
cues are represented as embedded gestures, as bringing context into the
formal fabric of the work itself. This process is always inevitably incomplete and, to one degree or another, obtuse; "misfires" of the satiric cues or
signals are to be expected. It can even be said that something of the social
situation and context of any satirical text is already "lost" from the incep-
tion of the work, because it functions through encoded or elusive gestures.
This is not to say that every satire is a private joke, only that all satire is
relational, public poetry, in particularly delimited and irrecoverable ways.
Its typical gestures take place in the public arena, as ephemeral social
transactions. The horizon of its reception is often multilayered: some in
the audience hear but do not understand, and only a select few are ever
fully in the know. Satire frequently works through the transactional mediations of sly gestures, innuendo, codes, and winks.

In this way it resembles the famous paradigm of cultural context derived by Clifford Geertz from Gilbert Ryle: the social gesture of winking.[7]
To wink is always to gesture within a particular social context. Simply
lowering one's eyelid in the proper social context counts as winking, but
that is only the beginning. Following Ryle, Geertz asks us to imagine one
boy parodying the wink of another. "Here, too, a socially established code
exists (he will 'wink' laboriously, overobviously, perhaps adding a gri-
mace—the usual artifices of the clown); and so also does a message. Only
now it is not conspiracy but ridicule that is in the air" (pp. 6–7). Moreover, there are innumerable contexts within which to understand and read
a parodic wink: a simple "misfire," in which the parodic intent is misin-
terpreted; a rehearsal before a mirror; a "fake wink" intended to mislead
with false irony; and so on. The point of the example for Geertz is that it
reveals the need for a thick description of culturally embedded events—a
kind of interpretation derived in the first place from hermeneutics, and
therefore not surprisingly picked up as a rallying cry by the first wave
of New Historicist literary critics in the 1980s. It is highly significant
that Geertz's call for interpretive ethnography (which influenced the New
Historicists' call for ethnographic interpretation) turns for its key paradigm to *satire*. Satire is a mode in which cultural embeddedness cannot
be ignored or denied by invoking the ideal of historical transcendence. To

satirize is to make allusive, ironic, partly concealing gestures, and to do so within very particular, ephemeral social contexts.

To read satire therefore is to contextualize, in the teeth of all the hermeneutic difficulties of any contextual literary history—only magnified.[8] Even the choice of a delimited context within which to read an individual satire is always more or less arbitrary. The connections between or circulations among text and context are impossible finally to fix or "establish." This problem is only faced, not solved, by showing that the context could plausibly have been mediated through the author's intellectual and biographical experience. The interrelations of what we think of as context go beyond the simplicities of influence; the most interesting connections are almost always "in the air." But particular mediations, where they can be constructed, are an important part of any contextual reading.

Accordingly, in a later chapter of this study, Shelley's aristocratic background and his insinuations of a duel provide me with a basis for reading his violent satire on Robert Southey as analogous to the social practice of dueling. Less directly, the apparent ties between *The Mask of Anarchy* and various popular satiric media—pamphlets, ballads, and cartoons—lead me to posit in several chapters yet another analogue from this same popular milieu: the dramatic pantomime. Such connections, admittedly provisional, are meant to point to cultural contexts that help to explain and form part of the effective field of Shelley's satires and his construction of a satiric persona. Because satire demands this kind of complex contextualization, it usefully resists essentialist definitions of genre: there is nothing "in" satire *but* its complex web of relationships to particular social contexts. This is no more true of satire than of any other kind of literature, of course, but the satiric mode foregrounds the situation in an obvious and inescapable way.

When in this study I speak of "satire" in general, as a genre or mode, I refer not to some timeless spirit or generic "form" but to the collective conventions and effects that specific satires have built up in layers during its history, a kind of repertoire of recognizable gestures. This is the same spirit—essentially a pragmatic, anthropological one—in which I appeal to the work of René Girard in this book. I would suggest that selected aspects of Girard's theory of violence as the founding principle of culture (given certain limitations) fit the evidence on satire.[9] Satire's "gibbets, axes, confiscations, chains" (to use the terms of one of Shelley's satires) amount to a weaponry the community as a whole would just as soon deny.

Thus satire—when read in social contexts—offers a valuable, ambivalent, and self-reflective record of the barbarism inherent in civilization.

• • •

In attempting to (re)construct some possible contexts for Shelley's satire, one is faced with the prevailing constructions of English Romanticism, including the notion that "the satiric" and "the Romantic" are naturally polar opposites, that "Romantic satire" is a contradiction in terms.[10] In the introduction to his extremely influential study, *Natural Supernaturalism* (1971), M. H. Abrams explained that Byron was to be omitted altogether, "because in his greatest work he speaks with an ironic countervoice and deliberately opens a satirical perspective on the vatic stance of his contemporaries."[11] Byron simply did not fit Abrams's paradigm of the "Romantic," it is clear, because he wrote *satire*. If Romantic poetry is defined as inward-turning, idealizing, solipsistic, sublime, and transcendent (even in its irony), then satire, with its socially encoded, public, profane, and tendentious rhetoric, is bound to appear un-Romantic. Jerome McGann has argued that satire represents an antithesis to Romantic poetry's "paradigm mode"—expressive sincerity—and that Byron's poetry is thus particularly valuable because it "opens itself to the horizon of its antithesis," to a kind of anti-Romantic public voice.[12] Elsewhere McGann proposes that "Romantic ideology, which privileges conventions of 'sincerity' over conventions of 'premeditation,' has all but obliterated our received sense of the satiric traditions that were being worked between 1790–1832."[13] Few would still subscribe to the tenet that English satire died with Pope (or perhaps lingered for a while, diminished, in Churchill—to flicker for a brief, decadent moment in Byron).[14] But few are ready nonetheless to acknowledge the workings of powerful "satiric traditions" as a dialectical force *within* Romanticism.

The workings of critical oppositions between the Romantic and the satiric, sincerity and insincerity, are perhaps best illustrated by an example on the verge of the Romantic period: the story of Thomas Chatterton and his reconstitution by literary history. The "marvellous Boy" (Wordsworth's famous epithet) was a Bristol apprentice who forged medieval poetry (complete with an invented context) at the age of fifteen (1768) and committed suicide in a London garret two years later. By the 1790s the poets who would come to be labeled "Romantic" began to claim him as their forerunner and precursor.[15] The powerful myth of Chatterton as a proto-Romantic, a sensitive genius and martyr to imagination crucified by the cold world, was codified in the works of the major Romantics, especially Shelley's *Adonais* and Keats's "Oh Chatterton! how very sad thy fate." By the later nineteenth century, Dante Gabriel Rossetti could write: "Not to know Chatterton is to be ignorant of the *true* day-spring of modern romantic poetry."[16]

One of the earliest and most influential tributes was Coleridge's sentimental "Monody on the Death of Chatterton" (1790), which—in defiance of the opprobrium of his suicide—describes the death throes as an apotheosis, while identifying Coleridge with the "fire divine" of his heroic genius.[17] Not just Bristol but England as a whole is chastised in the poem for failing to recognize the young prophet in its midst: "Is this the land of liberal Hearts!/Is this the land, where Genius ne'er in vain/Pour'd forth her soul-enchanting strain?" (ll. 13–15). And Chatterton's career is told in epic language, with the forged Rowley poems as the peak production of this visionary imagination. Interestingly, the poem refers briefly to Chatterton's late satiric writings: "And now he punishes the heart of steel,/ And her own iron rod he makes Oppression feel" (ll. 38–39).

The "Monody" tells a significant story. In it the dead young poet is mythologized—that is, romanticized—by emphasizing the sentimental and downplaying the satiric side of his career. In fact this is how literary history has continued to present Chatterton. It is a paradox that his most sincere expressions were forgeries and lies, whereas his acknowledged publications were freethinking and partisan satires whose "sincerity" is in doubt.[18] This dichotomy informs the master plot of Chatterton's career as a tragic fall: the youthful, imaginative genius, once squelched, turns cynically to public satire; rebuffed by the world, he dies. Madness or the pressures of poverty are invoked to explain the otherwise irreconcilable divisions in his authorial personality. Conventional literary history is unprepared to believe that the quintessential proto-Romantic poet could have chosen to write couplet satires in the tradition of Pope and Charles Churchill. The satire is inevitably figured as a comedown or a throwback, is in effect suppressed in the service of Romantic myth.

In point of fact, Chatterton was always a satirist. He began his brief career with a clever and competent squib (considering he was only eleven years old when he composed it), *Apostate Will* (1764), on Methodism and religious hypocrisy: "Apostate Will just sunk in trade,/Resolv'd his bargain should be made/Then strait to Wesley he repairs,/And puts on grave and solemn airs . . . ."[19] He ended in London, after trying his hand at political satires and journalism in the service of John Wilkes and the

Patriot party, a freethinking burletta for the stage, and the topical couplet satire, *Kew Gardens* (1770). The medieval-Romantic qualities of the Rowley poems are undeniably important, part of a tradition reaching from Ossian to the Lake School's landscapes. But they represent only a portion of Chatterton's "authorship," his self-projection as a poet, and form only an interlude in what would otherwise appear to be the career of a conventional eighteenth-century satirist. Even the Rowley poems can be seen as compatible with the masks and ironies of the satiric stance—especially once we recognize that the link between satire proper and any hoax is a shared aggression toward and manipulation of the audience. In each case someone is targeted for (at the very least) a kind of ridicule.

The key to reuniting the Romantic Chatterton and the satiric Chatterton in one personality and one career is to see that both involve the idealization of an autonomous, "independent" stance. The Romantics idealized him as the quintessential outcast, the emblem of neglected genius—and in his satires he often strikes this pose himself.

> Damn'd narrow Notions! notions which disgrace,
> The boasted reason of the human race.
> Bristol may keep her prudent Maxims still;
> I scorn her Prudence, and I ever will.
> Since all my Vices magnify'd are here,
> She cannot paint me worse than I appear,
> When raving in the Lunacy of ink,
> I catch the Pen and publish what I think—[20]

Exiled and rejected, the satirist rails against the community which has cast him out—notice that this description could equally well fit the *prophetic* stance of a number of High Romantic poems. As William Blake (and, from a very different perspective, Robert Burns) well knew, prophecy and satire share a position of authority grounded in moral indignation. What satire reveals, however, in the transparent violence of its representations and utterances, is the reciprocal aggression that is often implicit in such authority. This is precisely what is suppressed in many of Romanticism's self-representations and in literary history's received notions of the Romantic. In one sense, the prophet is the morally sincere double of the satirist, and thus the preferred self-characterization of the vatic Romantic poet. Just as Chatterton is made over into a Romantic by suppressing his satire, so Romanticism as a movement is constructed in part by setting it in binary opposition to the satiric. The satiric becomes in the nineteenth century one form of Romanticism's Other—a mode which negatively defines the contours of the Romantic.

Of course the Romantics were well aware of Chatterton's satire, as the two lines from Coleridge's "Monody" on the "iron rod" make clear. But in acknowledging it, they recast the satire in terms of the individual heroic imagination. Chatterton "punishes the heart of steel" from the position of *feeling*, as Coleridge says, and chastises Oppression from an outsider's stance of independent liberty. His outcast status is thus turned into a sublime virtue, the justification for his moral scourge. Coleridge and his contemporaries would have associated this moral voice with Juvenal's sublime style of satire.

Chatterton himself associated it with a gadfly's kind of Opposition, as practiced by Charles Churchill and the widely influential, anonymous political correspondent of the 1760s known as "Junius." The letters of Junius to *The Public Advertiser* (1769–72) attacked the Duke of Grafton and King George III himself, but his true importance is revealed by the fact that many suspected him of being Edmund Burke—the great Whig proponent of "independence" in the parliamentary sense.[21] To these charges Burke was compelled to reply, "I could not if I would, and I would not if I could." But he paid the satirist high tribute as "the mighty boar of the forest," and added, "Kings, lords, and commons are but the sport of his fury."[22] This may seem ambivalent praise indeed from the opponent of the "swinish multitude," but it is a significant picture of the satirist as an untamable, independent outsider whose very autonomy is the ground of his rage.

In both Junius and Churchill this kind of independent stance, an anti-authoritarian authority, was central to the projected satiric persona. Both writers—along with Chatterton—wrote in support of John Wilkes, who styled himself as the independent champion of liberty, based on the ideal of a free press. Not coincidentally, Wilkes was also a satirist. He was convicted and imprisoned in 1763 for publishing (with Churchill) a seditious journal, *The North Briton*. Then, prefiguring the widespread political charisma Queen Caroline would later embody (in 1820), he returned from exile to become a symbolic rallying point for demonstrations in opposition to the government—to become, in fact, a popular representative.[23]

• • •

Shelley has long been associated with the proto-Romantic Chatterton and his peculiar brand of narcissistic, persecuted genius. Shelley licensed this by linking himself ("one Frail form") simultaneously to Keats and to Chatterton in *Adonais:* "Chatterton/Rose pale, his solemn agony had not/ Yet faded from him . . . ."[24] When Dante Gabriel Rossetti (or, for that matter, a twentieth-century critic) looks back, this is the lineage he discovers: Shelley's Chatterton leads directly to Shelley himself, the two appearing as fellow Romantics, "inheritors of unfulfilled renown" (*Adonais*, l. 397).

Shelley was not, as Chatterton was, primarily a satirist, but he claimed the political legacy of the 1780s and 1790s, especially as it reached him through the early radical writings of Southey and Coleridge. Moreover, Hogg reports that Shelley "would often exult in the successful forgeries of Chatterton," and that these were at least indirectly connected with Shelley's and Hogg's own publishing hoax, *Posthumous Fragments of Margaret Nicholson*.[25] These poems applied the hoax to political ends, and it is important that we remember the late-eighteenth-century nexus of political satire—at the crossroads where the hoaxer Chatterton (along with Junius) wrote for Wilkes and party—as a context for understanding Shelley.[26] It has been said that Chatterton followed Churchill's lead in elevating the satiric persona to the role of self-conscious subject and in questioning the ground of satire's moral authority, a trend now conventionally recognized as fulfilled in Byron.[27] I would argue that Shelley, too, was part of this trend, and that the trend is actually part of a larger sociopolitical process: the valorization of the independent self, a kind of rearguard action in the face of the growing dominance of party and institutional collusion and of political reaction.

Shelley grew up in a time when the most widespread forms of satire were the graphic print and the partisan journal, and they were very widespread indeed. The most famous satirical journal of the 1790s (with an afterlife well into the nineteenth century) was the Tory organ, *The Anti-Jacobin*. Its clever poetic parodies, sometimes of actual works and sometimes of imagined ones, were embedded in an editorial and journalistic format, but they were also published separately in book form. By the sixth number (18 December 1797), the editors were claiming with justice that "The fashion of admiring and imitating these Productions has spread in a surprizing degree." The polemical tone and some of the parodic techniques of satire written during the Romantic period can be measured against this most polemical of sources.

The prospectus of *The Anti-Jacobin* had in 1797 come out on the side of

"Law," "usage," and "Prescription," as moral alternatives to "that new and liberal system of ETHICS, whose operation is not to bind but to loosen the bands of social order; whose doctrine is formed not on a system of reciprocal duties, but on the supposition of individual, independent, and unconnected rights . . . ." This statement provides a highly significant mirror image of the proclaimed values of the polemical writers on the other side (Shelley's side), the side of parliamentary reform. Despite the polemic, we must take seriously the criticism of *The Anti-Jacobin*, as many of the reformers did. A new radical ethics based on individual and independent rights (and autonomous authority) *did* have its dark side—the deep-seated fear of disconnection, of the loss of "reciprocal duties," and of the ultimate loss of community itself. Shelley's satires are important in part because they so vividly dramatize the dilemmas growing out of this threatened loss of community. This is perhaps clearest in his simplest kind of satire, invective curse, which I examine in the next chapter. In these poems he strikes out at lost leaders or tyrants in a way that reveals his own Romantic satirist's situation: impotently railing against the community that has failed him, an outcast who would prophesy, this satiric persona is like Chatterton come back from the grave to punish the "heart of steel" that could have cast him out in the first place.

Shelley's development, his self-fashioning as an author, took place in an especially polarized and conflicted period of English history, in which, to paraphrase Juvenal, it *should* have been difficult *not* to write satire. His (negative) success in that regard—that is, his success in avoiding conventional satiric modes—is fairly well known. What is less commonly acknowledged, and what it is the purpose of this book to examine, is the other side of the story: the significant extent to which Shelley indulged in satiric writing, sometimes reluctantly and sometimes with obvious glee, and the extent to which this writing sheds light on crucial literary, political, and ethical problems in his work and in the Romantic period as a whole.

2 Learning to Satirize

The Outcast's Curse

THOMAS JEFFERSON HOGG'S *Life of Shelley* tells us that the poet was known at Eton for performing dramatic, ritualistic curses against his father and the King. As an adult, Hogg says, Shelley was once asked by some former schoolmates to repeat the performance for old times' sake. After a little resistance, he "delivered, with vehemence and animation, a string of execrations, greatly resembling a papal anathema; the fulmination soon terminated in a hearty laugh, in which all joined."[1] This strange anecdote of Shelley's cursing and laughing performance is a vivid reminder that the satirical side of his personality was closely connected to his fascination with the language of violence (and the violence of language). Exactly where cursing leaves off and laughing begins in the story it is hard to say, and in fact it may be difficult to hear in Hogg's somewhat untrustworthy narrative the true tone of Shelley's laughter—which may well have been more diabolical than "hearty."

This chapter will focus on Shelley's poetic experiments in satiric cursing, beginning with an invective "To the Lord Chancellor"—a personal curse played out against the public backdrop of the Court of Chancery—and concluding with an imprecation against the Lake Poets, calling on them to reverse their reversals, to return from public apostasy. These writings are satires in the simplest, most "primal" sense—ritualistic uses of language to represent and to perform the harm or destruction of another. My purpose will be to demonstrate that the basis of Shelley's satire is in violence rather than in laughter, and in violence of a particular kind: the self-protective attack of the outcast, the curse of the accursed.

• • •

Shelley's stated antipathy toward violence is better known than his propensity for it, and it is therefore necessary to confront from the start the aggression in his poetry, which is most obvious in his poems of direct personal attack. The writings I have grouped together here range from conventional invective to a subtler form of ironic incantation, but in each case Shelley begins with the ancient supposition that satiric language is the language of power, a means for exercising control over others. In literary terms, cursing satire is—or would be—performative, a social transaction of verbal violence. In practice, however, the curser who would wield that power usually confirms his own status as a social pariah, becomes an outsider railing against his enemies, as the performative transaction serves mainly to highlight the distance between him and his target, the lack of a shared context within which his words could possess real power. In other words, the cursing satirist is frequently himself satirized, revealed as accursed, which is to say, isolated from the community.

A curse is language expressing the desire for power over others. An imprecation for the harm or destruction of another, it links "magic" with "rhetoric"—in fact, it reveals the magical pretensions of much rhetoric. Robert C. Elliott has argued that the literary genre of satire has retained traces of its ancestry in traditional cultural practices such as ritualistic cursing.[2] Archilochus and Hipponax, he proposes, were the earliest practitioners of the mode in Western literature, writing in a primal context in which magic could still be attributed to words. According to tradition, the hated Lycambes was killed by Archilochus's iambic verse.[3] The truth or falsehood of this story is of little concern. What is interesting is its perpetuation as part of the satiric tradition, how it has been used by literary satire to enhance its rhetorical and cultural power. Elliott's subtitle, *Magic, Ritual, Art*, suggests a linear genealogy that is part of the genre's constructed history, one of the key "fictions" or self-representations of satire itself. Satire is powerful in part because it projects itself as such, because of the rhetorical effects of its own history as a genre.[4]

The idea that satire's origins lie in magic remains a powerful one, rhetorically speaking. For this reason, and not to search for some origin or "primitive" source for satire, it is useful to follow up the quite plausible historical connections between verse satire and the Old Comedy, between the Old Comedy and the iambic tradition, and between iambic verse and ritualistic cursing.[5] Such a genealogy may be fictional, and is perforce heuristic and provisional; but it is important that we realize that satires have been written assuming such "roots," and that satirists have repeatedly behaved *as if* their art were linked in some way to magic. So the story bears investigating.

One advantage of such investigation is that it focuses the critical discussion on cultural practices, rather than on literary history per se, as the context of generic conventions. These practices, in turn, are usefully viewed in light of broadly "anthropological" studies like those of Tobin Siebers and René Girard, which can provide ways to frame the question of "the power of satire" as a question of *social* power.[6] We can begin by looking at the shared assumptions of curse and satire as social practices, the fact that both are grounded in a kind of superstition. Magic and rhetoric are in one sense different names for the same kind of sociolinguistic wish fulfillment; when the wish is for another's harm, satiric invective and curse turn out to have a great deal in common.

The context of superstition is important for understanding Shelley's behavior in the anecdote which began this chapter, notwithstanding its patina of urbane irony. And Shelley's work as a whole is full of the language of magical imprecation, with examples ranging from poems in the *Esdaile Notebook*, to "Hymn to Intellectual Beauty" (and the various gothic boyhood rites it recounts), to "Ode to the West Wind" and *Prometheus Unbound* (the whole "action" of which turns on a curse). His interest in magical language can be seen as an outgrowth of his youthful enthusiasm for the gothic, but this in turn is closely linked to the search for rhetorical power, for modes through which he might reach a wide audience. Ultimately, it is difficult to separate Shelley's interest in magical language from his general obsession with poetic authority and influence over an audience.

As in the case of the other Romantics, Shelley's interest in rhetoric is psychological, bound up with questions of belief in the supernatural and the social phenomenon of superstition. One of his favorite poems was Robert Southey's *The Curse of Kehama*, which builds a family melodrama out of recent orientalist scholarship, a tale of passion and vengeance set in an exotic, imaginary Islam. The work begins with a curse, an expression of "gathered vengeance" that is "uttered from the heart" of the Rajah Kehama.

> And thou shalt seek Death
> To release thee, in vain;
> Thou shalt live in thy pain
> While Kehama shall reign,

. . . .
And the Curse shall be on thee
Forever and ever.

(II.160–69)[7]

What is striking about this poetic curse is its straightforward naturalism, the way it makes no claim of supernatural power but openly represents itself as having a *psychological* effect on its target. The imprecation of Kehama is meant to force its victim, Ladurlad, into a self-destructive psychosomatic internalization, to induce him to *believe* in the curser's powers. He listens, "miserable," transfixed by his own fear, an effect reinforced by his superstitious dread of the evil eye: "Kehama's eye that fastened on him still" (II.184)

Southey's tale is in one sense yet another Romantic revision of Milton's Hell, following Satan's interpretation of damnation as fundamentally psychological: "The mind is its own place, and in it self/Can make a Heav'n of Hell, a Hell of Heav'n" (I.254–55).[8] Later in *Paradise Lost*, of course, Milton turns Satan's meliorism against him in the ultimate self-directed curse. "Me miserable! which way shall I flie/Infinite wrauth, and infinite despaire?/Which way I flie is Hell; my self am Hell . . . " (IV.73–75).

It has become commonplace to observe that, beginning with Blake, the Romantics intentionally misread *Paradise Lost* in order to secularize Milton's theological evil, turning it into a sublime case study in rebellion and related forms of psychopathology. For these writers, Satan is right to argue that his Promethean torments occur within the sublime space of his own mind, as a painful internalization of the structures of persecution and exclusion.[9] Southey's curse merely relocates this kind of social-psychologizing of the Christian myth to the exotic realm of "heathen" religion and superstition. In *The Curse of Kehama*, the passions of hatred and vengeance are rhetorically persuasive because they lead to a sympathetic, psychosomatic reaction on the part of the recipient, turning his mind into a hell at least partly of its own making.

Readers of Shelley are familiar with the same complex of ideas in *Prometheus Unbound*, where the hero's defiance of Jupiter takes the form of transparently self-destructive language ("Rain then thy plagues upon me here" [I.266]),[10] which cannot escape reflexively invoking the same on others associated with him.

Let thy malignant spirit move
Its darkness over those I love:
On me and mine I imprecate
The utmost torture of thy hate . . .
. . . .
Heap on thy soul by virtue of this Curse
Ill deeds, then be thou damned, beholding good,
Both infinite as is the Universe,
And thou, and thy self-torturing solitude.

(I.276–79, 292–95)

In the lyrical drama the Titan may be seen in some measure to repent, since he says, in the end, "I wish no living thing to suffer pain" (I.305). But part of the difficulty with reading *Prometheus Unbound* lies in the problematic question of just how far Necessity alone and how far Prometheus's oracular curse work to effect the downfall of Jupiter. The exact combination of moving causes remains obscure. The tyrant would seem to be a "living thing," and as a figure he does "suffer pain" at the moment of his climactic fall, his last words being the classical dramatic cry of "woe": "Ai! ai!" (III.i.83). Prometheus (and the reader) has in the end both the pleasure of hearing the curse voiced and the moral superiority of its denial, as the play's structure seems to suggest that escape from the original curse requires a countercurse. Like Southey's *Kehama*, *Prometheus Unbound* explores the nexus of ethics, powerful rhetoric, and invective curse, all of which draw upon the period's empirical fascination with the social psychology of superstition.

As Alan Bewell has shown, Wordsworth's poems about peasants, mad mothers, and other marginal figures can usefully be seen as ethnographic case studies in the developing tradition of Enlightenment anthropology.[11] A lyrical ballad like "Goody Blake and Harry Gill" versifies Erasmus Darwin's study of *mania mutabilis* in *Zoönomia*, the processes by which (in Wordsworth's words) the "power of the human imagination is sufficient to produce such changes even in our physical nature as might almost appear miraculous."[12] Harry Gill is a victim of Goody Blake's vengeful curse ("O may he never more be warm!")—or, rather, of his own belief that her words are powerful, capable of magical effect. It was Robert Southey himself who complained that the poem would be likely to "promote the popular superstition of witchcraft."[13] Southey was concerned about the intersubjective, contagious power of superstition (which he seems to feel is especially dangerous in the case of English peasants)—but this is also arguably the theme of Wordsworth's poem. Harry Gill's victim, the poor woman gathering firewood, becomes his punisher through a vengeful "magic" that may well be the product of his own unwitting collaboration with community norms and beliefs. As Bewell puts it, "Harry's disease" is both "*accusation*" and "projection of his own cold-heartedness upon the old woman," a bodily manifestation of "*punishment*" in the form of guilt (p. 156).

The most famous and fully developed exploration of the psychopathology of magical curse as both accusation and punishment is found in another lyrical ballad, one of the poems its author claimed was written as an experiment in the emotions that accompany experiences of supernatural situations—"The Rime of the Ancient Mariner." Its supernatural incidents, according to Coleridge, were to be treated as "real"—"And real in *this* sense they have been to every human being who, from whatever source of delusion, has at any time believed himself under supernatural agency."[14] Although this critical perspective was offered many years after the composition of the "Rime," it is important to consider when interpreting the fantastic in the fable—for example, the collective curse of the crew as the result of the Mariner's action, and then the reflective turning of their multiple evil eyes back upon him.

> An orphan's curse would drag to Hell
> A spirit from on high;
> But O! more horrible than that
> Is the curse in a dead man's eye!
> Seven days, seven nights, I saw that curse,
> And yet I could not die.
>
> (Part IV)[15]

This curse of the evil eye—a sign of penance on the brink of damnation—is still reflected in the "glittering eye" of the Mariner himself as he stops the wedding guest and forces him to hear the tale, thus depriving the guest of the social communion of the wedding feast.

The conjunction of verbal curse with the evil eye, and its result—social isolation—is no accident. In context, it reveals itself to be based on the relentless logic of superstitious associations, as Tobin Siebers outlines them in *The Mirror of Medusa*. "The pronouncing of compliments and curses has always been intimately related to the cause and cure of the evil eye" (p. 41), Siebers explains, because the evil-eye superstition "thrives by attributing a supernatural difference to accused individuals . . ." (p. xii). In other words, both cursing and superstitious belief are manifestations of a larger *social* dynamic of collective aggression and accusation. Siebers suggests that the evil-eye superstition and the related belief in efficacious curse are linked to the cultural propensity to scapegoat, the group's tendency to select a victim as an outlet for the energy of what is ultimately collective violence. Once someone is cast out in this way, a kind of superstitious logic paints the person as magically accursed, dangerously threatening but set apart to isolate the threat. In this sense, superstition is society's reaction to the misunderstood threat of mimesis, the process through which violent behavior leads to more violent behavior, one mechanism for limiting its own mass aggression through focused acts of prophylactic violence (p. 56).

But what is most important for my purposes is the circular, reflexive way in which the curser is bent on protecting *himself* against a curse he already feels. That is, the curse serves a talismanic purpose: through a form of sympathetic magic, it attempts to mirror a feared accusation, reflecting it back upon the potential accuser before the fact, in what Siebers calls the "logic of the amulet" (p. 10). This dynamic provides a perspective from which to understand curses like Shelley's invectives, a way to place their language in a social context where public and personal violence overlap and fuel one another.

• • •

At the end of 1816 and the beginning of 1817, Shelley faced first the death of his wife, Harriet Westbrook, and then Chancery proceedings begun by her family to prevent his custody of their children, Ianthe and Charles.[16] The plaintiffs' brief, drawn up in the names of the children on 8 January 1817, petitions Lord Chancellor Eldon on the basis of Shelley's being an unfit parent, living an immoral lifestyle, and manifesting radical opinions (in this case conveniently recorded in print). Both the somewhat notorious *Queen Mab* and the unknown *Letter to Lord Ellenborough* were introduced as evidence of Shelley's radical social theories, especially his atheism. The final decision against Shelley was based on the volatile combination of his published views and his alleged immoral conduct. The Westbrooks did not immediately succeed in their ultimate aims, but Shelley's children were placed in the guardianship of a third party.

Early in 1817, in the midst of these legal proceedings, Shelley composed a sixteen-stanza poem, "To the Lord Chancellor," at once venting his personal anger and attempting to place it on a national basis.

> I
> Thy country's curse is on thee, darkest crest
>   Of that foul, knotted, many headed worm
> Which rends our Mother's bosom—Priestly Pest!
>   Masked Resurrection of a buried Form!
> II
> Thy country's curse is on thee! Justice sold,
>   Truth trampled, Nature's landmarks overthrown,
> And heaps of fraud-accumulated gold,
>   Plead, loud as thunder, at destruction's throne.
>
> (ll. 1–8)[17]

The public pretensions of these bitter lines are remarkable. On behalf of the country, Shelley claims to cast a spell. This most intensely personal utterance—a "father's curse"—is pronounced in the voice of society as a whole (or so he would claim).

As if to caricature his own writing—then being held up by the Westbrooks for condemnation—Shelley opens the curse with virulently "radical" imagery, an inversion of the conventional Hydra image. More often used to symbolize the threat posed by the people (the Hydra-headed multitude), the Hydra was occasionally appropriated by reformers and radicals as an emblem of the conspiracy of power (see Figure 1).[18] In Shelley's poem, the "many-headed worm" stands for Eldon's network of tangled alliances—his role as a member of the government and thus, by extension, of the Holy Alliance. Thus Shelley manages to be both blasphemous and seditious at the same time. The combined power of Church and State is figured as a "Masked Resurrection"—a fraudulent representation of what is dead—the "buried Form" of both Christ/Christianity and the ancien régime the current government would help restore. Fraud is the vice Shelley always associated with Lord Eldon—the name of the allegorical disguise he wears in *The Mask of Anarchy*, for example—and this must have been in part because it works so well as a satirical inversion of his legitimate legal role: cases of fraud were among those Chancery was likely to hear. The Lord Chancellor is thus made the personification of the evil he has been appointed to combat.

THE

POLITICAL SHOWMAN—AT HOME!

EXHIBITING HIS CABINET OF CURIOSITIES AND

Creatures—All Alive!

BY THE AUTHOR OF THE
POLITICAL HOUSE THAT JACK BUILT.

" I lighted on a certain place where was a *Den*."   *Bunyan.*

WITH TWENTY-FOUR CUTS.

" The putrid and mouldering carcase of exploded Legitimacy."
Mr. Lambton.

LONDON:
PRINTED FOR WILLIAM HONE, 45, LUDGATE-HILL.

1821.

ONE SHILLING.

FIGURE 1. Title page from *THE POLITICAL SHOWMAN—AT HOME!* (British Museum 14148). Hydra with the heads of European monarchs; Vesuvius, a symbol of the threat of revolution, erupts in the lower-right corner.

Shelley makes much of the Chancery Court's legal charter as an institution to serve as the "general guardian of all infants, idiots, and lunat-
ics."[19] Guardianship—the care and proper education of the children—
was the purpose of the proceedings, the Westbrooks' point of contention. The Lord Chancellor hears petitions on matters directly related to
the King's role as *parens patriae*. Shelley deliberately frames his "father's
curse"—all twelve stanzas of repetitious vitriol—with an appeal to the
judgment of the country, in order to put his accusers on the defensive
and to suggest that in the court of public opinion, at least, the Lord
Chancellor (and by implication the King) is an unfit guardian of *his*
dependent wards. His language ("Thy country's curse is on thee") echoes
the proper legal terminology as found, for example, in Blackstone's
Commentaries: "The chancellor cannot try [a cause], having no power to
summon a jury; but must deliver the record . . . into the court of king's
bench, where it shall be tried by the country, and judgment shall be
there given thereon" (III, 48).

To have Eldon "tried by the country" is precisely the aim of Shelley's
curse, his purpose in speaking as a father, delivering his "father's curse"—
a phrase we might more readily associate with a curse *on* the father's
children, as in the famous examples in *King Lear*. First, the King's initial
curse of Cordelia:

> For by the sacred radiance of the sun,
> The [mysteries] of Hecat and the night;
> By all the operation of the orbs,
> From whom we do exist and cease to be;
> Here I disclaim all my paternal care . . . .

$$(\text{I.i.}109\text{–}13)^{20}$$

Later, his even more bitter denunciation of Goneril: "Hear, Nature, hear,
dear goddess, hear!/Suspend thy purpose . . . . /Th' untented woundings
of a father's curse/Pierce every sense about thee!" (I.iv.275–76, 300–01).
Here the "father's curse" is performative of the King's act of disinheri-
tance. This is the starting place for Shelley's unequivocally evil version
of such a curse in *The Cenci*. In Shelley's occasional satire, however, the
allusion supposedly redirects the curse, turning it against the King—in
the immediate person of his Lord Chancellor—for the loss of the persecuted father's rights.

IV

Oh, let a father's curse be on thy soul,
    And let a daughter's hope be on thy tomb;
Be both, on thy gray head, a leaden cowl
    To weigh thee down to thine approaching doom!

V

I curse thee by a parent's outraged love,
    By hopes long cherished and too lately lost,
By gentle feelings thou couldst never prove,
    By griefs which thy stern nature never crossed . . . .

(ll. 17–24)

This sounds extremely personal, of course, and the reader is surely justified in thinking of Shelley's cursing *his* father at Eton, for example, as the
displaced and troubled psychological background to this expression of
"outraged love." But the lines are deliberately public as well, addressed to
the country as at once the jury for Shelley's case and his literary audience.
This makes sense, given their setting in Chancery, the forum for a public
airing of private conflicts, and given the doctrine of the "patrimony" of
the King.

The incantatory formula, "By . . . [I curse thee]," is repeated twenty-
two times in this poem of sixty-four lines, a resounding index of the
speaker's desperate desire for potency. He curses "by" everything from
"a parent's outraged love" (l. 21) and various images of the children's
innocence, to the indirect punishments that *they* are sure to suffer under
guardianship: "the dull constraint and bitter heaviness" (l. 34) of their
conventional care and "the false cant" (l. 37) of their religious educations.
The latter stanzas shift to curses "by" the Lord Chancellor's own evil
qualities, beginning with his religious sanction of "Hell, and all its terror"
(l. 41) and culminating in "the hate which checks a father's love" (l. 53).
At this the poem turns explicitly *inward* for its sanctioning objects, to
curse "by" both the speaker's "despair" and the paternal "blood" running
through his children's veins (ll. 57–59). The appeal to the children is an
obvious attempt to tap the power of innocence, like the "orphan's curse"
in "The Rime of the Ancient Mariner" that can "drag to Hell/A spirit
from on high." But to curse by one's own children is (ethically and rhetorically) a risky business, at best, reminding us inevitably of the destructive
cry of Shelley's Prometheus: "Let thy malignant spirit move/Its darkness
over those I love:/On me and mine I imprecate/The utmost torture of thy

hate . . . ." There is something uncomfortably Medea-like in Shelley's representation of the children in his vitriolic invective, something too willing to exploit them as mere figures for the effects of his personal "sorcery," too ready to indulge in images of their persecution as an act of self-dramatization or self-pity.

The long series of objects upon which to predicate the curse calls attention not so much to the injustice committed against the children as to the extreme anger of the curser, foregrounding his frenzied search for the most negatively powerful "ground" for hatred that he can find. In one sense, this merely echoes the ancient either/or construction of primitive prayers and curses, which often invoked in their imprecations more than one god or name for a god: "The curser must exhaust all possibilities as he searches for the essential agency of power, the god's 'right' name."[21] But read rhetorically, this name-magic recalls the structure of multiple similes in "To a Sky-lark" ("What is most like thee?") and the "Hymn to Intellectual Beauty"—where it becomes clear that the "power" the poems seek to invoke cannot be covered in a single act of naming or comparison. As in these poems, Shelley's catalog of curses calls attention to the speaker and the constructed, literary nature of his utterance, its origins in the rhetorical power of imagined subjectivity.

Considered linguistically, the formula ("I curse thee by . . .") is probably best understood as performative: rather than stating something about the world, such an utterance does something, or at least represents the act of doing something; and that something is fundamentally social and contextual. The utterance "I curse," like the phrase "I promise," depends for its successful illocutionary force (and later "perlocutionary" effects) on mutual agreement, a social acceptance of certain conditions and sanctions for such utterances.[22] In this light, it is important to see not just verbal curses but also other expressions of "magical" or "superstitious" violence as socially constrained speech acts, predicated on a power which must be granted by those who are to be affected. But the question of shared context for such a performance is a complex one. If one were to say "I promise" or "I curse" in solipsistic isolation, the utterance would simply misfire or fail, except as a futile representation of the speaker's own desire.

Shelley's performative poetry highlights this ambiguous status of some poetic utterances that can be seen as performative, the equivocal way in which the "acts" they perform may work to deconstruct their apparent purposes. A curse can function apart from its author's intentions, to call into question the social agreement and discursive situation upon which it is founded. In such a case, the latent possibility of failure contained in the language of the act is what is most interesting, the fact that there may be *no* social setting in which the performance can be given meaning. The inflection of a curse can express the fear that the curse will fail. In so doing, it highlights the mutual isolation — rather than the community — of the rivals or opponents.

Shelley's invective seems at least partly aware of this possibility of isolation, and even self-consciously extends the possibility of failure as part of its effect, suggesting that any power the Lord Chancellor might have to condemn is likewise based in an absent context, a deficient set of conventions, and is thus open to potential subversion. For a condemned man to curse his torturer represents a threat to authority because it calls attention to the conventional source of that authority — its reliance on some degree of community assent or collaboration. We see this most clearly in the stanza on the Lord Chancellor's "Hell" (a stanza about which Shelley seems to have had second thoughts).

XI

By thy most impious Hell, and all its terror;
  By all the grief, the madness, and the guilt
Of thine impostures, which must be their error —
  That sand on which thy crumbling power is built —

(ll. 41–44)

"Cursed" is another term for "damned," of course, but "Hell" is here invoked primarily in order to allow it to deconstruct itself. The "sand" figures the weak foundation of such religious doctrines — the "fraud" or "error" on which the edifice of Eldon's hypocritical power is constructed, the ideological source of the concept of eternal punishment, and the conceptual "ground" for his authority. The Chancery suit is a kind of inquisition, Shelley implies, a way of terrorizing him with his own sense of guilt, the legal analogue of a religious threat of damnation. In response he offers an infidel's counterthreat, hinting that the structure of such authority will eventually fall of its own reified weight. By the same token, however, Shelley's procedure inevitably calls attention to the dependence of his *own* performed curse on similar conventional structures, its reliance on mutually acknowledged sanctions of self-directed guilt. The social determination of satiric power works both ways.

In the manuscript Shelley apparently drew a line through this stanza XI, and Mary Shelley subsequently marked it for deletion before she first published parts of the poem in 1839 (stanzas V–IX, XIV).[23] She also omitted the opening stanzas (I–IV) on the "country's curse"—presenting only the more personal expression of paternal woe; most important, not only in this edition but in the second edition of 1839 (in which the poem was printed in full) she tellingly omitted Shelley's title and its explicit naming of the target. Having said this, it is not clear why Shelley would have crossed out the "Hell" stanza—especially when so much else in the poem remained to offend. Perhaps it was to augment rather than to diminish the punishing effect, because the structure of the stanza revealed too clearly—made too transparent—the poem's central rhetorical strategy. This strategy clearly involves the exploitation of superstitious fear, casting the target of the curse in the role of self-damning demon. The poem ends with a surprising reversal:

> I curse thee—though I hate thee not.—O slave!
>> If thou couldst quench the earth-consuming Hell
> Of which thou art a daemon, on thy grave
>> This curse should be a blessing. Fare thee well!

(ll. 61–64)

This closing abjuration of hate seems at first more perplexing than convincing, coming as it does after fifteen bitter stanzas. But following the line of explanation I have been developing, we can see that Shelley is attempting here (however unconvincingly) to separate personal hatred from the public curse—to put his curse on the *public* footing claimed in the opening stanzas: "Thy country's curse is on thee!" Through a kind of rhetorical sleight of hand, he would articulate the curse while washing his hands of it, would claim that it grows reflexively out of the target's own hellish status as a demon, independently of the speaker's obvious personal animosity. Again, however, this move merely serves to remind us of the reflexive qualities of the act of cursing itself. It is conventional wisdom that curses, especially those of questionable justice, return upon the head of the curser—or (as in Shelley's last stanza) turn into a blessing.[24] As the proverbial epigraph to *The Curse of Kehama* reads: "CURSES ARE LIKE YOUNG CHICKENS, THEY ALWAYS COME HOME TO ROOST."[25] Shelley's manipulations in the end only serve to highlight the uncertainty of his position, to undermine the ground of his vituperation.

It is a widespread critical observation that bitter satire is inevitably reflexive, that it reflects back upon the satirist as much as it holds up a mirror to reveal its target's deep flaws.[26] This reflexive nature of satire is part of the satirist's marginal yet "normative" borderline existence in relation to society. The satirist is always the outsider with inside knowledge, crying out in the desert of isolation. In this sense the satirist is like the prophet, of course, but is also like the *pharmakos*, the ancient Greeks' "sacrificeable victim" maintained at society's expense, and like a priest of the sacrifice, set apart and always tainted by the poison he handles, implicated in the collective aggression of which he is the focus and reflection.

Satire of this kind can usefully be read in terms of René Girard's theory of mimetic desire.[27] It is frequently based on a kind of parodic relation to its target, through the mechanism that Shelley's fragment of "A Satire upon Satire" refers to as "the mirror of truth's sunlike shield"—what I have been arguing is satire's exploitation of its target's self-reflective and self-destructive internalizations of another's aggression—its "superstition." The language of Shelley's fragment (which I examine in detail in Chapter 4) suggests a very specific and thoroughgoing sense of aggressive "reflection," one that in many ways anticipates the insights of Girard's theory of violence and cultural formation. The satire is directed against Southey; it begins with a kind of rehearsal of possible violent curses, then refers to "truth's sunlike shield" as a surface for reflecting Southey's own worst nightmares: "Flash on his sight the spectres of the past/Until his mind's eye paint thereon."[28] Clearly this is yet another example of the use of satiric language as a psychological (superstitious) spur to self-damnation.

Moreover, the "sunlike shield" in Shelley's fragment must be seen as an allusion to another famous shield that was simultaneously protection and weapon, the shield of Perseus, the mirror of Medusa. In Ovid's account, Perseus approaches the Gorgons warily, knowing that he must avoid Medusa's gaze: "But he himself had looked upon the image of that dread face reflected from the bright bronze shield his left hand bore; and while deep sleep held fast both the snakes and her who wore them, he smote her head clean from her neck. . . . "[29]

Just as in Shelley's imagery, here the shield functions as a dangerous mirror, reflecting destructive magic back upon itself. In this way it both shields or covers Perseus from malevolence and kills Medusa, bringing about what is (technically speaking) a *self*-destruction. Like Shelley's "sunlike shield" of truth, this shield enables its bearer to commit an act of violence while shielding himself from the harmful effects of (and responsibility for) that act.

Like the shield, the severed head becomes an amulet, in part because Medusa was herself accursed. The myth of Medusa is a paradigm of superstitious self-protection. Shelley's fragment "On the Medusa of Leonardo da Vinci" (1819) exemplifies the dark Romantic fascination with the image: "Yet it is less the horror than the grace/Which turns the gazer's spirit into stone" (ll. 9–10).[30] This combination of sublime terror and fascination in the amuletic gaze is also found in another mythic figure that fascinated Shelley: Narcissus. In both cases, the element of reflection (in Perseus's shield and in Narcissus's pool) is "narcissistic" in the *social* sense. Both characters are outcasts who lash out. The violence of Perseus's mirroring—his causing Medusa to curse herself—is prophylactic and talismanic, an attempt to displace an already present danger or a prior "curse."

Narcissus, the beautiful but cold Boeotian youth, is the victim not only of self-love but also of the projections of supernatural difference, a curse put on *him* (via the agency of Nemesis) by one of the many youths whose desire he had spurned: "So may he himself love, and not gain the thing he loves!"[31] Narcissus is thus marked as different or accursed, and it is possible to read the *myth* of Narcissus as a back-formation, functioning to displace this accursedness by replacing it with a "cover story" that blames his fate on his self-love rather than on the curse. Among the Romantics, Shelley is particularly obsessed with Narcissus, associating him with artistic self-knowledge and a radical autonomy of vision based on alienation from the community. This is probably most familiar in *Alastor*, but a new dimension in Romantic narcissism is opened up when we connect it to the idea of the satiric curse—as Shelley himself did in another poem directed against an enemy, "Lines to a Reviewer."

This sonnet was published posthumously and inconspicuously in Leigh Hunt's *The Literary Pocket-Book* in 1823, a fate that belies the text's basic rhetorical intentions as a topical reply. It shares these basic intentions with "To the Lord Chancellor," but its tone is very different, almost Horatian, almost sincere. I quote it here in full:

> Alas, good friend, what profit can you see
> In hating such a hateless thing as me?
> There is no sport in hate where all the rage
> Is on one side: in vain would you assuage
> Your frowns upon an unresisting smile,

In which not even contempt lurks to beguile
Your heart, by some faint sympathy of hate.
Oh, conquer what you cannot satiate!
For to your passion I am far more coy
Than ever yet was coldest maid or boy
In winter noon. Of your antipathy
If I am the Narcissus, you are free
To pine into a sound with hating me.[32]

Like the final stanza of "To the Lord Chancellor," this poem attempts to return hatred while denying that it hates, a rhetorical tactic that we might call passive-aggressive resistance. A cruder version of the same technique is also at work in another poem of retort, "Lines to a Critic":

Hate men who cant, and men who pray,
    And men who rail, like thee;
An equal passion to repay
They are not coy — like me — .

(ll. 5–8)[33]

Each of these poems depends upon the attitude of self-righteousness; this one ends with an especially unconvincing dismissal.

A passion like the one I prove
    Cannot divided be;
I hate thy want of truth and love —
    How should I then hate thee?

(ll. 13–16)

Just as in the "Lines to a Reviewer," here Shelley poses as the persecuted, saying in effect, "You say that I am," supposedly heaping coals of fire on the head of his enemy but in reality revealing his own burning desires and aggressive impulses.

The "Reviewer" sonnet, however, reveals more interesting fault lines, running into the deeper ambiguities of the myth itself. For example, it cleverly exploits the view that reviewers are inherently parasitic, mere "echoes" of true writers. The reviewer, the lines suggest, is secretly enamored of the writer/speaker's beauty and potent creativity. The idea of the infatuated reviewer pining away to a mere sound—the echo that is his whole substance—is witty enough, but as an allusion it also contains a suggestion of fundamentally violent imagery. In Ovid's account, Echo's pining away is presented starkly and vengefully: "she becomes gaunt and wrinkled and all moisture fades from her body into the air. Only her voice and her bones remain: then, only voice . . . ."[34] The tone of Shelley's poem may for a time conceal the fact that it wishes harm on its unnamed target; but this is its wish, just as surely as in the curse on Eldon.

In "Lines to a Reviewer," however, Shelley fully engages the mythic complications as he writes in the voice of the accursed who would curse. If the myth of Narcissus has buried within it the story of a victim or outcast, Shelley's use of the myth would turn that outcast's status into a platform for counterattack. Once we have opened a critical perspective on the myth, the sonnet can be seen as effecting an exchange of accusations. Line 12's enjambment results in the syntactically awkward phrase "Of your antipathy," modifying the conditional identification of the speaker as Narcissus. The suggestion is that "antipathy" is only a negative form of sympathetic magic and identification, that the speaker's alleged narcissism is really only a "reflection" of the reviewer's own image, a kind of photographic negative produced by narcissistic self-projection. In other words, the depiction of the poet as a type of Narcissus is the mirror image of the hater's jealous imagination.

But the mirror reflects both ways: Shelley's strategy of vengefully depicting the reviewer as Echo must adopt, at least temporarily ("If I am the Narcissus"), the fiction it would attribute to the target. In other words, the satire is predicated upon and depends upon a shared context of accusation. Seen from this perspective, Shelley's sonnet begins to look like a complicated tautological attempt to return or counteract the curse of isolation and self-pity, to use the speaker's outcast status as the grounds for accusing his accuser. Such satire works by a kind of martyrdom of the satirist, who makes a point of accepting his represented isolation and pariah status in order to reflect persecution away from himself.

• • •

We find a remarkably similar strategy—claiming the position of accursed outsider in order to rail against the community—in Shelley's literary satires. One of these is also based on the monstrous figure of the Hydra ("that foul, knotted, many-headed worm"), which the speaker must face in heroic battle: an unpublished notebook fragment, "Proteus Wordsworth."[35] As in the "Lines to a Reviewer," the speaker of the "Proteus" fragment is caught up in reflexive patterns of linguistic aggression, closely bound up with the target of his invective. In "Proteus Wordsworth," however, the curse takes the form of a milder kind of invective, almost a childish chant or mere name-calling.

> ~~Water~~
>   ~~Then~~
>   Proteus Wordsworth who shall bind thee
>   Coleridge
>   Proteous ~~Southey~~ who shall find thee [. . .]
>   ~~Proteus~~ Hyperprotean Proteus, Southey
>   shall   shall
>   Who ~~can~~ catch thee, who ~~can~~ know thee
>   Hecate & the Trinity
>   Are but feeble types of thee
>   Thou polyhedric polyglot
>   And polymorph~~ic~~ I know what
>   Hundred headed lump of change
>   ~~Never~~
>   Aristeus, Menelaus

The fragment invokes the political and literary context of "apostasy" among English writers, the widespread shift from revolutionary sympathies to Toryism, exemplified for Shelley and Byron and Hazlitt by the Lake Poets. There will be more to say about this issue in the chapters to come, but here it is important to see that it affected Shelley's sense of his own public role in a way that seemed to him to call for sometimes scurrilous "personal" satire. This fragment's name-calling of the elder poets can be seen as a displacement of Shelley's need for prophetic power, his need to reverse the curse of isolation and silence under which he suffers.

Shelley employs the loaded name of the highly mutable sea god, already a proverb for moral slipperiness, as a figure for the elder poets' "polyhedric" duplicity. Each of the poets is simply *called* "Proteus" or "Protean"—or "Hyperprotean." But the incantatory rhythms suggest a kind of curse, a suggestion reinforced by the mention of Hecate (one of the three "persons" of Diana Triformis—her name when in Hell—she "was supposed to preside over magic and enchantments"),[36] and of typology and the Holy Trinity. The poets are the true "fulfillments" of these various prefigurations, Shelley says, and these lines are a spell for commanding them to clarify their identities.

The most likely source of inspiration for this sketch is a "satiric ballad" by Thomas Love Peacock, "Sir Proteus" (1814).[37] That satire mocks the Lakers' (and other modern poets') pretensions to immortality, following one Sir Proteus through the manifold transformations he undergoes, into first one and then another of the satire's chosen multiple targets. Southey is one of these targets, and Peacock notes that *The Curse of Kehama* had displayed this motto (from Nonnus): "Let me the many-changing Proteus see,/To aid my many-changing melody." It is to be expected, Peacock quips, "that a man, under a process of moral and political metamorphosis, should desire the patronage of this multiform god, who may be regarded as the tutelary saint of the numerous and thriving sect of Anythingarians." Peacock offers instead this revised motto, one more fitting to Southey: "Before my eyes let changeful Proteus float,/When now I change my many-coloured coat."

Shelley shared Peacock's views, but his use of classical allusion goes beyond that of his fellow classicist in exploring the problem of apostasy, as the last trailing words of the fragment suggest. He alludes syncretically to Virgil and Homer as dual sources for Proteus, and his key terms, "bind" and "catch," suggest that he is drawing on the conventional association of the god with prophecy and poetry. Lemprière's popular *Classical Dictionary* provides one well-known account: Proteus, according to Lemprière, "had received the gift of prophecy from Neptune because he tended the monsters of the sea, and from his knowledge of futurity mankind received the greatest services . . . ."

> He was difficult of access, and when consulted he refused to give answers, by immediately assuming different shapes, and if not properly secured in fetters, eluding the grasp in the form of a tiger, or a lion, or disappearing in a flame of fire, a whirlwind, or a rushing stream. Aristaeus and Menelaus were in the number of those who consulted him.

Two of the attributes of Proteus given here are essential to Shelley's satire: his power of metamorphosis and his power of prophecy, a power that can serve "mankind" as a whole. It was this role as seer (along with his pastoral occupation) that caused Proteus to be associated through the Renaissance and beyond with poets and poetry.[38] Aristaeus and Menelaus must capture the god and seek a prophecy from him in order to learn how to bolster their own lagging personal fortunes—to find the source of their troubles. Both predicaments imply that isolation from the community is part of their suffering. In *The Odyssey*, Menelaus is stormbound due to the gods' anger, unable to get home, to reach a place of belonging; in *The Georgics*, Aristaeus loses his swarm of bees and what they symbolize—a peaceful, cooperative agricultural existence—again a punishment from the gods. In both cases (cited by Shelley as well as Lemprière) the heroes must ambush, hold, and consult Proteus because they themselves are set apart or accursed.

From Shelley's point of view, the fragment is a public satire on the erstwhile radical Lakers which names their problem (their shifty lack of commitment) and the desired corrective (they must be held fast, then made to prophesy). This would return the poets to what Shelley sees as their true roles—forcing them to speak oracles and to serve society as a whole (just as "mankind received the greatest services" from Proteus, according to Lemprière). But the satire is based on a mythic curse against the *speaker*, and the attempt to undo the curse through epithetic language. Though this language may seem playfully comic, "Proteus Wordsworth" is generically related to the more violent "To the Lord Chancellor." It is crucial to an understanding of Shelley's satiric impulse to recognize how much these two poems have in common. In both, personal anger is deliberately situated in the public sphere, as the accursed speaker problematically attempts to speak for the community as a whole through his own expressed bitterness.

The continuity of the two poems is clarified when both are compared with another poem on Wordsworth's shiftiness, "An Exhortation," which was published—and quite prominently—in the *Prometheus Unbound* volume of 1820, and which Shelley referred to as "a kind of an excuse for Wordsworth."[39] Significantly, it was drafted in the same notebook as the "Proteus" fragment. It addresses the same basic problem, but its title would seem to claim that it offers a positive rhetorical alternative to the satiric mode, hortative or *paraenetic* rather than admonishing or punitive. Its central device compares the poet to the chameleon—which was traditionally associated with Proteus, both being Renaissance symbols of changeability, prophecy, and poetry.[40] "Chameleons feed on light and air:/Poets' food is love and fame" (ll. 1–2),[41] so by analogy are poets bound to shift their loyalties and identities in the search for vital sustenance. But the final stanza offers a warning to those who would corrupt the vulnerable seers.

> Yet dare not stain with wealth or power
> A poet's free and heavenly mind:

> If bright chameleons should devour
> Any food but beams and wind,
> They would grow as earthly soon
> As their brother lizards are.
> Children of a sunnier star,
> Spirits from beyond the moon,
> O, refuse the boon!

(ll. 19–27)

The last three lines address poets directly, exhorting them to refuse the "sordid boon" (an allusion to Wordsworth's "The World Is Too Much with Us").

"An Exhortation" can be read as a kind of gentle Horatian satire (one advantage of which is that it allows us to see the intentional humor in the comparison of poets to lizards). But I would suggest that it stands at the other end of the satiric spectrum from a curse like "To the Lord Chancellor," and that "Lines to a Reviewer" and the "Proteus Wordsworth" fragment fall somewhere in between. The milder poems in effect submerge their animus in parody and humor, sublimate it in the overall effects of their rhetoric—but their animus never really disappears.

• • •

Shelley's satiric writings always highlight his position as an outsider, even when they depend upon inside jokes, in part because they are always written with a rhetorical undertone of desperation. To account for this, we can of course resort to his biography, with its stories of cursing his father, increasing alienation from English society and his audience, a deepening sense of exile, and frequent self-representations as pariah. All of this is epitomized in the Chancery case—public proceedings about the most personal of feelings. But in order fully to account for this curse complex, we also need to note that the genre of satire itself, especially in its most nakedly aggressive forms—curse and invective—is built upon the notion that the satirist is a dangerous outsider within, a pariah outside the pale who rails at folly and vice (or merely vents personal spleen). Satiric curse aims to be performative. Like other "superstitious" speech acts, it is based on an inherently social transaction, and takes place where personal animus finds a social context that can give it force.

One of the central fictions the genre has invented about itself is that of the satirist satirized—which can be read as the self-consciously reflexive power of the satiric curse coming home to roost, becoming self-inclusive in order to reveal the taint left by satiric exchanges. But what Shelley's satiric curses reveal in vivid detail is that to say that the satirist is satirized is only to address one side of a larger, open-ended cycle of linguistic and cultural violence. The satirist who curses is frequently himself accursed to begin with, and the motivation for satiric performance is not so much simple revenge (as has often been said) as a kind of superstitious logic of amuletic exchange: he curses in order to relieve his curse, and the act of so doing maintains a certain social equilibrium. Needless to say, this is true even in the absence of any supernatural belief, since, as we have seen, "superstition" for the post-Enlightenment poet is often a matter of invoking sympathetic (or, in the case of malediction, "antipathetic") affective responses to rhetoric. In this way satiric rhetoric claims a "magic" all its own.

Shelley saw himself as a true outsider, exile, and pariah. The Chancery proceedings only served to verify and solidify this self-image. His invectives draw upon and perpetuate this sense of himself and, more vividly than other satires, reveal the precarious status of the satiric persona. This gives even his crude experiments in the mode a real importance, both because they highlight the complexities of his search for a social role, and because they suggest that he saw the process of radical political change complicated by complex differential relationships, the circulation of reciprocal power between satirist and society, curser and accursed.

3 "Fond of the Devil"

Damnation in *The Devil's Walk* and *Peter Bell the Third*

SHELLEY'S PROBLEM WITH SATIRE was a problem of authority, a question of how to reconcile conventions of demonization with a hopeful program of reform. Nevertheless, from *The Devil's Walk* (1812) to *Peter Bell the Third* (1819) his satires seem determined to employ the traditional satiric figure of the Devil and its conventional effect—the demonization of a "target." The obvious ambivalence of *Peter Bell the Third* is the result of this contradiction, as it attempts to use the Devil to satirize the Devil, to represent a transformation that would go beyond the imagery of damnation. The poem sets out both to damn Wordsworth and to save him because Shelley knows that he shares in the responsibility he urges—and is never convinced that the authority of satire is compatible with that responsibility.

To understand this struggle with the Devil in Shelley's satire, we must first return to the beginning of his career, after his expulsion from Oxford and his marriage to Harriet Westbrook. A little more than one year after the London bookseller Daniel Isaac Eaton was charged with blasphemous libel (for publishing Part III of Paine's *The Age of Reason*), Shelley wrote *A Letter to Lord Ellenborough*, defending Eaton and arguing against the libel law. As we have seen, the 1812 essay was used as evidence against him during the 1817 Chancery suit. Only months after it was composed, Shelley's young Irish servant, Daniel Hill (or Healy), was arrested at Barnstaple for distributing a Painite tract—the *Declaration of Rights*—and a satirical poem—*The Devil's Walk: A Ballad*.[1] Hill was jailed in lieu of the fine of £200, and the confiscated materials led the local authorities to contact the Home Office, which recommended that Shelley be kept under surveillance. The authorship of the incendiary broadsides was never really in doubt, despite Hill's rather Coleridgean cover story about a man in black whom he met by chance on the road. Shelley had already been observed at Lynmouth, floating wine bottles and toy boats out into the Bristol Channel. When they were confiscated, the boats and bottles were found to contain copies of the *Declaration* and *The Devil's Walk*.

This familiar image—the young poet casting his poetry on the waters (or aloft in hot-air balloons)—has become an enduring feature of the Shelley legend, whether as an emblem of the idealized politics of the angelic youth or as an example of his tendency to treat writing as political action. It also serves as an emblem of Shelley's failure to find an audience, especially in this case: copies of the broadsides survive only because they were preserved in the official legal and political correspondence. Without the Home Office they would have remained ephemeral indeed. I recite the events again, but paying close attention to what is usually passed over rather quickly: the specific generic contents of those bottles, the fact that they contained not just vaguely "radical" writings but a satire. This satire was openly aimed at a popular audience, with its double entendres, topical allusions, and grotesque, cartoonlike imagery, in a broadside ballad of thirty stanzas. But it was also presumably among the works Shelley memorialized at the time in a sonnet as "Heavenly medicine!," enlightening "Knowledge" for which the poet asks a blessing from the goddess of Liberty.[2] This chapter will highlight and examine the apparent incongruity in this moment of textual dissemination—between the high claims of the sublime apostrophe ("Heavenly medicine!") and the low tone of the satire itself, the tension between Shelley's aim (a benevolent revolutionary poetry) and his chosen means (broad popular satire). I want to consider exactly what kind of action Shelley's broadsides and bottles represent, to read not just the texts but the *situation* of his early satire.

• • •

Shelley's reaction to the highly publicized Eaton case is useful to keep in mind, first because it highlights the distance between London and Barnstaple when it came to government prosecutions, but also because it reminds us of just how badly Shelley wanted to bridge that distance, to project his local activities in Devon into national events at the center of society. *A Letter to Lord Ellenborough* argues against the social foundations of the charge of blasphemy in terms that idealize the public role of intellectuals: "Surely the individual who devotes his time to fearless and unrestricted inquiry into the grand questions arising out of our moral nature ought rather to receive the patronage than encounter the vengeance of an enlightened legislature."[3]

Shelley sent a copy of this essay to Godwin and perhaps even to Viscount Sidmouth (although it is unlikely that the latter actually saw it).[4] His ironic wish for the patronage of the legislature covers a real desire to enter the political fray in 1812—a time of some danger surrounding writings such as the *Letter*, however provincial their publication. Even the bottles and balloons represent more than mere self-indulgence or private symbolism, more even than a practical means of distributing propaganda. They should be seen as a kind of self-conscious performance—if for a very small audience (or even for an imagined, internalized one)—a display meant to puzzle the authorities and intrigue others. If we shift our focus a bit, the events of Hill's arrest and the production of Shelley's first satire appear as the logical culmination of a full year of intense political activism in Ireland, Scotland, Wales, and England, activism which received its initial impetus from Shelley's visit to Keswick, Cumberland, in late 1811.

There he met the famous poet Robert Southey (and just missed Coleridge and Wordsworth). Almost from the first, his reaction was divided; he was both impressed with the famous elder poet (soon to be Laureate) and prepared to "reproach" him for his political "tergiversation."

> He to whom Bigotry Tyranny and Law was hateful, has become the votary of these Idols, in a form the most disgusting.—The Church of England it's Hell and all has become the subject of his panegyric. . . . I feel a sickening distrust when I see all that I had considered good great & imitable fall around me into the gulph of error.
>
> (*Letters*, I, 208–09)

This letter contains the germ of all of Shelley's later satire: his reaction against Southey's apostasy on matters of Church and State (especially "Hell and all") and his struggle to find (and this is a telling juxtaposition) another "independant," yet "imitable," poet on whom to model himself. His intense political fervor is bound up with the need to forge an independent identity by pushing away from his precursor-models, because the "gulph" of their "error" threatens Shelley, too, if he cannot successfully set himself apart. Especially in his satires, he does so by returning to what remains "imitable" in the work of the apostates: their own earlier poetry.

One month after the letter about Southey's change, Shelley began a correspondence with a new mentor, William Godwin. In one letter he explicitly compares the two men: "Southeys conversation has lost its charm, except it be the charm of horror, at so hateful a prostitution of talents. I hasten to go to Ireland" (*Letters*, I, 232–37). As if in one breath Shelley revealingly moves from Southey's "prostitution" to his own plans for an Irish crusade. Near the end of the letter he says: "Here follows a few stanzas whic[h] may amuse you. I was once rather fond of the Devil" (p. 235). An early version of *The Devil's Walk* follows, a direct imitation of a 1799 newspaper squib coauthored by Southey and Coleridge, which Shelley had probably seen on a visit to Southey's library. He refers to his own imitative stanzas as a mere "trifling" and "a most teasing thing if you are not in a laughing mood" (p. 237); but if we read beyond the poem's contents, read the whole situation of its drafting, expanded composition, printing, and flamboyant distribution, we can see the ballad as an important event marking Shelley's serious effort to establish his difference from Southey and what he represented, to provoke the very kind of political conflict Southey was just beginning to put behind him. And we see how vital to this effort was the mode of satire.

This sort of combination of personal need and public urgency shaped other parodies by Shelley as well, including a parody of another newspaper squib Southey may have shown to Shelley in 1811, Coleridge's "Fire, Famine, and Slaughter" (1798). Shelley appropriated this poem for his own allegorical skit, "Falshood and Vice"—but the details of the imitation are less important than the very interesting fact that, as late as 1815, Mary and Percy Shelley had memorized and were known to recite Coleridge's satire on social occasions—along with his later, sublime "France: An Ode." The two poems were even copied together in one manuscript in Mary's hand.[5] These dual recitations may well have been intended as "satirical," parodic juxtapositions that called attention to the distance Coleridge had traveled—so Shelley would say—to forsake his ideals. These ephemeral squibs were generated quickly, in the heat of political controversy, but Shelley seems to have treated them with surprising respect, as documents of a youthful vitality and poetic power that the elder poet had lost and Shelley wished to claim. The two poems are juxtaposed in one manuscript in order to play one off against the other: one a passionate recantation by Coleridge of his support for France, the other an example of his most subversive Jacobinical tendencies.

Given this context, it becomes clear that "derivativeness" is precisely the point of a work like *The Devil's Walk*. Shelley declares himself to be derived—from what he sees as the best in the earlier work of the elder poets. By appropriating the radical mode now (in 1811–12) abandoned by Coleridge and Southey, he implicitly satirizes the present in contrast with the 1790s, a patently defiant gesture in 1812. He claims an integrity his models can no longer match; but they remain his models. Parody is characteristically an ambivalent mode, one which walks the line between homage and satire. Often, a writer chooses to parody precisely what is most interesting and most disturbing in an original, and this ambivalent relationship of parodied and parody—as "a form of imitation . . . characterized by ironic inversion, not always at the expense of the parodied text"[6]—has become a prevalent topic in the postmodern era. In Shelley's case—and this is crucial—the ambivalence of parody is experienced as an ethical problem. The question is, how can he project a poetic role that is at once in the lineage of and yet discontinuous with his powerful models?

Coleridge and Southey's "The Devil's Thoughts" (1799) satirized the government, the slave trade, and a random mixture of additional targets (including conventional types, lawyers and clergymen), using a comic Devil as a convenient kind of shortcut *picaro*, a mobile observer. Shelley translates this same picaresque Devil into his poem, but emphasizes the figure's hypocrisy.

> Once, early in the morning,
>   Beelzebub arose,
> With care his sweet person adorning,
>   He put on his Sunday clothes.[7]

He then takes specific targets from the original, some that were perennial clichés and others that could be easily adapted to the times. Here is the 1799 Coleridge-Southey stanza on lawyers:

> He saw a lawyer killing a viper
>   On this dunghill beside his stable
> Oh-oh; quoth he, for it put him in mind
>   Of the story of Cain and Abel.[8]

Compare with this the following stanza from Shelley, as an example of just how close the imitation could be.

> Satan saw a lawyer a viper slay,

> That crawled up the leg of his table,
>   It reminded him most marvellously
>   Of the story of Cain and Abel.
>
>   (ll. 84–87)

Most of Shelley's poem is not quite so directly imitative as this; but the closeness of the two ballads, Shelley's open dependency on the newspaper poem, is a primary fact of his satire. For one thing, it tells us a great deal about the generic "register" of Shelley's squib, its family connection to the ephemeral, incendiary, "Jacobinical" newsprint writing. Shelley's speaker indulges in a kind of gossipy, cartoon version of Swiftian ire as he responds to the universal evils represented by the comical Devil.

The Devil, "the prince of liars and imposters," belongs in satire, the genre which claims to expose the ugly truths behind society's false fronts.[9] Shelley's Devil gets dressed for his tour by disguising his identity beneath the lies of banal fashion, but he does so as a matter of course, with absolutely no sense of ceremony, no sublime diabolical mystery.

> He drew on a boot to hide his hoof,
>   He drew on a glove to hide his claw,
>   His horns were concealed by a Bras Chapeau,
>   And the Devil went forth as natty a Beau
>   As Bond-Street ever saw.
>
>   (ll. 5–9)

This sneers at the anthropomorphism of the orthodox *and* the moral hypocrisy of London dandies. And not only them. It suggests that *all* quotidian social customs and manners, especially those tied to class distinctions, conceal evil. Deception is the norm. The earlier poem, "The Devil's Thoughts," had Satan swishing his tail when he walks, "As a gentleman swishes his cane." In Shelley's ballad Beelzebub gossips all night and moves freely at court.

Shelley's *Peter Bell the Third* (1819), in which the Devil also plays a leading role, develops the same theme, as we shall see.

> The Devil, I can safely aver,
>   Has neither hoof, nor tail, nor sting;
>   Nor is he, as some sages swear,

> A spirit, neither here nor there,
> In nothing—yet in every thing.

> He is—what we are; for sometimes
> The Devil is a gentleman . . .

(ll. 76–82)[10]

Even when dressed up, this demon is only a poor relation to the most widely influential Devil in European literature (after Milton's Satan): Goethe's Mephistopheles.[11] Shelley later translated part of the Prologue to *Faust*, in which Mephistopheles speaks like a polished gentleman, but the sources for his balladic Devil could be found closer to home. Old Nick has a long tradition in English popular culture, from medieval drama, to Punch and Judy, to rural ballads, to popular prints. From the eighteenth century on, high art self-consciously mined this popular vein, including Robert Burns's balladic "De'il" and (even more relevant in spirit to Shelley's satire) the numerous Devils of graphic satires, which were often identified with (or as) various political targets. George Cruikshank's famous 1815 caricature (with George Humphrey) of Napoleon as *The Devil Addressing the Sun* is an exemplary case in point (see Figure 2).[12] The "Sun" in the print is the Prince Regent, a blasphemous allusion to Milton's "Son" (the design includes text from Book IV of *Paradise Lost*); and St. Helena is Hell, where the Emperor has been cast down by his adversary. The comic bluster of the expression on Napoleon's face is countered by his ludicrously withered wings, horns, and cloven hoofs.

It is interesting to note that during the blasphemy trial of Cruikshank's infamous collaborator William Hone (1817), this print was offered as proof of parody's safely transparent qualities. Obviously, it was argued, the Devil is targeted in the print, but not Milton's canonical text. By the same token, parodying the liturgy did not mean satirizing the canonical religious source, but only the secondary political targets against which the pamphlet was aimed.[13] But the argument was needed in the first place precisely because the effects of parody are *not* so univocal or containable. Milton's devout use of the Devil *is* to some degree debased or trivialized by this satiric appropriation. Indeed, debasement of this sort is traditionally one of the subversive intentions of popular diabolism—to stand conventional powers (including the powers of darkness) on their heads. Whatever Hone's legal arguments, the demotic Devil had a kind of life of

BONEY'S meditations on the Island of St Helena — or —
The Devil addressing the SUN.

FIGURE 2.   George Cruikshank's *Boney's Meditations on the Island of St. Helena — or The Devil Addressing the Sun* (British Museum 12593). A colossal Napoleon as the Devil and a plumed Prince Regent as the Sun; the speech is from *Paradise Lost* IV ("To thee I call . . . to tell thee how I hate thy beams, that bring to my remembrance from what state I fell").

its own. Even when employed against an enemy of the nation like Napoleon, it carried with it a legacy of carnivalesque inversion, of the temporary license for mockery, against or through the persona of the Devil or devilish characters. In some older versions of the Punch puppet plays, Punch was allowed to defeat the Devil in the end rather than being carried off to Hell, and in morality plays the Vice (to whom Punch is closely related) often struggled with the Devil in broad comedy.[14]

Satiric Devils like Coleridge's and Shelley's tap into these volatile popular conventions. An overlooked feature of Romantic satanism, such satiric or comic Devils arise as a kind of light effervescence from the deeper cultural phenomena of Miltonic rebellion and the Romantic agony.[15] Even more broadly, the satanism is part of the period's widespread intellectual fascination with the adversarial and the repressed, which reaches a peak in Byron and culminates in Baudelaire. In this broad context, Shelley's fondness for the Devil differs only in the lack of aesthetic success of its representations from Blake's stronger satirical advocacy in, say, *The Marriage of Heaven and Hell*. In both cases the intent is in part to destabilize conventional oppositions by exposing the demons at the top, those who maintain the status quo. Or the strategy is to exploit what Shelley called "the weak place of the popular religion—the vulnerable belly of the crocodile,"[16] the waning belief in the Devil among modern believers, which seemed to him a perfect inroad for subversion. Satire was well prepared, given its long history, to expose the displacement function of the orthodox Devil, to collapse the comfortable distance between humankind and its projected accuser.

As historians have noted, 1811–12 saw a revival of opposition to the blasphemy law, an opposition helped along by Eaton's prosecution.[17] When the Unitarians challenged the law in 1813, Lord Eldon countered by pushing through an act that repealed the law of 1697 but retained the common-law prohibition against blasphemous libel. In subsequent decades, ultraradical groups deliberately made strategic blasphemy a common practice. The defiantly blasphemous sermons heard in some radical chapels ultimately had ties to the anticlericalism of seventeenth-century Dissent, but such violations were given a new currency by the struggle over the law. In 1819, for example, Robert Wedderburn's Spencean congregation voted "to reject the idea of the existence of the Devil because it 'could be of no use except to the clergy of whom he was the principle [*sic*] support.'. . . "[18] Blasphemous opposition sometimes took the form of satirical or burlesque "theatrical buffoonery," as in the case of

Wedderburn's writings and oratory, or the popular radical Samuel Waddington, who printed hoaxing publications and staged various public performances — protests involving costumes and props. "Waddington was a
committed and able radical, respected by associates and opponents alike,
but his style of radicalism was saturnalian and burlesque" — and in this he
was not merely a colorful anomaly.[19] Satire, like blasphemy and noncon-
formity in general, was a natural component of such subversion.

Shelley never fully shared the politics of this radical underworld. As we
have seen, his one known appearance among the radical orators at the
British Forum may have been something of a lark (see Chapter 1). But as
his interest in Eaton, Cobbett, Hone, and Richard Carlile indicates, he
followed the movements and occasionally drew upon the tactics of this
milieu — especially when young and styling himself a fervent combatant
of "superstition." Such radical blasphemy is part of the context for his
1812 satire. His Devil is domesticated to the extent that (like "farmer"
George III, who was known for his interest in gardening) he becomes a
"man" of the soil, an "agriculturalist."[20] Shelley exploits the satiric potential of this idea by making the Devil tend "cattle" who collude in their
own subservience, behaving as if they did not want to penetrate his disguise.

> He peeped into each hole, to each chamber stole,
>   His promising live-stock to view;
> Grinning applause, he just showed them his claws,
> And they shrank with affright from his ugly sight,
>   Whose work they delighted to do.

> (ll. 23–27)

This kind of double entendre ("Satan poked his red nose into crannies
so small" [l. 32]) is only distantly related to *The Rape of the Lock;* it more
closely resembles an obscene schoolboy joke. But its ostensible purpose is
to expose the corruption behind the appearance of the "innocents" in the
Devil's stable. Public exposé is the poem's primary and oft-repeated trope,
from the priest who denies "the Tempter" — but sups and rides with him
(VIII), to the corrupt and corpulent court (IX; XIV–XV), to the brotherhood of the lawyer and the viper (XVIII), and the bishops and lawyers
protected by their habiliment (XXI). The ballad points a finger at the
numerous bedfellows of "Satan," and its political message is that such

alliances have evil consequences—war, inequality, and poverty—because the Devil always feeds his favorites on the blood of the oppressed. The social world, as seen by the satire, amounts to one great underground economy, with the Devil in control. Everyone thrives because "every gown, and every wig,/Hides the safe thrift of Hell within" (ll. 103–04). The paradox is further illustrated in lines that foreshadow Shelley's final satire, *Swellfoot the Tyrant*.

> Thus pigs were never counted clean,
>   Although they dine on finest corn;
> And cormorants are sin-like lean,
>   Although they eat from night to morn.

> (ll. 105–08)

In the end, the Devil throws *off* his disguise as a signal for his servant to do the same. There will come a day of truth when the statesman and the apostate poet ("Pale Loyalty, his guilt-steeled brow/With wreaths of gory laurel crowned") will be seen for what they are, in the company of demons, fiends, and "the hellhounds, Murder, Want, and Woe" (ll. 114–27). At this point in the ballad (ll. 128–31) there is an abrupt tonal shift, from satire to a kind of crude sublimity, a portentous rumble that only briefly postpones all Hell's breaking out of its "adamantine limits" (l. 135). The poem concludes: "were the Devil's sight as keen/As Reason's penetrating eye," he could see that his days were numbered (ll. 136–37).

Equivocation as to the duration of the current regime will become in Shelley's later poetry a crucial skeptical strategy against the uncertainties of history—part of the complex orientation Jerome McGann has referred to as his "futurism."[21] But it is important to recognize that Shelley in 1811 has already discovered something like this strategy and that he is deliberately experimenting with the abrupt intrusion of a positive prophetic voice into an otherwise cynical, satirical description of Hell on earth—and Hell looks a great deal like London on any given day. This kind of visionary medley finds its ultimate expression in *The Triumph of Life*, and the dialectical mixture of tones and modes becomes one of Shelley's most important satirical devices, especially in *The Mask of Anarchy*.

Shelley's next major satire after *The Devil's Walk* was *Peter Bell the Third*. Composed in 1819, just before *The Mask*, it is much less dialectical and more fundamentally ambivalent in its mixture of tones. But *Peter Bell the Third* fully shares the earlier satire's conviction that Hell *is* everyday social hypocrisy, that the Devil is the gentlemanly projection of those with a controlling interest in the social order. Sometimes he is also "a bard bartering rhymes/For sack" (like Southey), or a "statesman," or a "swindler," or a "thief," or even a "slop-merchant"—never anything so magnificent as a fallen angel (ll. 82–92). The point is that "He is—what we are" (l. 81). As the preface dryly comments, "it is not necessary to consider Hell and the Devil as supernatural machinery" (p. 324). The Devil is "no uncommon creature," but "A toadlike lump of limb and feature,/With mind, and heart, and fancy muddled."

> He was that heavy, dull, cold thing
>   The spirit of evil well may be:
> A drone too base to have a sting;
> Who gluts, and grimes his lazy wing,
>   And calls lust, luxury.

> (ll. 338, 341–42, 343–47)

These lines inevitably echo traditional satires (Pope's "Epistle to Dr. Arbuthnot," for example), but this should not obscure their topical depiction of the Regency as a rule of evil more banal than sublime, a Hell that is banality itself. Such evil is all too human, not attributable to a metaphysical agent—or scapegoat.

• • •

It is only logical that Shelley should think once again of the Devil when confronting the fact of Wordsworth's *Peter Bell: A Tale in Verse*, the conversion story of a North Country potter who is frightened and reformed by a confrontation with the joint forces of Nature and Methodism. Begun in 1798, it was not published until 1819, and the delay became a separate subject of ridicule after Wordsworth claimed that he had been working on the poem all those years in order to "fit it for filling *permanently* a station, however humble, in the Literature of our Country."[22] By 1819 Wordsworth made a broad target. Even the hint of a forthcoming poem could provoke satire. John Hamilton Reynolds parodied *Peter Bell* before it was published, in a skit entitled "Peter Bell. Lyrical Ballad," a parody which Shelley probably read before writing his own in the early autumn of 1819; at that time, however, like Reynolds, he probably had not yet read Wordsworth's poem.[23]

Peter Bell the Third was therefore Shelley's response to Wordsworth's work in general, but it was directed by Reynolds's and Leigh Hunt's responses to target especially *Peter Bell*'s supposed religious cant and metaphysical supernaturalism. Ironically, Wordsworth's poem was then published with a prose dedication and a verse prologue that made a point of its naturalism; like earlier lyrical ballads, it was composed to show that the imagination could work without the "intervention of supernatural agency," Wordsworth said (p. 331). In the prologue the narrator rejects a tempting flight in a crescent-moon boat and comes down to earth to tell his tale of a "sympathetic heart" and a "soul of power," qualities opposed to the magical powers of romance (ll. 139–40).

Although later readers can appreciate Wordsworth's ethnographic experiments with popular beliefs, these would have seemed objectionably disingenuous to Shelley, coming as they did in a poem whose action is effected through the agency of "Dread Beings" (l. 774), the "Spirits of the Mind" (l. 783), or the psychological force of fear and a Methodist preacher shouting "Repent! repent!" (l. 946). Part of the effect of the poem's use of popular ballad conventions was to ally it with popular superstition. In fact, Wordsworth deliberately allied the poem with evangelical Christianity—a conventionally English kind of "supernatural intervention."

> "A potent wand doth Sorrow wield;
> What spell so strong as guilty Fear!
> Repentance is a tender Sprite;
> If aught on earth have heavenly might,
> 'Tis lodged within her silent tear."

> (*Peter Bell*, ll. 146–50)

As I argued in Chapter 2, Shelley's own most aggressive satirical writings draw upon the Romantic interest in superstition to naturalize (and socialize)—but still deploy—curses. Wordsworth's *Peter Bell*, like "Goody Blake and Harry Gill," for example, pursues a similar anthropological interest in superstition.[24] Shelley's use of superstition in his early satires is uncomfortably close to Wordsworth's use of superstition in *Peter Bell*—a fact of which Shelley was (probably) ironically unaware when composing *Peter Bell the Third*. This makes all the more significant and revealing the antisuperstition of Shelley's satire, suggesting even more strongly Shelley's inherent closeness to the "Wordsworthian" qualities he would attack. Only the ends, not the means, of the two poets actually differed in this regard: Harry Gill is scared sick by the magic of a cursing prayer; Peter Bell is frightened by the curse of damnation in the form of Methodist sermon rhetoric; Shelley's satiric targets are terrified into psychologically "damning" themselves. The antipathetic magic in both cases is remarkably similar.

Shelley would also have objected to another feature of *Peter Bell:* its implied opposition of sublime imagination and religious piety. Shelley privileged imagination as the force that keeps alive political hope, the link between the esoteric and the mundane. An instructive counterexample to *Peter Bell* in this regard, though not a parody in the manner of *Peter Bell the Third,* is "The Witch of Atlas," probably a more direct answer to Wordsworth's uses of superstition than *Peter Bell the Third.*[25] The witch is essentially amoral, flying beyond guilt or sorrow, good and evil, a figure for the free play of the mind over and above the inevitable sufferings of humanity. Shelley implies in this response that Wordsworth had made a fetish of suffering and guilt, rather than seeing them as psychosocial evils to be eventually overcome. But behind this stands Shelley's awareness that his own curse poems—and by implication any satire—might be accused of committing the same error, of reifying another's tendencies to self-destruction by relying on the social dynamic of "superstition." In his critique of Wordsworth, Shelley walks a fine line, accusing him in effect of having rejected the wrong *kind* of transcendence. "The Witch of Atlas" makes it clear that Shelley wishes to substitute his own kind of rhetoric, his own psychological manipulations of the reader, for Wordsworth's— those he deems imaginatively stimulating rather than piously dulling.

Belatedly following Reynolds's protagonist Peter Bell (the "First") and Wordsworth's own (ironically, forced by Reynolds's into "Second" place), Shelley's Peter Bell is therefore the "Third," and his dedication makes a blasphemous joke of this dubious lineage: "if you know one Peter Bell, you know three Peter Bells; they are not one but three, not three but one" (p. 324). This kind of mock typology we have already encountered in "Proteus Wordsworth," but in this case the mockery also comments on the uncertain relation of parodies to parodied, the question of which is prefiguration and which is fulfillment of the type. The verse prologue strains the joke a bit, concluding with a denial of orthodox metaphysics.

> And the third is he who has
> O'er the grave been forced to pass
> To the other side, which is,—
> Go and try else,—just like this.

(ll. 23–26)

Shelley's Peter is converted after having been "With fresh-imported Hell-fire warmed" (l. 2), but his election is, at best, an open question. First a pious Methodist, he is "predestined to damnation" (l. 20), which allows Shelley to send his picaresque antihero to Hell to serve the Devil—first as footman and later as Poet Laureate. The poem is divided into seven sections, beginning with "DEATH," and culminating with "DAMNATION" and "DOUBLE DAMNATION." Most of the action takes place in a Hell that it is only a thinly veiled contemporary London, with its society, literature, and—worst of all—reviews.

Much of this mockery is aimed at Calvinist theological doctrine, but as it was commonly associated with Methodism's social influence. Historian Elie Halévy is usually credited with the thesis that Methodism worked to co-opt dissent among the poor and working classes in England, and thus prevented radical change.[26] Recent revisionist historians have questioned the hegemony of this interpretation, suggesting that it is "Whiggish" in its assumption of inevitable progress (toward radicalism).[27] Nineteenth-century Methodism was obviously a complex social phenomenon that changed over time, had *multiple* and sometimes contradictory social effects, and was related to changes outside the established Church as well as to developments within it. It was even for some the religion of the radical underworld.[28]

It is clear, however, that Shelley (along with a great many of the most ardent political reformers) saw Methodism in simpler terms, as a prop for power and monarchical orthodoxy. This perception, whatever the actual effects of preachers and meetinghouses, must be treated as an important historical fact. The term "Methodism" was often used rather loosely by radicals, to refer to a range of diverse evangelical practices supporting the dominant "political theology" of Church and State.[29] It was in this mode that Shelley remarked on the sad fate of James Montgomery, the Sheffield poet who first went mad, and only *then*, Shelley said, was truly prepared to become a Methodist.[30] In satirizing the "enormous folly" of Peter Bell the Third's "Baptisms, Sunday-schools and Graves" (ll. 614–15), Shelley is merely joining an already vocal anti-Methodist chorus. But there is little question that his satire followed the immediate example of Leigh Hunt, who had written a series of articles (eventually turned into a book) on the subject, "An Attempt to Shew the Folly and Danger of Methodism" (1808).[31]

Significantly, in the first of these articles (8 May 1808, pp. 301–03), Hunt attacks the Methodists for their intolerance and "supernaturals" (p. 301), their "vulgar and vehement" preaching, and their recourse to the threat of damnation and "violence" in the service of persuasion (p. 302). In fact, the charges Hunt levels against the sect bear an uncanny resemblance to the negative effects of satire as Shelley saw them. In this context, for Shelley to write a satire of Wordsworth's literary Methodism was a delicate exercise, a matter of fighting fire (and brimstone) with fire. Hunt's essay paints the Methodist preachers as indulging in a kind of hypocritical—and basically satirical—rhetoric.

> I confess that I have not vowed, like Mr. Wesley, never to laugh; and if some of these opinions should rouse in me a spirit of ridicule, I beg leave to remind the candour of the Methodists that all their great preachers and patterns have indulged in a raillery rather boisterous than otherwise. . . .
>
> (p. 301)

One such preacher was known as "a Theological Buffoon," says Hunt; others have pronounced those who would not be converted "damned fools and sinners"; and "Calvin himself called his opponents all sorts of beasts and devils" (p. 301).

The importance to Shelley of Hunt's writings in *The Examiner* can hardly be exaggerated. By the time of *Peter Bell the Third*, these appeared as part of the larger context of an ongoing battle between partisan journals. In an article in *The Examiner* on 2 May 1819 (pp. 282–83), Hunt calls Wordsworth's *Peter Bell* "another didactic little horror . . . founded on the bewitching principles of fear, bigotry, and diseased impulse." He then quotes the stanza from *Peter Bell* that Shelley used for the ironic epigraph of his satire:

> Is it a party in a parlour—
> Crammed just as they on earth were crammed,
> Some sipping punch—some sipping tea;

> But, as you by their faces see,
> All silent and all—damned!

Hunt construes this as evidence of Wordsworth's antisocial tendencies, and quips that—based on this stanza, at least—Peter Bell's crime seems to have been that he was too social. In one sense, Shelley's poem simply elaborates on this criticism. Wordsworth's ballad, Hunt goes on, supports Methodism and thus supports "the philosophy of violence and hopelessness. It is not teaching ignorance but scourging it" (p. 283). Note how Hunt links violence (even the moral violence of the righteous "scourge") with the social effect of hopelessness. This will pose very serious problems for Shelley when he comes to join the battle in satire, a mode whose conventional violence, its moralistic scourge, is at odds with Shelley's program of reform. This problem is at the heart of *Peter Bell the Third*'s ambivalence. How can it wield a rhetorical scourge like Wordsworth's— and like the Methodists'—and still claim to incite hope and promote change?

The following week's *Examiner* (9 May 1819, pp. 302–03) raised the stakes, explicitly accusing Wordsworth of a kind of literary Methodism, teaching submission and making his readers "timid, servile, and (considering his religion) selfish" (p. 302). Shelley is then held up as the contrasting example, championed for *improving* his readers by making them "infinitely social." "You might be made to worship a devil by the process of Mr. Wordsworth's philosophy; by that of Mr. Shelley you might re-seat a dethroned goodness" (p. 303). The reviewer's real complaint against Wordsworth is that he "has become hopeless of this world, and therefore would make everybody else so," but he ends by claiming to regret the "odious" opposition between the two poets who should have been allies. *The Examiner* sets up the same oppositions—Shelley versus Wordsworth, the social versus the selfish—which Shelley's satire adopts and then must struggle with.

These oppositions were being exploited on the Tory side, as well, in *The Quarterly Review*'s infamous article by John Taylor Coleridge on *The Revolt of Islam* (21 April 1819, pp. 460–71). The reviewer observes that Wordsworth's "religious mind" must be wounded to see the abuse of his philosophy by the Byron-Shelley-Hunt circle, "this miserable crew of atheists or pantheists" (p. 461). Shelley's radical bent is to blame civil and religious institutions for evil, the reviewer notes, when in fact those institutions "are designed to regulate the conduct of man here, and his hopes in a hereafter" (p. 463). In both *The Examiner* and *The Quarterly Review* the issue is hope and reform—whether poetry should encourage its readers to place their hopes in this world or in the next. Shelley, the reviewer says, can offer only dangerously heretical counsel to his readers, as he does in *The Revolt of Islam*.

> "Reproach not thine own soul, but know thyself;
> *Nor hate another's crime, nor loathe thine own.*
> It is the dark idolatry of self
> Which, when our thoughts and actions once are gone,
> Demands that man should weep, and bleed, and groan."[32]

The reviewer quotes these exhortative lines (the italics are *The Quarterly*'s) in order to accuse Shelley of selfishness and of inducing hopelessness in his readers—precisely the claims Hunt sets out to reverse. The ironic inversions of Shelley's dramatic lines (their paradoxical charge, for example, that it is actually *self-idolatry* to demand repentance of oneself) are easily twisted against their author, so that "know thyself" and "dark idolatry" are made, ironically, to seem unwitting self-chastisements. The attack is brought home by further innuendo about Shelley's private life, and then the review ends with a hyperbolic admonition equating the atheist poet with the Egyptians drowned by God's wrath in the Red Sea.

My purpose in quoting from these reviews is to situate Shelley's satire—and his public authorial identity—in the milieu of partisan journalism at its most specific and personal point of contact for him. Shelley wrote *Peter Bell the Third* in part to enter these controversies over selfishness and social good, and in so doing he placed the poem in a magnetized field of binary oppositions. Even *The Examiner* reviews, which set themselves against the religious doctrine of damnation, work rhetorically by opposing Shelley (whose poetry "may re-seat a dethroned goodness") to Wordsworth (whose poetry might lead the reader "to worship a devil"). In Shelley's poem these adopted oppositions become a formal and thematic problem to be wrestled with, but they nevertheless remain a determining force in its makeup. Shelley referred to *Peter Bell the Third* as a "party squib."[33] But instead of using this remark to dismiss the poem, as many critics have followed Shelley in doing, I want to suggest that we emphasize his word "party" as a way to see how the satire in fact focuses the conflict between Shelley and Wordsworth on the basic problem underlying partisan polemic, on what the poem figures as the problem of "damnation."

Damnation is obviously the satire's theme and obsession, from the mocking section titles ("Part Sixth: DAMNATION," "Part Seventh: DOUBLE DAMNATION") to the epigraph, Wordsworth's party-of-the-damned stanza. To understand this, we need to remember that Byron's satire on Southey and the other Lake Poets, "The Vision of Judgment," also turns on the question of salvation and damnation, mocking Southey's own magisterial last judgment of George III while itself refusing to damn anyone—except, of course, figuratively: in literary and political terms.

13.

"God save the king!" it is a large economy
  In God to save the like; but if he will
Be saving, all the better; for not one am I
  Of those who think damnation better still:
I hardly know too if not quite alone am I
  In this small hope of bettering future ill
By circumscribing, with some slight restriction,
The eternity of Hell's hot jurisdiction.

14.

I know this is unpopular; I know
  'Tis blasphemous; I know one may be damned
For hoping no one else may e'er be so. . . .

(ll. 97–107)[34]

Readers are accustomed to finding the tone of Byron's poetry complexly self-referential, canny in its deployment of the self-regarding speaker. But Byron may in this instance owe something to Shelley's example. These lines recall Shelley's conception of the ideal meliorist who resists orthodoxy by rejecting damnation, one of those who are condemned for rejecting the doctrine of absolute condemnation. In fact the two satires, *Peter Bell the Third* and "The Vision of Judgment," grow out of the same polemical milieu in which Leigh Hunt produced his journalism. "The Vision" was published after Shelley's death by Byron and Hunt in *The Liberal*. In reviewing it, *The Examiner* (13 October 1822) again draws the familiar battle lines, arguing that Byron allows the King into Heaven, whereas Southey would be sure to send Napoleon straight to Hell.

In 1816 *The Examiner* reprinted Coleridge's "Fire, Famine, and Slaughter" in order deliberately to taunt the poet. Coleridge then reprinted the poem in *Sibylline Leaves* (1817), where its "Apologetic Preface" explains that he had never intended *literally* the poem's closing damnation of Pitt, in which "Fire" is allowed the last joke (she will "Cling to him everlastingly").[35] On the contrary, Coleridge claims, he would not wish to damn the Devil himself. But this defense restricts itself to the charge of literal damning. A satirical poem makes possible the pleasures of a nonliteral damnation. Like a parody of Dante's perfect literary Hell, this kind of satiric caricature offers a perpetual arena of imagined retribution.

Peter Bell the Third declares outright, " 'Tis a lie to say God damns!" (l. 222), and asserts instead that in polite London, at least, all "are damned by one another,/By none other are they damned" (ll. 220–21). In Shelley's poem the very term "damned" keeps slipping, following the vagaries of popular usage, to function first as an oath, then as a mere expletive or empty epithet, then as a synonym for "doomed," or a figurative explanation of psychological torment. But it refuses to mean (as Shelley had noted elsewhere) what Dr. Johnson said it meant, that is, simply "Sent to Hell and punished everlastingly."[36] Damnation is universally distributed here, and it takes effect immediately, in this world. Most important, the poem makes it clear that damnation is fundamentally a self-inflicted condition—a way of casting oneself out of any possible paradise.

> Statesmen damn themselves to be
>   Cursed; and lawyers damn their souls
> To the auction of a fee;
>   Churchmen damn themselves to see
>   God's sweet love in burning coals.

> (ll. 227–31)

In each case self-damnation puts one outside and at odds with the benefits of community. The key question is whether belonging to a community is seen as a potential paradise or an irredeemable hell.

> And some few, like we know who,
>   Damned—but God alone knows why—
> To believe their minds are given
>   To make this ugly Hell a Heaven;
>   In which faith they live and die.

> (ll. 242–46)

Shelley obviously means to include himself in the beleaguered insiders' club ("we know who") of the "few" reformers and meliorists. Elsewhere he names Coleridge as a lost leader.

> This was a man who might have turned
>   Hell into Heaven—and so in gladness
> A Heaven unto himself have earned;
> But he in shadows undiscerned
>   Trusted,—and damned himself to madness.

> (ll. 383–87)

The price of working to ameliorate suffering may be personal despair.

The line between the reformers' "faith" in perfectibility and Coleridge's trust in "shadows undiscerned" is a fine one. There is something in Shelley's temperament that gives him a special affinity with this philosophical elder poet, and the danger of idealism—like the danger of self-sacrificing meliorism—is one to which Shelley is always prey. The following lines are attributed to Coleridge in Shelley's satire, but with minor adjustments, they could easily describe Shelley's own attitudes:

> He spoke of poetry, and how
>   "Divine it was—a light—a love—
> A spirit which like wind doth blow
> As it listeth, to and fro;
>   A dew rained down from God above

> "A power which comes and goes like dream,
>   And which none can ever trace—
> Heaven's light on Earth—Truth's brightest beam."

> (ll. 388–95)

"A power which comes and goes . . . " obviously echoes the "Hymn to Intellectual Beauty" and "Mont Blanc," and Shelley's relationship to the target of his satire here is extremely close. His attitude toward Coleridge has become a great deal more complicated since imitating "Fire, Famine, and Slaughter" and "The Devil's Thoughts." In 1819, Shelley knows very well that in a sense his own poetry also encourages a reliance on "shadows undiscerned"—on what is yet "unapprehended" and must therefore be projected or imagined.

Shelley's close affinities with his targets, the sense that in the satire he has "turned upon Wordsworth the critical scrutiny which one poet turns upon another who can help him—whose problems bear on his own," was first noted by F. R. Leavis and has been discussed again by William Keach, as Shelley's "reflexive dilemma."[37] Both critics imply that Shelley at least partly recognized the closeness, yet (as a result) sought to establish the difference between himself and the other poets. The passage to which both refer comes in "Part Fourth" of Shelley's satire, "SIN," after we have seen the ridiculous Peter Bell the Third damned and made "a footman in the Devil's service" (l. 264).

> All things that Peter saw and felt
>   Had a peculiar aspect to him;
> And when they came within the belt
> Of his own nature, seemed to melt
>   Like cloud to cloud, into him. . . .

(ll. 273–77)

In Peter, the "outward world" blends into himself, leading to egotism and scorn for more mundane persons.

> Such were his fellow servants; thus
>   His virtue, like our own, was built
> Too much on that indignant fuss
> Hypocrite Pride stirs up in us
>   To bully one another's guilt.

(ll. 288–92)

The gestural "like our own" recalls the identification of the Devil as "what we are" and would seem to include Shelley in his own critique. For the satirist to include himself in his own satire has been conventional at least since Horace, and Byron made it his primary satiric stance. But Shelley's passage seems to be questioning satire as a genre, to be testing the limits of *Peter Bell the Third*'s ability to escape from the role of "bully."

One way it attempts to escape is through mixing encomium with its satire, praise with its punishment.

> He had a mind which was somehow

> At once circumference and centre
> Of all he might or feel or know;
> Nothing ever went out, although
>   Something did ever enter.
>
> He had as much imagination
>   As a pint-pot:—he never could
> Fancy another situation
> From which to dart his contemplation,
>   Than that wherein he stood.
>
> Yet his was individual mind,
>   And new created all he saw
> In a new manner, and refined
> Those new creations, and combined
>   Them, by a master-spirit's law. . . .

(ll. 293–307)

These stanzas weave from praise to blame and back again in a way that requires close and subtle attention. On one level, Shelley joins the conventional attack on Wordsworth's choice of rustic subjects; Peter's imagination is compared to that of a "pint-pot"—the nickname for a *seller* of beer, as well a container for the liquor that is presumably the inspiration for (and the measure of) such coarse imaginations. But the rest of the passage suggests a more serious critique, which never denies what Shelley's own note calls Peter/Wordsworth's "strong but circumscribed sensibility" (p. 342).

The overdetermined figure of "circumference and centre" (which, in this form, has roots at least as early as medieval theology) was used by Shelley in seemingly contradictory ways. But after encountering it in *Peter Bell the Third*, it is striking to find him using it with such positive connotations in *A Defence of Poetry*, praising poetry itself as "something divine . . . at once the centre and circumference of knowledge."[38] Its concomitant ethical effect is that it promotes the "going out of our own nature" that is the prerequisite for morality (pp. 487–88). This expansive activity is paradoxically the result of the strong gravitational force of individual poetic thoughts.

Poetry enlarges the circumference of the imagination by replenishing it

with thoughts of ever new delight, which have the power of attracting and
assimilating to their own nature all other thoughts, and which form new
intervals and interstices whose void forever craves fresh food.

(p. 488)

This well-known passage is a positive inversion of Peter Bell the Third's
negative capacity to draw the world into "the belt/Of his own nature." Is
Shelley so respectful of Wordsworth's powers that he can only satirize
them in an image of positive poetic strength? Does this perhaps represent
a kind of failure of satiric nerve that becomes an excuse for the elder poet
instead? On the contrary, this would be to assume too much systematic
consistency in the circle figure, the significance of which in each case may
depend less on its simple valuation—whether it is to be read as "positive"
or "negative"—and more on the general dynamic of the figure itself as
Shelley usually employed it, that is to say, as an allegory of strong competing forces in opposition.

An illuminating use of the center-circumference figure occurs in Shelley's satirical essay "On the Devil, and Devils," which half mockingly
proposes a Dantesque cosmological scheme:

Shall we suppose that the Devil occupies the centre and God the circumference of existence, and that one urges inwards with the centripetal,
whilst the other is perpetually struggling outwards from the narrow focus
with the centrifugal force, and from their perpetual conflict results that
mixture of good and evil, harmony and discord, beauty and deformity,
production and decay, which are the general laws of the moral and material world?

(*The Complete Works*, p. 100)

Again we are reminded of the mind of Peter Bell the Third: "Nothing
went ever out, although/Something did ever enter." It would seem that
Peter/Wordsworth's problem is that his imagination is deficient in its
centrifugal effects: it draws the world it perceives into itself, as Shelley
believes all truly poetic minds must, but it cannot complete the cycle
and extend its own limited circumference back out into the surrounding
world—especially the social world.

Shelley remained concerned about the epistemological paradox that
the mind forms the subjective limit of the individual's experience of the

outside world.[39] But he always held that an ethical poetics must involve the gradual centrifugal expansion of that epistemological limit, and sought to replace the notion of mind as enclosure with a figure of mind as field of interaction with the world. He would supplant the image of a static container ("pint-pot") with that of an ongoing social process. His use of the center-circumference figure ought to be compared to Wordsworth's description of the mind of the autobiographical Wanderer (*The Excursion* IV), a mind/heart supposedly perfected by constriction, until it becomes a solitary still-point transcending the changes of the revolving world: "The centre of this world, about which/Those revolutions of disturbances/Still roll."[40] This comes close to making center and circumference signify "mind" and "world," respectively, and to setting the two in a static and balanced relationship ("just equipoise") of mutual exclusion.

This is precisely the distinction Shelley seizes upon in his satire: Peter Bell the Third retreats from disturbing social process into solitary stagnation—his poetry is paralyzing because his imagination cannot move outward from its own center of identity, and thus cannot move anyone else. In the poem this problem is figured, paradoxically, as a *negative* centrifugal effect on the surrounding world, spreading outward from friends to printers, to reviewers, like a plague or a curse. The paradox is that this is accomplished by a soporific "essence of his dullness . . . /Concentered and compressed" in Peter's verse (and prose), a "drowsy curse" or "contagious atmosphere," a "power to infect, and to infest" (ll. 733–37). Through the process of Peter's being published and read, what might have remained a personal problem in the "concentered" mind of the poet spreads out in widening concentric circles, to depopulate the community and finally to bring about an utter silence, the absolute negation of poetry.

> Seven miles above—below—around—
>   This pest of dulness holds its sway:
> A ghastly life without a sound;
> To Peter's soul the spell is bound—
>   How should it ever pass away?

> (ll. 768–72)

As in *The Dunciad*, here "dulness" stands for a chaos of uncreation that takes apart the life of the community. But whereas Pope blames the dunces out on the fringe, those who deviate too widely from the commonly accepted norm and pull away from the authorizing center of poetic values, Shelley blames the opposite cause: the widespread plague—reaching from the Lake Country to London—of adherence to the "norms" themselves, an increasingly *stable* consensus, loyalty to the center. Shelley's word for this is "dulness"—an ironic appropriation of Pope's term applied with the purpose of stimulating more imaginative, radical poetry.[41]

Wordsworth's "dulness" is a kind of self-damnation, the banal negation of poetic power. The final question of Shelley's satire ("How should it ever pass away?") is in this sense no more "rhetorical" than the similar question at the end of the "Ode to the West Wind." Or is it rhetorical in the sense that it is meant as a gesture outward, away from the poem itself and toward social effects? The question, at any rate, is implicitly aimed at poets. "Cursed" is also a synonym for damned, and since the curse of "dulness" is a self-inflicted damnation, the only cure must come from Wordsworth himself. In order to "defeat the curse" of epistemological limits in poetry, to write with anything like a beneficial social effect, one must reject the ideology of damnation for oneself and others. Shelley shares with Wordsworth the idealist Romantic assumption that the poetic mind is the emanating center of the social field. But he differs as to the direction poetic energy should flow: outward to widen the circumference rather than inward to draw everyone into an inclusive Self.

• • •

Shelley never suggests that Wordsworth's poetry has no public effect. On the contrary, Peter's dull verse moves out from the center of his limited imagination—the epicenter being the Devil—in ever-widening circles to anesthetize the entire community, in a kind of parody of Shelley's early aspirations for his own career: instead of "Heavenly medicine," Peter dispenses a destructive opiate. It dulls instead of enlivening imagination and thus turns out, in the long run, to be poison.

Peter's infectious "pest," in fact, recalls Wordsworth's very public celebration of "the God of peace and love" in the much-criticized "Thanksgiving Ode" on the victory at Waterloo (1816): "He guides the Pestilence . . . /The region that in hope was ploughed/His drought consumes, his mildew taints with death."[42] In Shelley's diagnosis the pestilence has its origin in the poet's perverted logos, the bad words and faulty reason of Peter, as exemplified in his own "Thanksgiving Ode"—written in this case "to the Devil."

> "May Carnage and Slaughter,
> Thy niece and thy daughter,
> May Rapine and Famine,
> Thy gorge ever cramming,
>   Glut thee with living and dead!"

(ll. 636–40)

This song comes at the climax of Shelley's satire, simultaneously alluding to Wordsworth's Waterloo ode and to Peterloo, a real-life example of poetic dullness and of the kind of social evil it supports.

Shelley was not alone in his disgust with Wordsworth's ode, especially with its infamous line on the holy necessity of war: "Yea, Carnage is thy daughter!" (*The Poetical Works*, p. 155). That Shelley was profoundly troubled by the "Carnage" line is revealed in other texts. He attempted a more ribald response in private, as it were, in the rough-draft notebook containing the "Proteus" fragment—the "Fragment of a Feast in Heaven." It is preceded in the notebook by these penciled lines:

> A Poet of the finest water
> Says that Carnage is Gods daughter
>   — ~~as~~
> This poet lieth as   I take
> Under an immense mistake
> As many a man before has
>   done
> Who thinks his spouse's child
>   his own.[43]

This provocatively puts the lie to Wordsworth (at least momentarily, until the meaning of "lieth" is stabilized with the following line's "Under"), and scatters other insults in the bargain. For example, Wordsworth may think he is godlike and yet be like a foolish cuckold (the patrimony of his Carnage being in question). Even in this doggerel Shelley's view of Wordsworth is obviously ambivalent. Such carnage could never really be the product of Wordsworth's mind, it implies, any more than it can be divine in origin.

As if this blasphemous gossip were not enough, Shelley drafted a fragmentary epithalamium on subsequent pages, using Wordsworth's Carnage and its suggestion of various unholy alliances, an inchoate depiction of a feast at the marriage of Heaven and Hell. Probably Carnage herself (God's daughter) was to have been the bride—and the feast recalls the "gormandizing" of the Devil/Moloch in *Peter Bell the Third*.

> ~~young~~ hydras hashed in
> ~~grilled~~
> Sucking
> ~~There was seraphym~~ & sulphur
> in Gods wrath wine
> Cherubs ~~& roast chains~~
> with [? some ~~bitters~~]
> stewed
> ~~Flakes of flame~~ that miss might
> Black-fire pies [? mull] for
> Syllabus of grace divine
> For the rose lipped Angel misses,
> ~~Coarser food~~ food
> Such coarse might spoil their
> kisses

(ll. 1–6)[44]

This is satire with the gloves off, but it veers away from personal attack and is thus free to be in bad taste.

Shelley's "Banquet in Hell," the fragment is traditionally satiric in an important sense. Since Juvenal and Petronius (and through Swift), satire has conventionally dealt in what is disgusting, especially in the spectacle of grotesque feasting and gluttony.[45] In Shelley's day this side of classical satire was usually expurgated, which would have made it even more attractive in his mind for the intended effect of shocking his readers. He must have known, however, that these lines could not have been published in Regency England. The fragment may have been originally intended, like the forbidden jottings of numerous other writers, as a personal outlet for himself and his friends; but this is also just the sort of writing Shelley might have imagined himself producing in blatant defiance of power, not so far from "Ode to the Devil" in *Peter Bell the Third*. The deliberate attempt to shock implies at least a desire for an audience; it depends upon going too far in some readers' eyes. It intentionally violates the normative standards of the community which could celebrate Wordsworth for his lines on "Carnage." All of this should remind us of the libel-baiting satire of *The Devil's Walk*, but its actual historical effect is to impress upon us how far Shelley restrained his virulence in the satires he finished, published, or tried to get published.

Shelley's "reflexive dilemma" when facing the older poets is emphasized by the apparent lack of subtlety of the "Feast in Heaven." Aimed at Wordsworth's poetic violence (and the sanctioning of political violence by his poetry), Shelley's unpublished fragment partakes of the violence it would attack. To satirize, as I have argued, is to invoke the very evil you would do away with and to engage it on its own terms, to replicate what you have targeted. In this sense, Shelley's dilemma is generic. It is not merely a problem of style but of the ethics of rhetoric, a problem bound up with his closeness to his primary targets, who are not moral monsters or literary dunces but poets very much like himself, especially in their idealizing poetic tendencies. The dilemma takes us back to *The Devil's Walk*, which attempted to transpose a mode of the 1790s, a mode associated with the older Romantics in their youth, into the very different Napoleonic era, to make "Heavenly medicine" (to be dispensed in bottles and balloons) out of old poison. Shelley's ambivalent closeness and resistance to the example of the older Romantics, which we first saw in his reaction to Southey, is reflected in his problem with satire as a genre. If Wordsworth is the Devil, and the Devil "is—what we are," then the satiric target, Wordsworth and all that he represents, also becomes "what we are." The reflexive dilemma complicates any easy polemical opposition, and it becomes difficult to distinguish between strong medicine and poison.

Both satires we have been examining accuse their targets of being too "fond of the Devil"—to apply in a slightly different context the phrase Shelley applied to himself in 1812. The Devil is satirized in both poems as an unacknowledged projection of human evil ("what we are"), damnation as a projection of the human propensity to displace this evil onto one another or into metaphysical space ("Hell is a city much like London"). In this sense both satires make recovery of projection their deeper purpose. But Shelley's own fondness for the Devil—his strategic advocacy of the enemy's chosen "Adversary"—traps him into adopting something of the mode of thinking he is attempting to overthrow, especially where his personal animus toward a poet such as Wordsworth is concerned. The basic opposition between election and damnation (of one sort or another) determines a large portion of satiric discourse, and makes extremely difficult any satiric project that would claim to question such categories.

Consider again Shelley's crucial "circumference and centre" paradigm.

Critics have been intrigued by the richness of mixed feelings it implies toward Wordsworth, but in the more blatantly satiric context of the "Essay on Devils," as I have shown, "centre" and "circumference" become metaphorical for a Manichaean opposition between "Devil" and "God." Rather than concluding that there is something inherent in this figure, much less in language itself, that lends itself to this mode of binary thinking, a kind of ineluctable linguistic violence, I would argue instead that there is something historically encoded in certain *uses* of language, in particular in the genre of satire, that implicates the satirist in polemical violence.[46] One of satire's most time-honored (that is, culturally sanctioned) practices is the demonization of the enemy, whether it be aristocratic women, parvenus, foreigners, or selected members of the opposing party. This is a device for reducing someone perceived as a threat, a device indispensable to much satire, broadly conceived, whether virulent propaganda or subtler literary evaluation. A characteristic or role is figured as an essential, inherent, irredeemable violation of the norm, which calls forth an ultimate communal condemnation. It is of course most obvious in the devices of caricature, in which the target ("Yahoo" or "terrorist") is made recognizable by an exaggeration that distorts him so as to render him not only ridiculous (as in the milder forms) but also marginal, ugly, subhumanly contemptible. But even in the loftier realms of literary dispute there is very little satire without some degree of demonization or damnation of this kind.

Now look once more at Cruikshank's graphic satire of Napoleon as the Devil (Figure 2). Superficially, it may resemble Shelley's satiric Devils insofar as it deflates the sublimity of Milton's figure of metaphysical evil. Merely depicting the Devil as vanquished and identifying him with the fallen Napoleon contributes to this effect, even though the iconography is employed with a "wink" that complicates its reception. Despite his cloven hoofs and wings, Napoleon wears his horns like an exotic and ancient helmet, and is in one sense just another inflated dandy. But the more obviously intended effects of the satire—which must be achieved in resistance to the ambiguous tendencies of parody as a mode—are based on unmistakably distinguishing Bonaparte from the Prince, the satirized from the celebrated. This is accomplished through stationing (high and low) and shading (light and dark) as well as less obvious allusions. This kind of popular visual form must be accessible on some level to immediate "reading," at a glance—perhaps in a shop window. Any confusion as to the basic target could blunt its polemic effects.

If Cruikshank's print had tipped the scales of the diminishing comparison too far to one side, if the Devil were humanized (made "what we are") more than the French Emperor were demonized (however comically), then the satire would have "failed" by being too complex, too parodically reflexive, not loyal enough (and it would not have served to refute the charges of blasphemy in the Hone trial). In this way the print merely exaggerates the binary structures of much popular satire, and seen in this context, Shelley's satire in *Peter Bell the Third* seems to be trying to exceed these conventional limits of the genre. But in attempting to have it both ways, his satire splits itself down the middle. It would demonize part of Wordsworth (as Peter) while humanizing the Devil as not just Wordsworth but all of us.

One side of Shelley, especially early in his career or later when facing some personal disappointment, was emotionally drawn to the broad polemical effects of demonization as a tactic of inversion. *Queen Mab* (which he had probably begun around the time *The Devil's Walk* was being distributed) has as its epigraph Voltaire's famous motto, *"Ecrasez l'Infame!"* which Shelley translated on at least one occasion (3 January 1811) as "Crush the Demon" (read: "Christianity").

> Yet here I swear, and as I break my oath may Infinity [*sic*] Eternity blast me, here I swear that never will I forgive Christianity! it is the only point on which I allow myself to encourage revenge. . . . Oh how I wish I *were* the Antichrist, that it were *mine* to crush the Demon, to hurl him to his native Hell never to rise again—I expect to gratify some of this insatiable feeling in Poetry.
>
> (*Letters*, I, 35)

This is the young Shelley at his intemperate gothic worst. He is writing to Hogg about the loss of Harriet Grove, but if we look steadily at this effusion, rather than dismissing it as an embarrassment, we can see that the intensity of his anger runs deeper than the moment, and was eventually to be transmuted into a serious philosophical and theological resentment. Usually this resentment was expressed in terms of ironic inversions, like the transvaluations of "Hell" and "Demon" in the letter.

This is merely one example of a problem central to Romanticism, in which the tactic of radical inversion replicates the polemical structure it would challenge, like Prometheus perpetuating his own torture, calling down a curse (his curse) on himself and those he loves. Too much self-consciousness about the limits of this process and the dangers of such replication, I would suggest, can inhibit conventional satire, which depends upon polarization and the violent projection of personal animus or community ills onto the chosen target. This is the double bind of most of Shelley's satire. On the one hand he would reject demonization as ideologically untenable and rhetorically counterproductive. On the other hand, he is temperamentally attracted to the strong tactic of demonization. His satires, therefore, frequently become awkward experiments in just how far ironic inversions can go before becoming damning of others or themselves. Thus Shelley's satire raises the question of the poet's social responsibility. His satire on Wordsworth is ambivalent, not just because of his mixed feelings for the elder poet but also because of his skepticism toward the authority of the genre itself, his uncertainty as to whether the violent medicine (or poison) of satire can ever contribute to that responsibility.

4 "Paper Warfare" and Single Combat in "A Satire upon Satire"

DURING THE REIGN OF GEORGE III (1760–1820) there were 172 reported duels in England—and a great many more probably went unreported.[1] Weapons were unreliable, and the combatants' intent to harm varied, but 91 of these 172 cases resulted in death. Less than twenty of these murders were ever prosecuted, and only two prosecutions led to the allowable penalty of execution. This officially illegal but ubiquitous practice (begun in its modern form in the seventeenth century) was obviously widespread during the late eighteenth and early nineteenth centuries, and was at least partly sanctioned, sometimes simply winked at by judges (and more often by juries).

By Shelley's time, dueling was not only commonplace, it was highly fashionable. Special dueling pistols had become a status symbol among aristocrats and gentlemen by the 1770s, and sermons and pamphlets campaigning against the fashion proliferated for decades thereafter, as did codes or guides to the proper etiquette and numerous anecdotes of horrifying or interesting duels. An Anti-Dueling Society was formed in 1843,[2] but by then the practice had probably peaked in England and had begun to decline, becoming first an occasional, flamboyant display on the part of a few—including prominent public figures—and eventually a quaint archaism of the old order by the early twentieth century. During its vogue dueling seems to have remained primarily an activity of the upper classes, but it surely included a certain number of the obscure as well as the famous, and it is impossible to generalize about so clandestine an activity. It seems probable, however, that the "vogue" of dueling came after its statistical peak, that the spread of the fashion to some aspiring duelists from the middling and even working classes, for example, marked its decline as a functional, classbound ritual; when the code began to be widely published, it must have lost some of its hold over those who had first created and lived by its unwritten form. The recorded incidents are probably only the tip of an iceberg, only the publicized duels, many of which involved famous politicians and writers or journalists (later in the period they included the occasional tradesman or shopkeeper).

Historically, polemical writing and dueling have been closely related social practices. The era that saw the peak in dueling was also, perhaps not coincidentally, the great age of polemical journalism and partisan reviews. *The Edinburgh Review* was founded in 1802 as a Whig organ; *The Quarterly Review* was begun in 1809, as William Hazlitt said, "not as a corollary" to *The Edinburgh*, "but in contradiction to it."[3] Its Tory founders included the satirist and former editor of the famous *Anti-Jacobin*, William Gifford. Numerous journals joined these two in an unprecedented flood of publication, much of it with pecuniary connections to one party or the other.[4] Even a cursory examination of the period reveals that politics and writing—especially personal satire and libelous journalism—were united in a rich context of public controversy and private revenge. The histories of polemical writing and of the duel form an overlapping context of classbound social conflict, one that is crucial for understanding Shelley's satire, and particularly its concern with the ethical problem of coercion. Between 1818 and 1820 Shelley engaged in a bitter quarrel with Robert Southey, whom he had imitated in his first satire and who had now become Poet Laureate. The conflict led Shelley to draft another satire and—it would appear—to hint at a duel. In what follows, I will focus on this quarrel as it is represented in the poets' correspondence and in Shelley's fragment of "A Satire upon Satire." My purpose will be to situate the personal conflict in the wider social context that includes both satire and dueling, two comparable, culturally sanctioned forms of ritual violence.

• • •

Stories of famous duels form a subgenre of their own in the eighteenth and nineteenth centuries. I will relate a few of these narratives in this chapter because they provide a concrete sense of the rituals involved and the contexts out of which they arose. Many prominent political duelists of the late eighteenth and early nineteenth centuries turn out to be connected to literature or journalism, in many instances including those covering duels for the press as well as those involved in controversies. Take, for example, the case of the famous 1762 battle between John Wilkes, the politician and libelous pamphleteer, and one of his targets, Lord Talbot.[5] Talbot became incensed over an anonymous article in *The North Briton*, the satirical Opposition paper published by Wilkes and Charles Churchill. Wilkes refused to acknowledge the article, so Talbot called him out. After firing his horse pistol and missing, Wilkes approached his opponent, admitted authorship of the disputed article, and the two went to a nearby inn for a drink. A year later Wilkes fought a similar duel with Samuel Martin over another article in *The North Briton*. The quarrel carried over into the House of Commons, Martin challenged Wilkes (with some goading from the latter), and in the ensuing duel Wilkes was wounded. Churchill wrote a political satire on the incident, "The Duellist" (1764), in which Martin is represented as the tool of a cabal in the Commons bent on luring his opponent into an assassination attempt.[6] Wilkes's connections to a partisan publication, the charges of libel, and the involvement of the satirist Churchill (not to mention the notorious "Junius," who also wrote in support of Wilkes) place this kind of duel in a volatile milieu where journalism, satire, and politics overlap.

The most celebrated duel of the era was fought 21 September 1809 (when Shelley was at Eton) between two of England's leading statesmen: George Canning (Foreign Secretary) and Viscount Castlereagh (War Minister). The story of their conflict highlights the ethical nature of debates on dueling.[7] Coleridge lamented that this "disgrace to the nation" was taken so lightly by the press ("not a Breathing of it's hideous Vulgarity & Immorality in any one of the Papers!"), and felt compelled to assure another correspondent (and perhaps himself as well) that the "Country at large" was "a moral Country," despite its misrepresentative government and press.[8]

The actual cause of the dispute was political intrigue, but the impetus was gossip and slander leading to disgrace. Castlereagh discovered that Canning had been maneuvering behind his back over the mishandled Walcheren expedition. When report of this inter-ministerial deceit reached him, Castlereagh called Canning out; they met on Putney Heath, Canning was wounded on the second shot, and the government fell over the ensuing publicity. Both men, having preserved their honor, were out of office (though both later came back in). Coleridge was not alone in his moral revulsion at the event: the Evangelical leader William Wilberforce recorded a similar reaction.[9] Wilberforce's response, like Coleridge's, focused on the deleterious public effect, especially given the notoriety of the participants. Castlereagh and Canning played to a large and interested audience—notice that Coleridge is appalled as much at the press and its readers as at the two combatants, and his reiterated moral protest reminds us that debates about dueling turn on the basic questions of moral philosophy: duty, truth, coercion, and freedom. Dueling was often treated as a kind of extreme test case—played out in the public arena of the courts and the press—for ethical debates.

Three years before, in 1806, the Irish poet (and satirist) Thomas Moore had challenged Francis Jeffrey, editor of *The Edinburgh Review*, over an article.[10] The review called Moore "the most licentious of modern versifiers, and the most poetical of those who, in our times, have devoted their talents to the propagation of immorality"; his work was "a public nuisance."[11] The following month Jeffrey met Moore at Chalk Farm, but just before the men could fire, Bow Street runners intervened. A story soon appeared in the papers that Jeffrey's pistol had been found to be unloaded. Moore was humiliated and signed a public statement denying this "falsehood"—and the implication that he had rigged the encounter. Moore and Jeffrey soon made peace (the former later contributed to *The Edinburgh*), but the botched affair was ridiculed for years thereafter. Byron mocked it in *English Bards and Scotch Reviewers*:

> Can none remember that eventful day,
> That ever glorious, almost fatal fray,
> When Little's leadless pistol met his eye,
> And Bow-street Myrmidons stood laughing by.
>
> (ll. 458–61)[12]

Byron later said that the satire here was aimed primarily at Jeffrey (he even gives the empty pistol to Moore—whom he renames "Little"—rather than to Jeffrey), but his note had joked that "the balls of the pistols, like the courage of the combatants, were found to have evaporated." The overall effect was humiliating for Moore, a challenge to his credentials as a gentleman, so he wrote a letter to Byron that was itself only a thinly veiled cartel of defiance. In Byron's satire, Moore claimed, "the *lie is given* to a public statement" he had made (denying the accusation that there was an unloaded pistol).[13] The letter goes on to speak of returning to London and to request "satisfaction" (albeit explicitly the satisfaction of hearing Byron respond) for the "insult." Moore conveniently underscores the key words in his letter: giving the lie to a gentleman was the most common provocation to dueling. Byron never received this challenge, but Moore reminded him of it three years later, in a way that carefully avoided any new challenge while repeating the original charge of giving the lie.

Eventually the two were reconciled through the mediation of Samuel Rogers, and Moore was flattered in 1812 when Byron chose him to act as a second in an "affair" of his own (a conflict, incidentally, based on writing and settled by deleting certain objectionable passages in the text of a letter). Byron incorporated the lore of dueling as a feature of his colorful public persona. One digressive stanza in *Don Juan* knowingly refers to the practice in the voice of experience.

> It has a strange quick jar upon the ear,
>   That cocking of a pistol, when you know
> A moment more will bring the sight to bear
>   Upon your person, twelve yards off, or so;
> A gentlemanly distance, not too near,
>   If you have got a former friend for foe;
> But after being fired at once or twice,
> The ear becomes more Irish, and less nice.

(IV.41)[14]

These anecdotes provide a sense of how widespread dueling was during Shelley's formative years, and emphasize the complications that could develop around duels and their public representations and narrations, when offensive words frequently led to physical violence. Wilkes and Junius, Coleridge and the newspapers, even Canning's earlier career as editor of *The Anti-Jacobin*, all underscore the central role of more or less public language in the circumstances of dueling. Satire and dueling share the same medium and social milieu—a field where public utterance can destroy someone's standing, and therefore can provoke revenge or become itself a kind of revenge in turn.

In 1822 Byron was involved in another near duel with his nemesis, Robert Southey. Again the conflict turned on a question of libel and slander—in this case gossip and poisonous reviews about Byron and the Shelley circle. In Italy by this time, Byron finally sought "satisfaction" in satire—the (suppressed) dedication to *Don Juan* and "The Vision of Judgement." As Laurence S. Lockridge has pointed out, this conflict shows how Byron "works his animus off in verse," and how "The vein of satire happily gets the better of his sense of honor; aggression takes a different tack from dueling and grants a qualitatively higher pleasure."[15] I am intrigued by Lockridge's way of putting the question, by his suggestion that there can be a kind of transfer of energy between dueling and satire, but I want to emphasize the cultural institutions and assumptions that make such an exchange possible in the first place. The larger economy of violence embraces both practices, and the transfer can work both ways; to someone like Byron, dueling and satire seemed naturally interchangeable forms of action.

Satire and dueling also have frequently been connected, at least implicitly, by anthropologists, who apply the term "duel" to various kinds of verbal contests, or exchanges of mutual invective, including the "song duels" of the Eskimos and the flytings of the Scottish or Scandinavian peoples.[16] A similar range of "primitive" practices has traditionally been connected with early comedy and satire, along with ritual cursing. Whether or not actual ritual practices can be genetically linked to later cultural forms of linguistic aggression, especially satire, it is clear that similar kinds of social rituals inform both. The link is based on the resemblances between verbal abuse and libel or satire, and on the difference between spontaneous violence and carefully controlled and ritualized single combat. In this sense, a duel is more like satire (both codified ritual practices) than either is like a spontaneous fight between two rivals. Satire shares with dueling conventional rituals of mutual verbal aggression. And for legal and practical purposes, satire is often a form of libel. It is always caught up in questions of truth and honor (or lies and dishonor).

In one discussion of "the spirit of honor" ("the shadow or ghost of virtue deceased"), Coleridge scorned the common definition of honor, which leads men to dueling and "may be allowed to the writer of satires, but not to the moral philosopher."[17] While he was at Cambridge, an undergraduate was killed in a duel, and he always despised the practice on principle, calling it "that gothic compost of Suicide and Murder."[18] The ancient Greeks, Coleridge argues, had avoided dueling altogether; and, he says, in a telling juxtaposition, they resorted instead to an ethically superior form of retribution: "ridicule."[19] The often satirical Old Comedy of Aristophanes is seen as an alternative to modern dueling; satire is implicitly linked with dueling. Satire was the most obvious literary form of "verbal affront" in Coleridge's day, and thus led in many cases to the ultimate resort of violence. Sir Walter Scott made the same connection years later when he commented on a particularly bloody duel (between Boswell and Stuart), wishing that the event might "end the species of personal satire and abuse" which had so tainted "political discussions" in his era.[20]

The individual motive of revenge or resentment plays such an obvious part in so many duels that it can distract us from their extrapersonal nature, the fact that they are social transactions not unlike the performative curses discussed in Chapter 2. Duels, like legal disputes over libel, usually take place to determine some socially acceptable "truth" in a case where lying is charged.[21] Dueling is always implicitly enacted before a court of public (but strictly class-determined) opinion. Of course secrecy is necessary for legal reasons, and duels usually are explicitly treated as private affairs; but if *no* one ever knew the outcome of a duel, its purpose in an important sense would be defeated. Giving the lie is often the impetus and, in the absence of objective evidence, duels themselves become a judicial means of determining who is telling the truth. This makes dueling a Solomonic ritual relying on chance or Providence to decide the truth. "Honor" is one synonym for "honesty," and his "word of honor" is something upon which a true gentleman had to be ready to stake his life. Southey's reputed gossip in London circles about the Italian "league of incest" violated the gentlemen's code and gave Byron (and Shelley) the recognized right to respond belligerently.[22]

Byron had made remarks about dueling Southey as early as 1818. In a letter to John Murray, for example, he called the Laureate "a dirty, lying rascal," adding: "and [I] will prove it in ink—or in his blood, if I did not believe him to be too much of a poet to risk it."[23] In another letter he suggests that Southey is beneath dueling—"too powerless to require a 'vigour beyond the law' for his chastisement" (*BLJ*, VI, 104). Nonetheless, he sent a challenge via his friend Kinnaird in 1822, which the latter (using the diplomatic prerogative at the disposal of a second) withheld from Southey (*BLJ*, IX, 95n). Byron also drafted an inflammatory letter to *The Courier*, in answer to Southey's similar letter. Byron's was never sent, but it openly speaks of seeking "satisfaction" and closes with an outright challenge.

> I am as tired of this war of words as he can be—and shall be happy to reduce it to a more tangible decision—when—where—and how he pleases.—It is a pity that we are not nearer—but I will reduce the distance—if he will only assure me privately that he will not decline a meeting.

> (*BLJ*, IX, 99–100)

The easy shift from a "war of words" to a "meeting," as from the earlier "ink" to "blood," shows how Byron's satire was driven by displaced aggression, an expression and enactment of interpersonal violence. The aggression is, I believe, displaced rather than sublimated, in that both dueling and satire take place on a "surface level" of sanctioned but morally questionable cultural practices: there is not a transformation of violence into something else so much as a shift from one action to another in the shadowy realm where private revenge takes on the appearance—and the symbolic function—of public honor.

• • •

This is the context within which we must read Shelley's battle with Southey (in which he may have been prompted by Byron). Around the same time in 1822 that Byron was composing his challenges to Southey, Shelley wrote a letter to Leigh Hunt abjuring any vengeance against reviewers who had wronged him (which at this time could well have included the unnamed Southey).

> As to Reviews, don't give Gifford or his associate Hazlitt a stripe more for my sake. The man must be enviably happy whom Reviews can make miserable. I have neither curiosity, interest, pain or pleasure in [or] for any thing good or evil they can say of me—I feel only a slight disgust & a sort of wonder that they presume to write my name.—Send me your satire when it is printed—I began once a Satire upon Satire, which I meant to be very severe,—it was full of small knives in the use of which practice would have soon made me very expert.—
>
> (*Letters*, II, 382–83)

The weary tone of this renunciation cannot fully offset its intriguing report that Shelley had composed at least part of a satire, one intended to be "severe" and cutting. There is also the suggestion that he naturally associates the impulse to satirize (Hunt's and his own) with the polemics of reviews. The satire he names is almost certainly the fragment found in his rough-draft notebooks, now entitled "A Satire upon Satire." The elegiac way in which he refers to this project, as well as the deeply ambivalent nature of the fragment of "A Satire upon Satire" itself (as we shall see), has led many critics to assert that in composing it, Shelley rejected or renounced satire as a genre.[24] Obviously any account of Shelley's satire as a whole must deal with this question: Did he reject satire altogether at some point in his career?

The first difficulty we face is the highly uncertain date of the fragment. Shelley's tense ("I began once") would seem to place it further back than the recent past, from the perspective of 1822, but this is not much to go on. We do know that in 1818–19 Shelley was the victim of several negative reviews, as we have seen, reviews which probably provoked his composition of *Peter Bell the Third*. Through various channels, which remain obscure, he came to believe that Southey had been the author of the worst of these articles, an anonymous attack in *The Quarterly Review*. By 1820 he was engaged in a heated correspondence with Southey over this supposed calumny—as well as other, better-documented gossip and publications. Internal evidence alone would seem to suggest that Shelley's "Satire" fragment was composed around the same time as the letters, perhaps late in 1820 or early in 1821. If this date is correct, then Shelley may have published *Swellfoot the Tyrant* (December 1820), one of his most raucous and violent satires, just *after* drafting the fragment, the latter being, purportedly, his swan song of satire. But we cannot know without further evidence whether the chronological order was reversed: the fragment may have been written after *Swellfoot*, perhaps in 1821, and it may indeed amount to Shelley's final rejection of the satiric mode. Or, to propose a third alternative, Shelley may have "rejected" satire in the one draft (which he did not finish, let alone publish) while producing satire in the other poem (which he published).

Such speculation is ultimately fruitless, I think, and is in a sense misguided, because it is based on the assumption of an orderly or at least continuous progress in the poet's development. It mistakenly looks for consistency, an absolute rejection (or embracing) of the genre, when there is good reason to expect from Shelley a continued and unresolved ambivalence. There are also internal reasons to read the fragment as a more complex document, as reflecting Shelley's profound uncertainty about a genre that, nonetheless, held strong attractions for him. The very intensity of the poem's rejection of at least a certain *kind* of satire—vengeful personal invective—suggests the strength of that kind of satire's appeal.

"A Satire upon Satire" effectively dramatizes Shelley's ambivalence in structural terms, dividing itself in two. The first part displays the imagery of vitriolic Juvenalian invective, but in the subjunctive, hypothetically comparing satire to the tyrannical machinery of State and Church.

If gibbets, ~~confise~~ axes, confiscations, chains
~~And infamy & hatred   —if they pains~~
If
    ~~And~~ racks of subtle torment, if the pains
                    {   }
Of ~~everlasting Hel~~
        shame   burning
Of ~~infam~~y, if   Hell's tempestuous wave
Seen through the caverns of the shadowy grav
Hurling the damned into the murky air,
While the meek blest sit smiling— [. . .]

                                (ll. 1–8)[25]

Like *Peter Bell the Third*—but even more vehemently and explicitly—
this fragment attacks the violence inherent in the idea of damnation,
equating its use against "the damned" by the "meek blest" with other
forms of punitive inquisition. Even "infamy" is presented as a kind of hell
imposed on others by the self-righteous, as in Shelley's self-torturing
curses. All such tortures, the catalog suggests, including the more socially
acceptable practice of satire, are designed to discipline through threat of
punishment. Pope had written of satire as a "sacred Weapon," the possession of which makes the satirist understandably and justly proud: "To all
but Heav'n-directed hands deny'd,/The Muse may give thee, but the Gods
must guide./Rev'rent I touch thee!" (ll. 214–16).[26] Shelley's fragment
would debunk satire's ancient and often-repeated claim to moral purpose,
the "sacred" status of the satiric weapon, as only another form of cultural
displacement of basic aggression.

If such weapons are "the true secrets of the commonwealth," the poem
sardonically declares, then priests should be mobilized immediately, sent
out "To preach the burning wrath which is to come" (ll. 11, 17–18).
Instead, it seems likely that such sulfurous violence amounts to merely
"the sophisms of Revenge, & Fear/Bloodier than is Revenge" (ll. 15–16).
Shelley's draft refers first to the "statutes" (legal institution) and then
revises that to the "sophisms" (ideological foundation) "of Revenge, &
Fear." Bloody emotions motivate larger societal structures as well as individual actions, and in fact form a bridge connecting social with interpersonal conflict. Each case of personal sophistry is a function of ideology, an
ideology which it in turn reinforces.

Before we simply repeat the fragment's own dismissal of its "gibbets," "axes," and "rack" as mere hyperbole, only conventional figures of the satiric tradition, we should remember the recent reinstitution of the Inquisition in Spain, not to mention the new French device for capital punishment, the guillotine. Shelley's revulsion against public execution and torture is not merely automatic, though it became a kind of convention of sensibility during the Romantic period.[27] Shelley's movement from public forms of punishment to the feeling of "shame" in the prison of the self is in keeping with a movement toward internalizing torment in Romantic "men of feeling," who frequently became the source of their own worst punishments through the emotions of remorse and guilt. In this way the focus of Shelley's fragment eventually shifts from "gibbets" to the "mind's eye" and internal "spectres" of one particular target who seems to deserve the most extreme punishment available.

On another page the draft continues its rhetorical concession, but in a way that seems to relish the very violent language its subjunctive "if" calls into question. "If" only such counteraggression could actually correct viciousness like that of Robert Southey, it concedes, then anyone might accept the means of satire.

> . . . who that has & seen
>
> ~~cry~~
> ~~Both what he was~~   Exclaim
>   What Southey is & was, who w.^d not   ~~spare~~
> . . . Lash on, ~~lash him like the verse is bare~~
>   & be the keen verse dipped in flame
> Follow his flight on winged words, & urge
> The strokes of the inexorable scourge
> ~~Till it be broken on his flinty soul heart~~

                                    (ll. 27–32)

The temptation here is, significantly, to commit precisely the crime Shelley discovered in Wordsworth's *Peter Bell:* the teaching of hopelessness through fear. In the case of such crimes, satirist and damning priest are finally indistinguishable. The last line about Southey's "flinty heart" was canceled, and the fragment as a whole goes on not exactly to cancel but to countermand its own most excessive imagery, to turn away from such satire as counterproductive—and wrong: "This cannot be—[. . .]it ought not . . . /[. . .]Suffering makes suffering—ill must follow ill[.]" Instead of changing anything, such tactics merely play to the targets' "perverse antipathy of fame," their propensity to become what they are accused of being (ll. 43–45). In one part of the draft Shelley figures Southey's punishment as a forced self-examination in "the mirror of truths sunlike shield" (l. [3]), which, as I argued in Chapter 2, can be read as a superstitious reflection of a curse and in the end seems to reflect back upon the satirist himself. In so far as satire is violent, it cannot mirror truth, but only perpetuate—or reflect—its own projected image.

The second part of the fragment thus turns away from its own animus, proposing a surprisingly unexciting and (literally) pedestrian style of persuasion.

>   friend
> If any ~~one~~ would take Southey some day
>
> ~~It ought to be~~
> And tell him, ~~all the ill men say of him~~
>   in a country walk alone
>
>   friendship's
> ~~And~~ Softening harsh truths with ~~such a~~ gentle
>   tone
> [. . .]
>   How incorrect his public conduct is
>   it
> And what men think of ___ twere not amiss;
> ~~And all men should be friends & equals. So~~
> ~~Meanwhile to give a sort of specimen~~
> ~~Far better than to walk into his study~~
>   to make
> Far better than   innocent ink
>   stagnant
> With the ~~trite~~ truisms of trite Satire stink
>
>   (ll. 49–59)

This appeal to preserve "innocent ink" from the contamination of satire seems to come too late; surely satiric imagery has already muddied the pure stream of language. And Shelley's turn from writing (satire) to speech (conversation) may seem at first ripe for deconstruction. Upon closer examination, however, we see that it is "ink"—writing—which is said to be "innocent," and only the conventional accretions of traditional satiric rhetoric that are said to be polluting. Moreover, the poem's apparent logocentrism is pragmatic and provisional: confronting Southey in his study for a chat is only *relatively* "better" than the alternative of satire.

Finally, there is the further complication in the evidence of the draft that Shelley may have originally intended to continue the fragment with an imitative (written) example of its proffered speech to Southey, "a sort of specimen" of the ideal benevolent talk, in the form of an exhortation to a Godwinian brotherhood of "equals" (ll. 55–56). In fact, the concluding lines of the satire can be read to suggest that, because the priority of "innocent" writing is always already violated, one might as well resort to face-to-face encounters as the relatively less offensive kind of communication. Satire, historically among the most conventional and self-allusive of genres, is simply a repository of dead metaphors leading to the sort of linguistic entropy discussed in *A Defence of Poetry*, for example. It cannot be true poetry, in Shelley's terms, because it is not defamiliarizing, not "vitally metaphorical."

The fragment's final rejection of "trite Satire" may seem somewhat disingenuous, not so far from the denials of "To the Lord Chancellor" in its attempted cover-up of its own venomous opening.[28] Of course interpretation must remain even more tentative than usual in the case of such (materially) textual indeterminacy—a poem never finished certainly cannot be read as an organic whole. But the total textual evidence we have in the fragment does preserve (if only by chance) lines of intensely vitriolic satire alongside its brief, anticlimactic renunciation. It seems likely that "A Satire upon Satire" is *neither* a sincerely painful self-examination leading to epiphany *nor* merely an exercise in weak and shifty rhetorical casuistry, but is instead a deliberate—if ambivalent—dialectical experiment in opposing impulses toward Southey and what he represents. It first expresses real venom and only then attempts to overgo (but not deny) that expression. Shelley told Hunt that he intended this satire to be "very severe" and "full of small knives, in the use of which practice would have soon made me very expert," thus implying that cutting was a part of at least the original intention of the satire. The image of "small knives" is probably a self-reference to the "Letter to Maria Gisborne," in which Shelley praises Thomas Love Peacock, a satirist whose "fine wit/Makes such a wound, the knife is lost in it" (ll. 240–41).[29] In addition to a "fine," refined, or polite wit, this could signify an effective surgical violence that leaves no trace, even an untraceable weapon that conceals itself in the act of cutting. This is perhaps the way in which Shelley's satiric barbs get "lost" by the unwary target (and reader), are enfolded in the "frame" of subjunctive qualifiers and the final disarming line of the fragment, but are never really canceled out—remaining capable of a destructive effect as they are read and reread.

We have seen how the image of the shield in "A Satire upon Satire" becomes an amulet and aggressive weapon for returning aggression. Similarly, the idea of narcissistic reflection in "Lines to a Reviewer," as I tried to suggest, deploys a rhetoric of self-protective return, abjuring "hate" as a means to express it. (Shelley may well have had Southey in mind as the "Reviewer" in question.) Like the "Satire" fragment, it is based on interactions of moral "sympathy" and "antipathy" in literary conflicts, making use of a two-edged rhetorical sword (or small knife). The smug self-righteousness of the "Lines to a Reviewer" makes "A Satire upon Satire" appear complex by comparison.

Still, "A Satire upon Satire" also claims to be above its own satiric ire toward Southey, while its concluding gesture, ostensibly one of peace, cannot erase the imagery that has already impressed itself upon the reader. If these are the "stagnant truisms" of satire, then they are hurled with enough repetition and apparent hatred to seem a serious threat. Even the final line of the fragment concedes its ability to have made a "stink." Because it remained in rough draft, this fragment preserves even its cancellations, which provide traces of the development of Shelley's rhetoric. One case in particular stands out: Shelley replaced the drafted line "Far better than to walk into his study" with the final two lines attacking satire as trite and stagnant, a change that would seem to indicate that in his original plan, the satire was to be opposed not only to the "country walk" but also to another kind of face-to-face confrontation—perhaps one less benevolent and gentle, more "gentlemanly."

Perhaps the fragment reflects an ambivalence that extends beyond the central contrast of satire with talk, into the imagined encounter with Southey as well. Is it possible that the meeting between the two poets— which the benevolent chat is said to be "far better than"—was originally imagined as a menacing encounter, in which the angry adversary would walk (barge?) into the Laureate's study at Keswick to confront his opponent directly? Could the poem's focus on the institutional violence of the Inquisition be a displacement of a more personal kind of violence hovering in the background of the dispute? It does seem possible that one short-lived impulse of the projected meeting (one indicated by the "walk into his study" line but apparently supplanted by the draft's final call for a benevolent talk) may have been the desire to give a verbal affront.

This is just the sort of thing Shelley might well have imagined doing in 1820, when the fragment was probably drafted, the kind of confrontation the correspondence between the two poets seems to portend. I want now to turn to that correspondence and the interpersonal situation between Shelley and Southey that "A Satire upon Satire" seems to have been drafted to represent or (as the case may be) to revise.

Though mistaken about Southey's authorship of the vindictive review in *The Quarterly*, Shelley was right to be suspicious of the elder poet's representations of him back in England. He may have been aware of an earlier published review by Southey (in 1817) containing a thinly veiled attack on him.[30] One way or another, he came to believe that he had been libeled and slandered by the elder poet, that his honor had been impugned. Note that the original urge in "A Satire upon Satire" was to repay Southey's libels in an exchange of further calumny, to "tell him, all the ill men say of him" (l. 50). Shelley thought better of it, and canceled that openly retaliatory sentiment in the manuscript draft. In other plans for a public response to the offense, he first drafted an indignant legalistic letter to the editor of *The Quarterly* (the satirist William Gifford) in October 1819. It calls upon the anonymous reviewer or the editor, "his responsible agent," to prove the article's charges (of irreligion and immorality), but then trails off in anger: "or as you have thrust yourselves forward to deserve the character of a slanderer, to acquiesce also in"—and here the manuscript ends (*Letters*, II, 130). We can only speculate as to what Shelley intended when he drafted the letter: a lawsuit, a published rejoinder (perhaps "A Satire upon Satire" itself?), or some other retaliation—but he is clearly angry and ready to demand some form of satisfaction. The letter was never finished or sent. Only weeks later he wrote to Hunt that "the only notice it would become" him to take of Southey was to approach him face to face when he returned to England (*Letters*, II, 134).

When he realized, however, that he would have to remain in Italy for the time being, Shelley wrote directly to Southey, challenging him to deny the alleged libel. Taken together with the letter to Gifford, this missive bears a remarkable resemblance to the language building up to a duel in the letters of Moore and Byron.

> I had intended to have called on you, for the purpose of saying what I now write, on my return to England; but the wretched state of my health detains me here, and I fear leaves my enemy, were he such as I could deign to contend with, an easy, but a base victory, for I do not profess paper warfare.

But there is a time for all things. I regret to say that I shall consider your neglecting to answer this letter a substantiation of the fact which it is intended to settle—and therefore I shall assuredly hear from you.

(*Letters*, II, 204)

Byron, remember, had said in his letters that he was tired of the "war of words" with Southey and sought instead a more "tangible" battle in a "meeting." Later he decided that Southey was beneath dueling. Similarly, Shelley here declines to "profess paper warfare," yet writes ominously "But there is a time for all things," and closes by throwing down the gauntlet and demanding a reply from Southey. He also suggests that the writer of the review (whoever he may be) is already his "enemy," but one with whom it is beneath him "to contend." The similarity of language here may indicate that a shared code of behavior is being invoked in both letters. Southey, at least (not unreasonably), interpreted Shelley's language as hinting at a challenge to a duel, as he told another correspondent.[31] His reply to Shelley mentions this apparent threat or "menace,"[32] and Shelley's next letter is forced to deny any such implication—at least as it applied to Southey. In response Shelley again calls for a somewhat friendlier tête-à-tête: "I hope some day to meet you in London," he replies; "ten minutes' conversation is worth ten folios of writing" (*Letters*, II, 231).

In declining "paper warfare" in the first instance, Shelley may have been rejecting published satire but not private correspondence. Clearly his language and posturing in the first letter are belligerent. But it is possible to read Shelley's language in all of these letters, to *The Quarterly* and to Southey, as intentionally equivocal—open to interpretation either as a cartel of defiance or, alternatively, as a diplomatic overture to debate. This is not so different from the strategic ambivalence of "A Satire upon Satire." Such legalistic equivocation was often part of observing decorum in challenges, a kind of polite indirection as well as a way of giving one's opponent every opportunity either to back down and apologize or to seize the aggressive role in a counterinsult (which would conveniently make him an equal party to the conflict).[33]

It is not my purpose here to assert that Shelley actually intended a duel in this exchange. His second letter to Southey seems to obviate that *literal* possibility, at any rate. I merely want to show that the language he used, when placed in the larger context, reveals class assumptions which make a duel a real possibility—as a way to resolve a conflict that plays itself out in private while always threatening to go public. I am suggesting that Shelley's stance toward Southey in the affair, including the rhetorical stance of "A Satire upon Satire," can be explained with reference to the gentlemanly code of honor that regulated the practice of dueling. Although he explicitly rejected the standards of this code, Shelley's ethics—and his satire—inevitably retain the trace of the class interests that gave rise to the code in the first place.

We more readily expect dueling from Byron than from Shelley, who is better known as a precursor of political nonviolence and the tactic of passive resistance. In fact Shelley explicitly rejected dueling in a letter of 1811, on the occasion of his quarrel with Thomas Jefferson Hogg over Hogg's advances to Harriet Shelley (and only two years after the Canning-Castlereagh duel). Shelley tells another correspondent that Hogg has written to him "with some hints as to duelling to induce me to meet him in that manner," even though Hogg knows how much Shelley "despis[es]" the practice.

> I have answered his letter in which I have said that I shall not fight a duel with him whatever he may say or do—that I have no right either to expose my own life or take his . . . nor do I think that his life is a fair exchange for mine, since I have acted up to my principles, and he has denied his, and acted inconsistently with any morality whatsoever—that if he would shew how I had wronged him, I would repair it to the uttermost mite but I would not fight a duel.
>
> (*Letters*, I, 208)

This language is in keeping with the utilitarian antidueling statements made by Godwin, for example, who attacks the practice as illogical and not in the interest of the greater good. He exhorts his readers instead to aspire to that true courage which lies in "daring to speak truth"—even to the point of declining a challenge in polite but grim, rigorously logical terms.[34]

Shelley, however, possessed his own "aristocratic biases,"[35] and we cannot uncritically accept his conscious declarations of nonviolence as the last word on the subject. We must remember that, from his early days at Oxford, he always carried a brace of dueling pistols, even if he professed to abjure the practice of dueling.[36] His upbringing in the world of the patriarchal aristocracy would have guaranteed his exposure to competitive violence. Take, for example, his experiences with schoolboy violence at Eton.

His master there, John Keate, was infamous for flogging the boys and staging bloody boxing matches between them—complete with "seconds" and other accoutrements of the duel. Shelley spent the rest of his life reacting against this early experience, staking out a position firmly against violence—as the expression of either tyranny or enslavement. But later there were several crucial physical encounters: with the mysterious "assassin" of Tanyrallt (involving sword and pistols), with the indignant man in the post office at Florence (who reportedly knocked him down for being a "damned atheist"), and with the dragoon, Masi, at Pisa.

It is not the actual truth of these events—which in any case is in dispute—but Shelley's psychological response to their social contexts that is of interest here. Two of the three incidents were first narrated and shaped by Shelley himself. Each case recounts a remarkably duelistic face-to-face confrontation sparked by a threat to Shelley or to others of his party—often accompanied by slander, insult, or other breaches of social etiquette based on rank. The most violent, a kind of reenactment on the personal level of Peterloo, was a confrontation with a dragoon, Sergeant-Major Masi. This incident was perpetrated mostly by Count John Taaffe and Lord Byron, although Shelley was in the thick of things, and it culminated in swordplay and the probable attempted murder of the dragoon by one of Byron's servants.[37] The dragoon had ridden roughly through the Byron-Shelley ranks on the road to Pisa, and in the ensuing fray Shelley was knocked off his horse by Masi's sword blade while apparently confronting Masi directly—riding up to him in a characteristic act of what we might call passive-aggressive resistance. It is an interesting coincidence that this incident occurred around the same time that Byron was preoccupied with challenging Southey, back in England, to a duel.

In each of these conflicts Shelley apparently behaved admirably, acting only in self-defense and, even then, usually in a passive manner. But the stories are pivotal in his biography, and most of them have their origins as stories (whatever the truth of the original occurrences) in Shelley's imagination. One side of him is clearly drawn to the gothic, dramatic possibilities of conventional aristocratic displays of force, even, arguably, when he deliberately abjures such prerogatives, as in the Masi affair. This is merely to admit that ubiquitous, classbound codes must have shaped Shelley's attitudes toward violence, if only negatively, notwithstanding his explicit disavowals and serious convictions against violent behavior.

· · ·

Until the practice began to decline in the nineteenth century, dueling (especially in France and England) remained the prerogative of the nobility, and only after that, of gentlemen in general. (There are a few recorded cases of women dueling, but they are inevitably presented as freak occurrences far outside the male-determined norm.)[38] One well-known guide of 1790 makes explicit what was usually taken for granted in a section headed "A Gentleman not to meet any one but a Gentleman."[39] Even seconds, it was commonly held, should be of a social rank commensurate with the principals, and opposing seconds, like the primary combatants, should always be equals. The early French Revolutionaries predictably denounced dueling as among the corrupt practices of the ancien régime whose exclusivity was founded on inequality. Under the Directory and eventual counterrevolution, the vogue for dueling revived.[40]

Different explanations have been offered for the intraclass nature of duelistic violence and the unofficial tolerance of dueling during the period of its greatest popularity. For example, the warring governments of the time may have depended upon the duel to perpetuate the "ethos of the sword," or the duel may have offered a "regulated outlet for violent impulses" that would otherwise lead to anarchy, a way in which "impulses of private violence could . . . be made conducive to social stability, instead of disruptive."[41] Such explanations are governed by a theory of productive sublimation, by the assumption that "primal" endemic violence can be channeled and regulated by the codes of civilization. Dueling is nothing if not a highly civilized activity. The unity of class that supports the practice may be seen as a fruitful conspiracy among those powers who control society for the good of the whole.

Class unity is clearly central to the code of dueling, either a prerequisite or a consequence of the practice, depending on how one views the ongoing process of dueling and the sanctioning of duels. Collective sanctions in favor of it were extremely powerful. Dr. Johnson, when asked his opinion on dueling in 1772, replied that it was probably a justifiable or "lawful" resort, given the refinements of high civilization. In such a civilized society, he admitted, answering a challenge could become a moral duty on the part of the duelist and a means of self-defense, "to avert the stigma of the world, and to prevent himself from being driven out of society."[42] William Godwin argued that by his day the "despicable practice" had lost even the original motive of sincere revenge, and that "Men of the best understanding who lend it their sanction are unwillingly induced to do so, and engage in single combat merely that their reputation may sustain no slander."[43]

Dr. Johnson's phrase, "to prevent himself from being driven out of society," makes the duelist manqué who would refuse a challenge something like a ritual scapegoat figure.[44] The scapegoat or *pharmakos* must be randomly or arbitrarily selected in order to place him outside the cycles of retribution through the ties of kinship or other alliances—he must, paradoxically, be an outsider from within. Only then can the act of sacrifice redirect dangerous internecine aggression—the result of competitive "mimetic desire"—into a single channel, and thus unite the group while preserving the fabric of the community as a whole, which would otherwise be torn apart by its own escalating violence. One is sacrificed for the good of all. Unity, in this view, is not only a means of covering up group violence after the fact, it is itself the primary benefit to be derived from the founding act of sacrifice, its ultimate social (though not conscious) motivation. By driving the scapegoat out of the group and ultimately destroying him, the group reasserts its own threatened wholeness. This pattern is mirrored in later rituals of sacrifice, which in their earliest forms serve to reunify or reestablish the group in a repetition of the initial founding process, whose origins are now unconscious, concealed from the participants. Obviously, this is a functional explanation: sacrificial violence occurs at moments when it is most required, at moments of crisis and social disunity, as a mechanism for establishing social equilibrium.

There is a great distance between actual primal violence and "primitive" ritual reenactments, and an even greater, more problematic distance between those rituals and modern practices. We should be cautious about applying such a theory to specific and diverse cultural phenomena, especially modern phenomena far removed from sacred rituals themselves.[45] But the general social dynamics it implies are—at the very least—metaphorically suggestive when applied to the case of the duel. Duelists can fruitfully be seen as functioning as dual scapegoats for their class: first both become the focus of intraclass rivalry, then one or the other is made the "sacrifice" (the loser, whether fatally wounded or not) to defuse the rivalry. Chance is involved in the eruption of their interpersonal violence into the public, "judicial" sphere, and the chance of "equal hazard" usually is deliberately invoked in the form their battle takes, dating back to medieval trials by combat. A coin may be tossed to determine who fires first, handicaps are often equalized (if one duelist suffers from weak eyesight, for example, the other might be made to wear a patch), and when it became more likely that unequal *skill* would enter the equation—as with the rifling of gun barrels in the nineteenth century—the practice seems to have become less common.[46]

The effect of these customs and the dependence on chance is to make the selection of the actual "sacrificial victim" (the final one taken from the two who meet on the field) more random, more arbitrarily "fair," and thus less open to continued vendetta and counterrevenge (by seconds, or relatives, for example, not to mention the courts). In this way, intraclass conflicts can be channeled through the duel into a sanctioned ritual for destroying one (or, in rare cases, two) members of the dominant group instead of the whole fabric of civilized society in a cycle of escalating violence.

This is one way to begin to explain how duels over a sexual object and over public slander are related: in both cases it is the mutually desired object of "honor" or status within the group that is at stake (if only vicariously, through the reified and appropriated reputation of a wife or mistress, an objectification of woman as a projection of honor, and the object of triangulated mimetic desire). This enables us to read dueling in a way that goes beyond the level of interpersonal animus, or even individual resentment against society, to interpret it as functional in sociological terms. In this light, dueling appears as a ritual driven by the collective needs of class self-preservation. It also explains why dueling should be particularly viable during the period of the American War for Independence and the French Revolution, and the decades leading up to the first Reform Bill of 1832, a time when the old order was under new pressures from below and from without, and may have resorted to tighter controls on any behavior which threatened its stability and unity from within. The duel may be seen as a logical feature of the political and social reaction (and even counterrevolution) that characterized English society in the early nineteenth century. It is no surprise to come upon Jules Janin's assertion that "It is to duelling alone that we owe the remains of our civilization."[47] To adapt Walter Benjamin, the history of the duel is a document of civilization that is also obviously a document of barbarism.[48]

Not every work of satire fits the analogy, but the public satire of personal hatred is like the duel in that it is a codified, socially sanctioned, but legally (and morally) marginal way to seek revenge—or to deter the vicious. Too often we still view satire like Shelley's primarily in terms of literature, his conflict with Southey as a professional battle between writers. For gentlemen (even gentlemen writers) like Shelley and Southey, satire was not a strictly aesthetic "genre"—it was one means of enacting social conflict, and one not so different from pistols. Both cultural practices, dueling and personal satire, take place at the intersection of private disputes and public consequences, and both function as recognized means of establishing a public version of the "truth," to the truth teller's honor and the liar's dishonor.

Since the legendary iambics of Archilochus supposedly called down the laughter of ancient Greece on his enemies, driving them to suicide or exile, one kind of ad hominem satire has worked by destroying reputation, honor, or community standing. It can also be deployed (like the curse) reciprocally, to defend one's honor against such attacks. Such defenses of class-determined honor have the collateral effect of warding off the threat from outsiders or violators of the codes of the social group. Satire's conventional xenophobia and attacks on parvenus and upstarts function like the duel and other rituals to regulate "true" membership and deportment in "normal" society. Satire can usefully be understood in relation to dueling because the two practices share a certain space in culture, bounded by class prerogatives and the demands of social order, where conflicts between individuals take on social significance and interpersonal violence shades over into social violence.

• • •

For Shelley, the interpersonal and the political marked points along a complex continuum of social power. Following his mentor William Godwin, he insisted that politics should be understood as "the morals of the nation," ethics writ large, and that artificially to divide interpersonal morality from public politics was needlessly to diminish both spheres of action.[49] In one place he defined ethics, or "the science of morals," as "the voluntary conduct of men in relation to themselves or others."[50] The key word is "voluntary," implying an ethical imperative of free will directly opposed to coercion or violence in any form. In fact, Shelley's precise term, "voluntary conduct," invokes a long tradition in moral philosophy of examining the problem of volition and coercion, beginning with Aristotle and running through eighteenth-century moral-sense theorists to Hume and (especially for Shelley) Godwin.[51] For Shelley, as for other Romantics, the psyche (and hence the will) is never absolutely free, but is conditioned and—in part—determined by chains of causes (some of which lie below the level of conscious, rational choice). Thus coercion is always a danger, and the concept of "voluntary conduct" is made irreducibly problematic.

Shelley accepted the Godwinian conclusion that coerced virtue is a contradiction in terms.[52]

> My neighbour, presuming on his strength, may direct me to perform or to refrain from a particular action; indicating a certain arbitrary penalty in the event of disobedience within his power to inflict. My action, if modified by his menaces, can in no degree participate in virtue. He has afforded me no criterion as to what is right or wrong.[53]

On the social level, as Godwin had argued, coercion is finally counterproductive: it only reproduces itself mimetically in further aggression.

If rhetoric is to claim truly moral effects, according to this criterion, it must persuade without coercing, must avoid the unjust influence of another's volition. Like William Blake, Shelley posits an ideal community of strong mutual persuaders. But there is a fine line between suasion and coercion—and it is upon this distinction that writing's ethical justification depends. Shelley ultimately defined violence not impersonally or metaphysically but as the unjust use of force by human beings against other human beings. He maintained a belief in the possibility of rhetorical nonviolence over and against the potential of language to coerce nonethical, nonvoluntary actions.

In the preface to *The Cenci*—a dramatic experiment in the problematics of ethical principles in practice—Shelley wrote, "Undoubtedly, no person can be truly dishonoured by the act of another."[54] As revenge for lost honor, or as sacrificial ritual of normative self-protection, duelistic public satire would violate his stated ethical principles on several grounds. This is why, despite his class (and perhaps psychological) inclinations, Shelley never published the violent invective that "A Satire upon Satire" imagines—just as he never followed through with the implied challenge to a duel. Such satire (like dueling) would appeal to the private motive of revenge over the public consequence of utility and would fail to reform or correct the target. Where it did make a kind of appeal to usefulness, it would be the "utility" of maintaining social order through regulated ritual violence. Unethically, it would apply the "menaces" of violence or violent language (what "A Satire upon Satire" calls "the pains of shame") as a psychological deterrent, sacrificing the "target" for the good of the dominant community. For all of these reasons, to meet the opponent on the field of combative satire would be to disqualify any desired result as a truly voluntary action, as far as Shelley was concerned. It would be to coerce rather than to persuade, to escalate the ritual of "paper warfare" (and potentially of the more destructive kind) into further acts of insular, reciprocal violence that could only perpetuate themselves.

Hypothetically, satire can be seen as aligned with the comic, a mode of liberating subversive laughter, but for Shelley the history of the genre (especially in the wake of the eighteenth century) is dominated by cycles of oppressive, resentful, or retributive violence, by imposed authority from above rather than saturnalian license from below. He believes that the dominant conventions of satire are founded on unjust motives and social constructs, to the point that much of traditional satire must be discarded by an ethically sensitive poet. The satire that is to be kept and used, according to him, must be in some way offset or modified away from its dangerous tendency toward coercion. His most interesting satires can be seen as urgent experimental attempts to solve this problem, attempts to take seriously the etymological hint that satire's strength is its identity as *satura*, in order to produce mixtures of satiric and other rhetorical modes that might do something more than merely curse, damn, discipline, or punish, all tactics that Shelley believed merely deferred the possibility of social change. His dilemma concerns the violence of language—not in its essence but as a culturally embedded medium of social interaction. It is therefore an ethical as well as a rhetorical problem, and it is a problem by no means limited to satire.

5 Satire of Succession in *The Mask of Anarchy*

AFTER *THE DEVIL'S WALK* (1812), the satires we have been examining so far—from the early curse on Eldon (1817–1820) to later satires on Wordsworth (1819) and Southey (ca. 1820)—are more personal in their targets, though they remain situated in social contexts. With the present chapter and the following one, however, I want to turn to satirical poems that are more openly and thematically political, with relatively collective targets (the Liverpool Ministry and the Crown) and collective subjects (the people). Both *The Mask of Anarchy* (1819) and *Oedipus Tyrannus; or Swellfoot the Tyrant* (1820) are intensely concerned with the threat of public violence—both the violence of the state and its mirror in the violence of the people—rather than the interpersonal violence of a curse or a duel. Historical occasion and Shelley's own explorations into the ethics of poetry come together fruitfully in these next two satires (though in different ways) to produce complex satiric *medleys* directed toward active intervention in the processes of social change.

In the summer of 1819, an announcement was published in Manchester informing the public of a meeting to be held on 9 August in the fields by St. Peter's Church, for the purpose of considering "the most speedy and effectual mode of obtaining Radical Reform" of Parliament,

> being fully convinced, that nothing less can remove the intolerable evils under which the People of this Country have so long, and do still, groan: and also to consider the propriety of the "Unrepresented Inhabitants of Manchester" electing a Person to represent them in Parliament . . . .[1]

The chief signatory of the announcement was Henry "Orator" Hunt, invariably referred to as a "demagogue," clearly one of the more popular speakers and symbols of the reform movement. Among the others to sign was Sir Charles Wolseley, who had himself been elected a representative (or "Legislatory Attorney") for the unrepresented city of Birmingham. Such mass demonstrations and elections, looking a little too much like the prelude to a national convention, were decidedly illegal, and the threat of one at Manchester was one of the factors that prompted the local authorities (in consultation with the Home Office) to prohibit the announced meeting.[2] In a complicated and still obscure process of legal speculation and maneuvering, reaction and counterreaction, the organizers planned another meeting for the following week, and the government in turn made plans to disperse it, should it turn seditious—significantly, by attempting out-of-doors to elect illegal representatives.

These are some of the events leading up to the infamous "Peterloo Massacre" of 16 August 1819. The story of the preparations for the meeting, even more than the well-known story of the clash itself, usefully calls attention to the legal substrata beneath the events: the structural provisions for collective action and representation in England. This chapter will look at the events of Peterloo, and at Shelley's poem on the occasion, *The Mask of Anarchy*, in the context of the reform movement's language of "representation" and the "laws of England." I will read the poem as an ambivalent "succession satire"[3]—one which calls for change as the people's rightful inheritance but recognizes (uncomfortably) that the inheritance may have to be wrested away from the legitimate line. In the extraparliamentary sense, Shelley's poem attempts to represent the people and to legislate a reformed succession from the distance of an exile in Italy.[4]

• • •

The debate over exactly what happened in Manchester on 16 August 1819 and how to interpret it has become paradigmatic of controversies in the discipline of history. Long before there was a New Historicism, Peterloo stood as a case study of the single historical event as a field of contending readings.[5] What seems clear is that the local yeomen on horseback, called in to break up the meeting of approximately 60,000 people—and probably to arrest Henry "Orator" Hunt—became enclosed by the angry crowd after (many accounts say) a woman was knocked down and her baby killed. The hussars, coming to the yeomanry's support, rode into and attacked the crowd. Whether the yeomen are seen as inept victims of circumstance or part of a government plan, whether the crowd came armed and prepared for battle or peacefully defenseless, and whether the Home Office was behind the hussars' actions are matters of debate. But the results, everyone agrees, were deadly. At least eleven persons were killed and hundreds more were wounded. The bloody clash quickly came to be known as the "Peterloo Massacre," the term itself a satiric commentary on the war at home being fought by English soldiers and constables (some of whom were wearing Waterloo medals) against the English citizenry.

Questions for historians include the motives on both sides of the conflict: Did the protestors meet as a provocation, armed and prepared for violence? Did the Home Office, or at least the local officials in Manchester, allow the meeting with the prior intent to crush it violently, as part of a larger national campaign of reaction? One source cites an eyewitness account from the law enforcement side in order to argue that many in the crowd were armed and dangerous, and to suggest that the police forces were actually less organized than the demonstrators.[6] For decades, revisionist historians have challenged the arguments of E. P. Thompson and others that the crowd was largely peaceful and well-meaning; on the contrary, they say, much of the calculation—and the menace of violence—leading up to Peterloo should be located on the side of the reformers.[7] The revisionists accuse earlier historians of being influenced by the 1819 press and a relatively small group of radicals, who promptly mythologized the confrontation, exaggerating its violence and significance for propaganda purposes, taking it out of the context of long-brewing threats to the peace.

It is important to continue to question what had in fact until recently become the standard account of Peterloo: a perfect microcosm of class war.[8] But to point to the inevitable blindnesses of, say, Thompson's social history is not to debunk it or devalue its fundamental insights. One thing most revisionists miss, but which Thompson's Marxist perspective allows him to see, for example, is the degree to which ideological "mythologizing" was the very stuff of nineteenth-century reform battles—the atmosphere in which they took shape—on both sides. These political conflicts had already been mythologized, even allegorized, for quite some time when Peterloo occurred. To realize the extent of this mythologizing, one need only remember Edmund Burke's allegorical account of the French Revolution and English Jacobinism, with its ravished Queen and "swinish multitude."[9] The reform meetings, like the publications which announced

| THE CLERICAL MAGISTRATE. | THE RADICAL PULPIT. |

" *The Bishop.* Will you be diligent in Prayers—laying aside the study of the world and the flesh !——*The Priest.* I will.
? As Bishop. Will you maintain and set forwards, as much as lieth in you, quietness, peace, and love, among all Christian People !——*Priest.* I will.
¶ The Bishop laying his hand upon the head of him that receiveth the order of Priesthood, shall say, RECEIVE THE HOLY GHOST."
The Form of Ordination for a Priest.

The Brave. Will you neglect all prayers, laying aside all morality and industry, and attend only to Politics? *The Dupe.* I will.
The Brave. Will you disturb, as much as lieth in you, the peace of Society; and subvert by all means in your power, the Christian Religion? *The Dupe.* I will.
¶ The Brave laying his head on his Votary, shall say, YOU ARE ADMITTED A RADICAL.
The Form of Admission is Order.

———" The pulpit (in the sober use
Of its legitimate peculiar pow'rs)
Must stand acknowledg'd, while the world shall stand,
The most important and effectual guard,
Support, and ornament of virtue's cause.
* * *
Behold the picture ! Is it like?

THIS IS A PRIEST,
made ' according to Law',

The pulpit, in the sober use
Of its legitimate peculiar pow'rs
Will stand acknowledg'd while the world shall stand.
The most effectual and substantial guard,
Support, and ornament of Vintage's cause.
* * *
Beware !—This picture is not like it.

A RADICAL MAN,
who despises all Law,

FIGURE 3. *The Clerical Magistrate* (left) from William Hone and George Cruikshank's *The Political House That Jack Built* (1819) (British Museum 13303) and *The Radical Pulpit* (right) from *A Parody . . .* (British Museum 13689). In the first, the Form of Ordination is cited ironically; the parody mirrors the mockery and turns it against radical orators (the caricature may be of Gale Jones).

and commented on them, were already symbolic events, awash with red caps of liberty, allegorical goddesses (Liberty or Britannia), sprigs of oak, hearts, skulls, banners, broadsides, and cartoons.

In this context, the exchange of such signs was necessarily an exchange of power, part of a competition to establish the value and to define the meaning of political struggles.[10] After 1815, when restrictions on public meetings were loosened, layered gestural symbols like the Phrygian cap (or cap of liberty) regained their currency, though often in self-protective allusive disguise. The red cap was associated with republican Rome as well as ancient British constitutional freedoms, and—less openly—with the subversive, even regicidal forces of the French Revolution. In discourse, appropriating or parodying a sign became a means of engaging in (coded) ideological dispute and exchange. Displaying, defending, seizing, or capturing a banner or cap sometimes became the focus of violent physical struggle—which is precisely what happened at Peterloo.

Frequently the same symbols were appropriated and deployed in the parody and counterparody of literature and graphic prints—for example, the pair of plates *The Clerical Magistrate* (1819) and *The Radical Pulpit* (1820) (see Figure 3).[11] The first depicts the duplicity of the clergy as a literal doubleness—the sacred writ on one side and the inquisitorial tools of state violence on the other. The text immediately below the emblem is the Form of Ordination, and its juxtaposition with the picture is the most direct kind of mocking irony. The second print, a reactionary parody of the anticlerical satire, claims to expose the two-faced nature of the reform movement: the appearance of lofty, legal, and constitutional representation (mere "puff") really has behind it a radical orator, with banner and Phrygian cap of liberty. His pulpit is labeled with a reversed "Peace," his intention being to breach the peace. The (literal!) subtext, in the style of *The Anti-Jacobin*'s parodies, mocks a radical initiation. This pair of prints (within each and between the two) illustrates in a literal sense the mimetic violence of parodic satire. Note as well that the debate is over the law and its uses, in a mixed milieu of religion and politics, with the assumption that the battle takes place in the sphere of public oratory— from one pulpit or another.

The extent to which a semiotic milieu or a symbolic language was shared by graphic satires, in particular, is clarified by the example of a loyalist cartoon from 1 December 1819 by George Cruikshank, one which superficially resembles Shelley's poem in its imagery (British Museum 13279): DEATH OR LIBERTY, *or Britannia and the Virtues of the Constitution in danger of Violation from the grt Political Libertine, Radical Reform!* (see Figure 4). The central standing image, a Dance of Death skeleton, is part of a visual pun on the inverted slogan (one actually displayed at Peterloo), "Death or Liberty." It wears an idealized mask of Liberty, topped by a cap of liberty (turned fool's cap), and assaults the female figure of Britannia (who recoils). She has on her side the British lion, the rock of Religion, and the (wobbly, compromised) sword of the Laws. On the other side, behind Death-as-Liberty, is an onrushing mob of allegories, including Murder, Robbery, Blasphemy (carrying a copy of *The Age of Reason*), and Immorality. All are sheltered under the cloak of Death, which is labeled "RADICAL REFORM."

The striking iconographic resemblance of Shelley's poem to this print

FIGURE 4. George Cruikshank's DEATH OR LIBERTY! *or Britannia & the Virtues of the Constitution in danger of Violation from the grt Political Libertine, Radical Reform!* (British Museum 13279). The destructions under the cloak of Liberty are labeled Murder, Robbery, Starvation, Blasphemy (carrying *The Age of Reason*), and Immorality; on the ground, the pamphlet reads, "Radical Liberty—i.e.—To *Take Liberties.*"

and others is not a question of direct influence or specific single sources, but of a shared context, a symbolic language, that places Shelley's satire in the public realm of the conflicted discourse on reform. This kind of symbolic language was well established and available to him through various channels at the moment he first heard the news of Peterloo in Italy (as he wrote to his publisher, Ollier, on 6 September). It provoked in him a "torrent of indignation . . . . I wait anxiously to hear how the country will express its sense of this bloody murderous oppression of its destroyers. 'Something must be done . . . what yet I know not' " (*Letters*, II, 117).

It is highly significant that Shelley here quotes the ambiguous heroine of *The Cenci.* Like that work, his satire in response to Peterloo is concerned with the problems of reciprocal, escalating violence and revenge; but even more than the tragedy had, the satire aims for popularity, and speaks the language of reform (and antireform) discourse. *The Mask of Anarchy* is a ballad for reformers—of various stripes—and it exhorts them to non-vengeful action, though not, as I shall argue, to an absolute avoidance of all violence. It was probably among the group of poems Shelley planned (but never published) for a collection of "popular songs wholly political & destined to awaken & direct the imagination of the reformers" (*Letters*, II, 191).

Shelley, the heir (eventually of a baronetcy) and son of an M.P. who thought of himself as a practical reformer and orator as well as a poet, would put into practice his famous metaphor of the poet as legislator: not so much a lawgiver as a charismatic leader who could "awaken and direct" reform in the role of the people's "representative," one who could speak for or act on behalf of the people. The models closest to hand in the autumn of 1819 were reformers like Henry Hunt and Sir Charles Wolseley, out-of-doors representatives (Wolseley's unofficial title was "legislatory attorney") elected defiantly outside the bounds of the law, as a challenge to the established system of legal representation.[12] This kind of illegal represen-tative was an unrecognized, unlicensed, and therefore "unacknowledged" legislator.

Shelley's 1817 pamphlet, *A Proposal for Putting Reform to the Vote Throughout the Kingdom*, has as its first premise that "Every one is agreed that the House of Commons is not a representation of the people."[13] The rest of the essay is devoted to proposing a practical means for determining whether "the people" (propertied adult males) want a more "complete representation" (p. 64), whether they "ought to legislate for themselves" (p. 63), or whether the existing Members of Parliament can be rendered (by reform) "the actual Representatives of the Nation" (p. 66). Elsewhere Shelley declared that the Commons "actually represent a deception and a shadow, virtually represent none but the powerful and the rich."[14] He was well aware that the question of reform turned on the definition and boundaries of representation, "virtual" versus practical. In a telling 1823 speech the editor Francis Jeffrey said that Peterloo had converted him to the cause of reform.[15] Prior to 1819, he admitted, he had considered "virtual representation as equivalent to *real* representation," but the kill-ings in Manchester changed his mind: "In proof of the dangers which arise out of the imperfect state of the representation, there is one fact which speaks volumes. I allude to the transactions which took place lately at Manchester, an unrepresented town . . ." (p. 418).

It is in this context that we must read Shelley's attempted participation in this pivotal event, slightly after the fact of the confrontation but in the heat of the confrontational responses to it, which was to compose a poem calling for *yet another* mass meeting.

> "Let a vast Assembly be,
> And with great solemnity
> Declare with measured words that ye
> Are, as God had made ye, free —
>
> "Be your strong and simple words
> Keen to wound as sharpened swords,
> And wide as targes let them be
> With their shade to cover ye."
>
> (ll. 295–302)[16]

The "sharpened swords" of the reformers' words are of the same general category as the "small knives" of Shelley's "Satire upon Satire," except in this case the keen verbal weaponry is "solemn," open, and therefore presumably justified. Described as "targes," the "strong and simple" words are thus identified as an ancestral Anglo-Saxon shield or protection. Not merely defensive, they are "keen to wound." The people's language is implicitly associated with a mythical national heritage (as against the "Norman Yoke" or other "un-English"—that is, Hanoverian—oppressors), and the cause of the unrepresented is handed the sword of language—like that of *The Mask* itself. These wounding words serve to represent—to stand in for as well as to express—the needs and wishes hitherto suppressed by the established order. But their means of representation is deliberately figured as a dangerous weapon, not a reflection but an enactment, a "display" in the sense that combat arms are displayed. In effect, the poem attempts to transfer the social energy of Peterloo to a call for a new meeting, to represent the event and in so doing to enact another such event. Shelley wishes in this way to link his literary representation directly to the power of political representation. A meeting of the unrepresented is the climax toward which *The Mask of Anarchy* is aimed from the start, as well as its initiating occasion.

In order to support its basic aim, the poem presents itself as operating firmly within the discourse of the reform movement. Its embeddedness in reform discourse is most clearly demonstrated in the famous early stanzas, the satirical "masque" of Anarchy. The poem opens with a single framing stanza, which suggests a kind of improvised Dantesque dream vision ("As I lay asleep in Italy/There came a voice from over the sea . . ."), a form that Shelley would use to its fullest in "The Triumph of Life." This gives way to an allegorical procession which resembles the satirical prints and other popular forms of the day in its eclectic mix of medieval emblems, caricature, burlesque, and political rhetoric.[17] The speaker encounters figures of Murder, Fraud, and Hypocrisy, who are wearing the masks (or gowns or other icons) of (or "like") real politicians: Castlereagh, Eldon, and Sidmouth. The irony is that the reality is abstract evil; its appearance merely takes the form of persons. Shelley had done this before, as we have seen, in *The Devil's Walk*, and some of that early satire's targets reappear here.

> And many more Destructions played
> In this ghastly masquerade,
> All disguised, even to the eyes,
> Like Bishops, lawyers, peers, or spies.

> (ll. 26–29)

Just as the Devil had been disguised as a dandy and a gentleman, so impersonal forces of destruction and evil here wear the appearance of respectable members of society.

The language *imitates* simplicity, is stripped down to the point that it has been read as condescending to or patronizing the ballad tradition.[18] But I would suggest that the tradition on which Shelley is building has less to do with actual popular ballads (or with secondary developments like Percy's *Reliques*) than with Canning and Hone, the already parodic and even self-mocking forms of pamphlet balladry, whose singsong simplicity (e.g., "This Is the House That Jack Built") was part of its satirical effect. Shelley's awkward rhymes and metrical clumsiness often work to enhance the atmosphere of satirical absurdity; as usual, his ear for the music (however rough) of verse is good.

> Last came Anarchy: he rode
> On a white horse, splashed with blood;
> He was pale even to the lips,
> Like Death in the Apocalypse.

And he wore a kingly crown,
And in his grasp a sceptre shone;
On his brow this mark I saw—
"I AM GOD, AND KING, AND LAW!"

(ll. 30–37)

Shelley's rhyming "to the lips" with "Apocalypse" and mixing up, *satura*-like, the Dance of Death, Benjamin West's sublime painting, the Bible, and parodic political cartoons, all in the language of rousing popular songs, only reinforces in its cacophony the dissonant rule of Anarchy. This is a device in the tradition of the antimasque. Like the antimasque, these satiric stanzas take their effect from a pointed contrast with a dominant structure.[19] But where the conventional masque dramatizes potential subversion in order to contain it, Shelley's structure represents the eventual subversion of the established disorder by way of parodically inverted formal expectations: the first procession is formally disordered—anarchic—and it is eventually subverted by a formally controlled and measured "speech."[20] Through satiric contrast, the ludicrous masque of Anarchy is set against the poem's final solemnities, effecting a quiet exchange of power. The triumphal masque is first rudely interrupted, like a scene in a cobbled-together farce or a mechanical special effect in a loosely structured pantomime, by a kind of dramatic interlude in which a "maid," Hope, and a characteristically sublime "Shape" effect a transformation and transition to the famous rousing song to the men of England ("Rise like lions after slumber") that concludes the poem.

Structurally, then, the poem divides roughly into two parts, with a transition between them: the first twenty-one stanzas of the satiric masque, the transitional fifteen stanzas on the "maniac maid" and the indeterminate Shape, and the final fifty-five stanzas, an exhortation to material and intellectual "freedom." When Bertolt Brecht came to imitate *The Mask* in his "*Der anachronistische Zug oder Freiheit und* Democracy" (1947; pub. 1948), he tellingly chose as his model only the early stanzas, the "masque" or satire proper.[21] Even when using Shelley's poem in his 1938 essay on realism,[22] Brecht skips the opening stanza (which frames Shelley's *Mask* as a dream vision) and moves from the end of the procession of destructions (ll. 78–81), quoting only the famous lines 151–55 ("Rise like lions") as a transition to the stanzas (ll. 156–75) on material social conditions ("What is Freedom?"). Absent are the stanzas on Hope and the Shape, the central hinge or transformation scene of Shelley's poem.

Also missing from Brecht's quotations are Shelley's later, more positively exhortative stanzas (with their calls for an assembly and a confrontation); these stanzas subsequently did not figure in Brecht's imitation because they exude precisely the sort of meliorist optimism that his modern satire wished to call into question, particularly in the weary atmosphere of reconstruction and contemporary displays of "triumph" in the spring of 1947. In the German ballad, the refrain of *"Freiheit und* Democracy"—with the key word in English because it is an "anachronistic" concept accepted from or imposed by the West—is taken up by a chorus of seedy Berliner rats, concluding the ballad on a note of bleak absurdity, with imagery that could have come from a 1920s cartoon by George Grosz.

In our time, it is probably inevitable that we read Shelley alongside Brecht, as it were, despite the very great differences of temperament and politics between the two writers. Given intervening history, many of us are likely to view *The Mask of Anarchy* through a perspective closer to Brecht's than to Shelley's. Walter Benjamin's famous meditation on history, civilization, and barbarism is relevant here; it arose out of the same context of "triumphs" Brecht had in mind—from the Nazis to the Allied troops: "Whoever has emerged victorious participates to this day in the triumphal procession in which the present rulers step over those who are lying prostrate."[23] It is easy enough to understand how Shelley's hope (not to mention his imagery of violence) would seem inappropriate to Brecht's postwar context, and this sort of distance from Shelley's Romantic rhetoric is necessary for many in the late twentieth century as well. Skepticism toward Shelleyan hope and idealized "freedom" in general is a useful antidote for some tempting historical oversimplifications of *our* present. By the same token, Brecht can help us to appreciate what is truly strange, characteristically Romantic, in Shelley's satire: its admixture of represented violence and hope.

As Benjamin argued, Brecht was an important satirist in the tradition of Swift and—because his work stripped the illusions from things as they are—of Marx himself.[24] In Marxist terms, Shelley's satire can be read in light of Brecht's dramaturgical concept of *Verfremdung,* the "alienation" (or estrangement) effect, the immediate purpose of which is a kind of defamiliarization. Brecht himself said, "Estrangement means to *historicize,* that is, to consider people and incidents as historically conditioned and transitory. . . . [man] is conceivable not only as he is, but also as he might be—that is, otherwise—and the same is true for circumstances."[25] Brecht was able to claim Shelley as an exemplar of "realism," despite his use of figurative language (and seeming formalism), because Shelley's poem shares with Brecht the basic aim of unmasking the reified identities of society—and of encouraging intervention on the part of its audience. According to Brecht's view, true realism works by exposing the "causal nexus" (*Kausalkomplex*) of social relations, by "unmasking the dominant perspective as the perspective of the rulers . . . ."[26]

The absence in Brecht's poem of Shelley's bipartite structure serves to highlight the formal contrasts between his modern ballad and Shelley's— but it also emphasizes the *internal* differences between the two main sections of *The Mask of Anarchy:* how radically it shifts its own tonal registers, for example, and how Romantic (and "unsatiric") its primary exhortation may at first seem. How, exactly, is exhortation meant to function in this context? What is the exhortative mode doing in Shelley's most immediately topical political satire?

The Roman formal verse satire (as produced by Lucilius, Horace, Juvenal, and Persius) was conventionally bipartite in structure.[27] Usually a particular folly or vice was targeted in the first part and then, following an abrupt turn, the "opposing virtue was recommended" in the second part (Randolph, p. 172)—a fitting description of *The Mask of Anarchy*. In some cases, a "transition" leads to "a direct admonition to virtue or rational behavior couched in plain words" (Randolph, p. 175). Shelley merely exploits one side of the classical satiric tradition against the other, magnifying the importance of the positive "admonition" or exhortation against the negative attack. We have seen him working out this kind of strategy in "A Satire upon Satire," in which face-to-face plain talk displaces the weaponry of satire proper. Even in that draft the satiric weaponry is not completely canceled out, and the exhortative talk seems to be asserted against the poet's own deeper urge for a potentially more violent kind of meeting, a duelist's challenge. Still, Shelley clearly prefers the mode of exhortation to that of satire, for rhetorical as well as ethical reasons; and his satires, especially after *Peter Bell the Third*, always employ generic mixtures of negative and positive modes—while privileging, giving the last word to, the positive.

The exhortative mode is stylistically compatible with Shelley's prophetic poetry as well, which begins with a sense of perfectibility and ends in meliorism. Exhorting others to some imagined change is only the most direct form of his primary rhetorical imperative. To highlight what Shelley is about, here, Byron provides a useful counterexample.

> Oh pardon me digression—or at least
>   Peruse! 'Tis always with a moral end
> That I dissert, like Grace before a feast:
>   For like an aged aunt, or tiresome friend,
> A rigid guardian, or a zealous priest,
>   My Muse by exhortation means to mend
> All people, at all times and in most places;
> Which puts my Pegasus to these grave paces.
>
> (*Don Juan* XII.39)[28]

It is tempting to speculate that the "tiresome friend" referred to here is Shelley himself, the Shelley who is fictionalized in *Julian and Maddalo* as the idealist and (at least) verbal supporter of perfectibility—an ambiguous character whom Shelley ironically describes in the preface as "somewhat serious." At any rate, the point of Byron's satire is to deflate such earnestness: to question its claims. In contrast, Byron suggests a more profound and painful satiric correction.

> But now I'm going to be immoral; now
>   I mean to show things really as they are,
> Not as they ought to be: for I avow,
>   That till we see what's what in fact, we're far
> From much improvement with that virtuous plough
>   Which skims the surface, leaving scarce a scar
> Upon the black loam long manured by Vice,
> Only to keep its corn at the old price.
>
> (*Don Juan* XII.40)

This amounts to a complete repudiation of Shelley's attitude, as expressed, for example, in "An Exhortation." Byron's view is in fact closer to that of Pope, who remarked that "To reform and not to chastise, I am afraid is impossible . . . the best Precepts, as well as the best Laws, would prove of small use, if there were no Examples to inforce them."[29] Shelley's "muse" really does "by exhortation" expect to "mend," to persuade positively to right action, in the classical tradition of Ciceronian rhetoric.

Shelley refers to Cicero's *De Oratore* in the midst of his "Essay on Christianity," where he argues that Jesus was a reformer and rhetorical orator.[30] According to Shelley, the latter "did what every other reformer who has produced any considerable effect upon the world has done. He accommodated his doctrines to the prepossessions of those whom he addressed" (p. 242). Citing Cicero, Shelley explains that a "skilful orator" must take into account the "prejudices" of his audience, employing "professions of sympathy with their feelings" to gain their hearing (p. 242): "The interests therefore of truth required that an orator should so far as possible produce in his hearers that state of mind in which alone his exhortations could fairly be contemplated and examined" (p. 243). Shelley believes, however, that exhortation depends on a preparatory rhetoric, either a cooperative or a dialectically opposed mode that makes it viable for an audience. This is very close to Cicero's recognition that certain affective states, including "hope," will predispose the audience to receive the orator's message. Book II of *De Oratore* argues that

> the greatest part of a speech must occasionally be directed to arousing the emotions of the audience, by means of exhortation or of some form of reminder, to either hope or fear or desire or ambition, and often also to calling them back from rashness, anger or hope and from injustice, envy or cruelty.[31]

The ethical questions that surround such manipulations of the audience's emotions—even in the service of noble ends—press upon Shelley's somewhat apologetic discussions in this fragmentary essay of the reformer's need at times to dissemble. One view of the mode of exhortation is that it is appropriate only to political propaganda and religious sermonizing, forms meant to lead not to rational "consent" but to the irrational conformity of "conversion."[32] Shelley might not object to the term "propaganda," and he would probably agree that emotional excitement is necessary to rhetorical persuasion, but he would certainly have been chary of associations between the exhortative mode and religious enthusiasm. Indeed, some such concern may lie behind his essay's secularizing juxtaposition of Cicero and Jesus.

In early nineteenth-century England, the term "exhortation" was likely to bring to mind Evangelical (or vaguely "Methodist") sermon rhetoric. But this sort of exhortation to moral "reform" (or personal salvation) would in most cases have been more like *protrope* or *cataplexis* than *adhoratio*—more an admonishment backed by the threat of hellfire than a positive encouragement to ethical action.[33] This sort of subtle modal distinction is likely to have concerned Shelley. Clearly he was more interested in stimulating hope than fear, but he also follows the Ciceronian scheme in applying rhetoric to the task of dehortation, to calling back his audience from "rashness" and the "injustice" of public revenge. His use of Jesus as a reformer and orator in the fragmentary essay indicates his own involvement with the competing discourses of "reform" at the time; "reform" was a contested field in the early nineteenth century. Shelley, by his rhetorical ploy of treating Jesus as a canny reformer in the classical tradition, appropriates the exemplar of the pious, setting himself apart from the religious reformers by suggesting a kind of enlightened syncretic fusion of Ciceronian and Christian rhetorics—a secular *imitatio* for reformers, in which the ideal is not harangue but deliberate persuasion.

The germ of the exhortation section of *The Mask of Anarchy* seems to have been the famous stanzas Shelley wrote in 1819 and Mary Shelley published in 1839 as "Song: To the Men of England." Its picture of exploited (because alienated) labor made it a favorite text of later radicalism.[34]

V

The seed you sow, another reaps;
The wealth ye find, another keeps;
The robes ye weave, another wears;
The arms ye forge, another bears.

VI

Sow seed,—but let no tyrant reap;
Find wealth,—let no impostor heap;
Weave robes,—let not the idle wear;
Forge arms,—in your defence to bear.

(ll. 17–24)

In the sixth stanza each positive, imperative exhortation is balanced against a negative qualifier: productive actions are accompanied by acts of self-protection and class interest. The men of England are exhorted to sow, find, weave, and forge, but also to prohibit, withhold, and arm. The call to take a stand implies at least the possibility of defensive violence, and the precise meaning of "let not" is in any case unclear—it could conceivably include acts of retributive or repossessive justice as much as preemptive resistance.

This strategic space between passive resistance and active defense is where *The Mask of Anarchy*'s exhortation would enact its rhetoric as well. The implied threat of the chorus, "Rise like Lions after slumber/In unvanquishable number . . . Ye are many—they are few," is somewhat qualified by the series of six stanzas whose exhortations begin with a repeated passive: "Let the tyrants pour around," "Let the charged artillery drive," "Let the fixed bayonet," "Let the horseman's scimitars" (ll. 303–15). But after being told to let the tyrants in effect run over the assembly, the audience is exhorted: "Stand ye calm and resolute," let Panic "pass" (ll. 319–26), and depend on the final resort—the laws.

> "Let the Laws of your own land,
> Good or ill, between ye stand
> Hand to hand, and foot to foot,
> Arbiters in your dispute,
>
> "The old laws of England—they
> Whose reverend heads with age are grey,
> Children of a wiser day;
> And whose solemn voice must be
> Thine own echo—Liberty!
>
> "On those who first should violate
> Such sacred heralds in their state
> Rest the blood that must ensue,
> And it will not rest on you.

(ll. 327–39)

This appeal to law would claim the heritage of constitutional English Liberty for the reformers. It also suggests that the anarchic lawlessness of the state is outside the true, permanent structures of society. Shelley's rhetoric casts a blood curse on those in power and depicts the repression of reform as violence deployed to preserve the status quo.

But the depiction remains deeply ambivalent and unable fully to escape from the system it would subvert.[35] The ambivalence of *The Mask of Anarchy* toward popular violence reflects a profound ambivalence in the reform movement itself—which has since been mirrored in the historians' debates over Peterloo. The poem's equivocal call for passive resistance is not really a program of "nonviolence"—if by that we mean a strategy for avoiding violence altogether. Like Gandhi in India and King in the United States (and tragically unlike many in Tiananmen Square in 1989), Shelley in the England of 1819 clearly expects—though he hopes to defuse or divert—violence from the *other* side. The poem imagines this potential violence only too vividly. Its final oratory is introduced with images of the "indignant Earth" shuddering under the blood of her sons—the "sons of England"—as if the bloodshed had given rise to a primal chthonic utterance rather than a merely political protest.

The exhortative "speech" follows "as if" from the English earth—nation as nature—blood being made to cry out from the ground ("Blood is on the grass like dew"). This high prophetic language refers to what was by several accounts the initial act of real violence at Peterloo—the trampling of a mother and her baby by a yeoman's horse. This atrocity became the focus of many of the graphic representations and rhetorical denunciations of the clash, and Shelley himself drafted an even more indignant, bloodier stanza (but chose not to include it in the finished poem), in which a "red mist like the steam of gore" rises before the onrushing Anarchy: "And the earth where're he went/A cry Like a trampled infant sent . . . ."[36] He included other images of the hussars' bayonets thirsting "with . . . desire to wet/Its bright point in English blood" (Quinn, pp. 92–93), and in one canceled passage, drafted a disturbing speech that salutes and eulogizes those about to die.

> Bethink ye my beloved sons
> All things mortal [. . .] die once.
> There will come a destined day
> When the Earth must pass away [.]

> (Quinn, pp. 100–01)

These canceled lines emphasize something still present in the final draft: Shelley's poem can be accused of envisioning a kind of collective self-sacrifice of the people as the means to unmask their ongoing victimization. We cannot overlook that vision's own mimetic violence—its implication in the overwhelming system it desires to subvert by representing that system's horror. The poem itself represents this ideological implication; it does not merely wish away or dialectically supersede the potential bloodshed and the conflicts it signals; it embodies them in its own structure of images.

The bloodshed and the exhortative speech that follows come by way of fifteen stanzas of transition, stanzas in which the opening satiric grotesques are in effect wiped away, displaced by or transformed into a typically Shelleyan sublime allegory. This transformation scene is ushered in by the allegorical figure of Hope, a "maniac maid" in the guise of despair, who resembles the idealization of radical femininity seen, for example, in allegories of Liberty as well as in the actual Female Reformers of Blackburn, who one month before Peterloo, at another meeting, presented the male orators on the platform with a homemade liberty cap.[37] Shelley's Hope is similarly gendered; passively symbolizing the endangered purity of the movement, she is nonetheless willing to sacrifice herself for the future. But she also symbolizes the revolutionary appropriation and parody of the traditional feminine figure of Britannia, the same figure that is restored or rescued from appropriation in the Cruikshank print discussed earlier (Figure 4).[38] Prostrate, Hope lies down in the street in front of the horses, but is rescued by the intervention of "a Shape arrayed in Mail." When we next see her, she is "Ankle-deep in blood" but is "serene" and "quiet." Anarchy is dead, and its escaping horse tramples the antimasquers we had first encountered, clearing the stage for the Earth's newly hopeful utterance.

The allegorical relation of Hope to the Shape is intricate: just as hope is being sacrificed to violence, the indeterminate Shape rises up (not unlike Aeneas's divine protector) in "a rushing light of clouds and splendour" (l. 135)—to restore hope, but in an act of impersonal violence. It is significant that Hope's passive resistance does not exactly stop the hooves of the horses, but merely disperses the energies of Anarchy in a frenzied explosion that allows for a radical shift in scene and the destruction of the "Destructions." As in *Prometheus Unbound*, the actual moment of revolution is dispersed among several discrete actions and "actors," all of which it is possible to read as multilayered allegories. Hope gives way to the Shape, who gives way to the Earth; but the poem's words are not directly attributed to any one speaker (they are only heard "as if" from the earth)—they simply arise.

The pivotal figure in all this is the Shape, an anticipation of the "shape all light" in "The Triumph of Life." Its translucent amorphousness as an image is precisely its point; it first appears as "A mist, a light, an image" (l. 103) and then becomes the martial, armored anthropomorphic Shape that blends into the Turneresque landscape, the "sunny rain," the clouds, and the planet Venus. In Shelley's draft its initial appearance goes through a process of revision that resists specific or determinate references.

> A shape,   like like Day arose
>   dawn   arose
> [P]   like the ~~Angel of dawn~~
> [?] a mist,   a F[orm]
> { . . . }
>   [light]
> A mist,   a ~~shape~~,   an   image   rose.

(Quinn, pp. 54–55)

Apparently, as he revised, Shelley gradually rejected similes, choosing instead to blur the visible outlines of the figure so that it is visualized only vaguely, as superimposed on the sky—or even as consisting of the sky's chaotic and unpredictable weather, a mythopoesis of meteorological processes.[39] Ultimately, it becomes simply an overhead "presence" with unseen and unacknowledged influence. In an anticipatory parody of the destructive, lethean tread of the "shape all light" in "The Triumph of Life," this Shape's footsteps give birth to "thoughts." In this sense the Shape signifies the spirit of historical change itself, to figure the idea of history as a history of ideas.

On a material level, this vaporous Shape, with "wings whose grain/Was as the light of sunny rain" (ll. 112–13), is seen through as much as seen, and reminds us that the resemblances between *The Mask of Anarchy* and graphic satires include analogous modes of imagery and audience effect— for example, the popular "transparency." The device of the transparency was an elaboration on the popularity of prints and their potential "to give verisimilitude to slander."[40] Credited as the invention of George Townshend, the transparency was essentially a kind of print that exploited special effects of light, most interestingly by folding to superimpose or overlay multiple images. In the transparency, something hidden behind a veil or curtain could be revealed through this simple optical device, but ideal realities concealed behind appearances could also be allegorically "brought to light."[41] Transparencies were quite fashionable for a time, and were displayed on a number of special occasions. They both superimposed images and caused an image to "stand out" with a heightened vividness. A related form was the graphic medley, in which separate images were layered in a complicated collage.[42] Like the popular diorama, these forms exploit a taste for optical illusions or special effects and are based in manipulating the physiopsychology of perception and imagination.

These forms suggest ways in which the "textuality" of graphic satires—how their material forms of production and reception provoke certain ways of "reading" them—is analogous to Shelley's satire. The analogies go beyond simple iconography—they reinforce his poem's ties to such nonliterary representations and to their whole cultural milieu. Shelley also employs a technique of superimposing multiple images in order to cause his readers to perceive overlapping or substitutive "realities." Thematically, the imagined optical effects of *The Mask of Anarchy* are meant to figure the act of confronting and unmasking hypocrisy, the process of bringing hidden truth to light, through either the implied comment of juxtaposition or the imagistic device of enhanced "illumination."

Another example from popular satire may help to clarify the analogy. In one especially well-known transparency by George Cruikshank, exhibited in 1820 during the general illumination of London in honor of Queen Caroline, a "show-cloth" or theatrical curtain reveals Liberty, backlit by the glow of the free press, holding a pike and liberty cap in one hand and a portrait of Queen Caroline in the other (British Museum 14150; see Figure 5). The depicted radiance of the emblem disperses the clouds of murk surrounding a swarm of "vermin" with recognizable human heads—the accusers of the wronged Queen. (As the next chapter will show, Shelley attempted to enter the fray over Queen Caroline in a satire of 1820.) This "show-cloth" plate, reproduced in a pamphlet form, served to introduce a longer William Hone–George Cruikshank satire, a kind of sequential medley which bears a striking resemblance to *The Mask of Anarchy: THE POLITICAL SHOWMAN—AT HOME! EXHIBITING HIS CABINET OR CURIOSITIES AND Creatures—All Alive!* (title page, Figure 1; British Museum 14148). The series of plates opens with the Press as the "Showman," presenting an emblematic bestiary of "Creatures," including (in suggestive analogue to Shelley's iconography) a weeping crocodile and a Bishop's "MASK.—(an Incrustation—a Relique.)." A series or "procession" of these satirical caricatures culminates in a plate (British Museum 14168) showing the "EYE" of the Press shining down on the vermin—now revealed in their human forms—and scattering them in a confused rout.

If we turn for a moment from the graphic print to yet another resonant

FIGURE 5.   "The Transparency" from THE POLITICAL SHOWMAN—AT HOME! (British Museum 14150). A portrait of Queen Caroline is held by the Goddess Liberty; both are backlit by the glow of the free press, as enlightenment chases away caricatured vermin.

popular form of satire in Shelley's day—what Leigh Hunt called the time's "best medium of dramatic satire"—we find a further analogue in the pantomime.[43] Shelley was undoubtedly familiar with this most popular of popular entertainments (though he later disdained such subtheatricals): it was the height of fashion during the years before he left England, and we know that he saw pantomimes in London in 1809 and 1818.[44] Derived ultimately from the commedia dell'arte, it had become a traditional feature of the English stage by the Regency, especially on feast days, Boxing Day, or Easter, a vehicle for mildly topical or type-character satire by way of songs, caricature, conventional comedy, and a basic plot structure which could be varied indefinitely.[45] A short opening, usually based on classical myths, popular legends, or nursery tales, involves the story of frustrated love: a stern father or king preventing the union of his daughter and a suitor. This portion was often played in stylized costumes and cartoonlike "big heads"—oversized papier-mâché masks. At a key moment in the conflict the action is interrupted by the intervention of a "benevolent agent" (almost always feminine) who effects a "transformation scene," during which the masks and costumes are stripped off to reveal the conventional type-characters: Pantaloon, Harlequin, and Columbine. In the next section, the harlequinade, a slapstick chase ensues, filled out with comic or satiric songs and commentary, in which stage machinery and acrobatics provide startling special effects—mostly further transformations of persons, objects, or scenery into alternative identities or things. After a "dark scene" in a grotto or castle, there is a finale in an elaborate setting, sometimes including a grand procession, frequently brightly illuminated.

The pantomime is built around the trope of transformation—and it functions on every level. Grotesque gives way to comic, dark to light, ugly to beautiful, character to character, and object to object, by way of surprising dramatic optical illusions. In this, and in its asymmetrical, roughly two-part structure, as well as in its use of caricature masks, the pantomime obviously resembles *The Mask of Anarchy;* it is quite likely that it was one of the popular kinds of art Shelley had in mind when he wrote the satire. Perhaps the most compelling analogue, however, is the role of the feminine "benevolent agent," who arrives in a cloud or magical car, causes the pivotal metamorphoses and stripping away of masks, shifts the scene, and sometimes concludes by effecting an apotheosis of the characters. As Leigh Hunt said in the 26 January 1817 edition of the *Examiner,* the "sudden changes" of the pantomime were one of its unique pleasures (p. 57). As a writer, Hunt goes on to admit, he greatly envied the pantomime's ability thus to expose the truth about venal characters—"when transformed into their essential shapes." The transformations of pantomime seemed to him inherently unmasking, inherently *satiric* in their effects.

One satirical broadside from 1803 shows just how readily pantomime conventions—as well as visual transparencies—were associated with satire. As propaganda, its purpose was to arouse patriotism and to defuse fears of a threatened French invasion; in form, it parodies common pantomime playbills: "HARLEQUIN'S INVASION/or the/DISAPPOINTED BANDITTI/ With new Machinery, Music, Dresses, and Decorations . . . ."

> The whole to conclude with a GRAND ILLUMINATION
> and a
> TRANSPARENCY displaying BRITANNIA receiving the
> Homage of GALLIC SLAVES[46]

The broadside assumes familiarity with a layered overlay of popular modes and emblems: transparencies (in this case a theatrical curtain or show-cloth, of the kind often reproduced as prints), general illuminations, pantomime, print, Britannia, and triumphal procession. Again, this example only points to a broader discursive context, an idiom shared by various kinds of popular satire. The overdetermined two-part structure was in fact common in many popular media, in which dark grotesques are stopped, unmasked, and the scene transformed: sometimes from the grotesque to the comic—as in the first portion of the pantomime—and sometimes from the dark into a sublime display of an illuminated apotheosis.

The Mask of Anarchy's translucent, enlightening Shape rises out of this popular milieu, where overdetermined images take many forms with no clear boundaries between the forms. It has no single "source." The figure has obvious relatives within Shelley's work as well, repeated and overlapping images that include the "glorious phantom" which "may/Burst" upon the scene of relentless topical desolation "to illumine our tempestuous day" in the sonnet "England in 1819." That phantom's subjunctive status (or conditional status—only history, the poem implies, will determine which) is the reason for its indeterminate figuration—though it clearly suggests a range of possible abstractions, including Liberty and probably Britannia herself.

An earlier figure in Shelley's pamphlet *On the Death of Princess Charlotte* (1817) is actually named the Spirit of Liberty.[47] There, too, Shelley begins with a procession—in this case the funeral for the lamented daughter of the Regent—and then shifts registers suddenly to an unexpected triumph, a positive usurpation: "A beautiful Princess is dead:—she who should have been the Queen of her beloved nation, and whose posterity should have ruled it forever . . . LIBERTY is dead. Slave! I charge thee disturb not the depth and solemnity of our grief by any meaner sorrow" (p. 82).

The chief rhetorical device here, apart from the obvious appropriation of femininity, is the surprise of transformation—as the pamphlet asks the reader to transfer his or her emotional loyalties from the lost Queen to an abstract "sovereign," to allow the one to stand in the rightful place of the other. In this device the pamphlet images the psychological process of substitution necessary to the reception of radical reform. In terms of rhetoric, Shelley thus attempts to prepare his audience emotionally for his peroration, to accept as sublime and ideal his final antimonarchical image:

and if some glorious Phantom should appear, and make its throne of broken swords and sceptres and royal crowns trampled in the dust, let us say that the Spirit of Liberty has arisen from its grave and left all that was gross and mortal there, and kneel down and worship it as our Queen.

(p. 82)

This is also how *The Mask of Anarchy* works. The Shape, like the Spirit of Liberty—or the "benevolent agent" of the pantomime—supplants the caricatures of the Ministry, figuring a new order's uncertain shape, and it does so through an intervention on behalf of a noble, sympathetic female figure: the maid Hope, the daughter of Time. It is possible to read even in this phantom figure's contextual layers the image of the dead Princess Charlotte, the daughter of the Regent, as well as the very different character of Columbine in the pantomime. This is not mere speculation. For several years, in fact, Charlotte had been popularly associated with Columbine—the daughter of a tyrannical "Pantaloon"—and had been made to play the role of the nation's best hope.[48] The heiress apparent, she was beloved especially (but not exclusively) by those opposition forces who despised her father, and was made a symbol of the nation's brighter future. With the loss of her stillborn child and then her own death in 1817, the line of succession was broken. This was a moment of profound crisis: an heir was needed, and the descent was rapidly established with some maneuvering of a hasty marriage for the Duke of Kent, whose daughter Victoria was born in 1819 and reigned from 1837. The Regency itself can be seen as a structure of vicarious rule for ensuring the proper succession, a measure intended to avoid an interregnum and the accompanying threat of anarchy.

The whole Hanoverian line, in fact, leading to George IV, was the result of an earlier crisis of succession, resolved in the Act of Settlement of 1701. Interestingly, a 1702 poem praising the settlement, *Eusebia Triumphans*, provoked a response from Alexander Pope ("To the Author of a Poem, Intitled *Successio*")—part of which was worked into *his* later satire of succession, *The Dunciad*.[49] *The Dunciad* can be seen as "a succession poem for a kingdom that ought not to be," a kind of dark vision of degeneration (Seidel, p. 226), and canonical satire has frequently had as its focus problems of succession, descent, and inheritance. It is in this context that we can speak of *The Dunciad* as "a succession satire" (Seidel, p. 234), as a work typically satiric in its revelation of degenerative potential beneath the surface of orderly descent. This way of seeing satire is especially useful in the case of, say, Dryden's *MacFlecknoe* or, in another way, in *Absalom and Achitophel*.

The latter is actually a satire of *false* succession, with the popish plot the background to a struggle between heroic and satiric alternatives for the kingdom.[50] Of David's numerous progeny the poem explains, "But since like slaves his bed they did ascend,/No true succession could their seed attend" (ll. 15–16). The satire is clearly obsessed with legitimacy; the worst possible outcome is for a son to be "born a shapeless lump, like anarchy" (l. 172). Such issue must be cast out—or, what amounts to the same thing, satirized—in order to make way for heroes and their praise. The displacing of monsters by heroes, bastards by true heirs, is the basic narrative structure of the poem.

This description of Dryden's satire applies to *The Mask of Anarchy* as well, another poem that expels one line of rule—the 1819 government as the Ministry of Anarchy—to replace it with another, more ideally "legitimate" one—the "sons of England" under Liberty. Given Shelley's reliance on "the Laws of England," the specific laws of succession and their foundation in concepts of inheritance would seem relevant to the satire. Blackstone points out in his *Commentaries* that "The doctrine of *hereditary* right does by no means imply an *indefeasible* right to the throne."[51] The King, with Parliament, may "defeat this hereditary right; and, by particular entails, limitations, and provisions . . . exclude the immediate heir, and vest the inheritance in any one else." Particularly if the heir apparent "should be a lunatic, an idiot, or otherwise incapable of reigning," he could be disqualified and set aside. This section goes on to cite several famous cases in which the succession was altered, though always with the purpose of maintaining continuity. The whole point of English laws of inherited succession is to preserve order, to preclude the possibility of anarchy. "Where the magistrate, upon every succession, is elected by the people, and may by the express provision of the laws be deposed . . . by his subjects, this may sound like the perfection of liberty . . . but in practice will be ever productive of tumult, contention, and anarchy" (Blackstone, I, 217).

This danger of anarchic succession was fully appreciated by Edmund Burke. In *Reflections on the Revolution in France*, he discusses succession as a legal problem inherited from the Glorious Revolution and its aftermath. In the context of the French Revolution and English Jacobinism, Burke interprets this inheritance as standing against the popular election of kings and in favor of strictly hereditary succession by law (pp. 103–04).

Characteristically, he does so by arguing that "A state without the means of some change is without the means of its conservation" (p. 106), but also says that the provision for altering the succession does not open the legal possibility of republican revolution. He simply wants to "reconcile" peacefully, he says, "the sacredness of an hereditary principle of succession in our government, with a power of change in its application in cases of extreme emergency" (p. 105). Burke goes on to defend the Act of Settlement, which had established the Hanoverian line, as a preservation of this sacred principle.

> No experience has taught us, that in any other course or method than that of an *hereditary crown*, our liberties can be regularly perpetuated and preserved sacred as our *hereditary right*. An irregular, convulsive movement may be necessary to throw off an irregular, convulsive disease. But the course of succession is the healthy habit of the British constitution.

> (p. 109)

Shelley's poem joins a complex, ongoing conversation on reform by challenging this orthodox view of succession, challenging the established line with the concept of the people's alteration of succession—holding up an explicit, positive alternative to state "anarchy." His appeal to the old laws protecting the rights of Englishmen—the "heirs of Glory"—inevitably invokes the constitution as well as the legal issue of succession.

All theoretical discussions of succession turn on questions of inheritance and the legal doctrine of "representation," by which, as Blackstone says, the "lineal descendants" of a person "shall stand in the same place as the person himself would have done, had he been living" (II, 217). The battle for reform was a dispute over what constituted legitimate representation—over who could be said to "stand in the same place" as the English people; this was the central legal issue at Peterloo: whether " 'Unrepresented Inhabitants of Manchester' " would dare to elect their own representative. In a fundamental sense, the question of the right of representation in Shelley's day contained within it a potential challenge to the notion of hereditary, indefeasible succession itself. And it claimed to find this potential challenge in the constitutional tradition of English "rights." As Blackstone's cautious remarks and Burke's arguments reveal, the real threat lay in carrying the right of "altering the succession" too far, in supporting an elective monarchy—or worse, a popular, republican democracy—that would, in effect, wrest the succession from the royal line and vest it in the enfranchised populace.

On the other hand, Shelley was ambivalent about the idea of a people's succession or inheritance, especially when it came to questions of personal property, as an 1819 fragment drafted in *The Mask of Anarchy* notebook (and closely associated with "Song: To the Men of England") attests: "What men gain fairly—that they should possess,/And children may inherit idleness,/From him who earns it—This is understood."[52] This rightful line of inheritance, Shelley goes on to write, can be violated when the wealth is ill-gotten, "even as a stolen dress/Is stripped from a convicted thief . . ." (ll. 7–8). The radicalism of this defense of revolutionary expropriation is inevitably qualified by the tone of agrarian conservatism—the attitude toward matters of landed property—that is implied in the opening lines. This fragment, so closely associated with *The Mask of Anarchy* (in time and the material intertextuality of the shared manuscript), suggests, however, that Shelley's thinking after Peterloo about radical action on the part of the people was inevitably bound up with questions of inheritance—and the grounds for "purchase" or expropriation of the legal descent. This included the possibility that an inheritance could be transferred away from the heir—that the line of succession could be redrawn—in the pursuit of justice.

This is the significance of Shelley's formal mode of representation as I have explained it: the larger design of *The Mask of Anarchy* is based on a shift of figures, each succeeding figuration standing in the place of another, amounting to a trope of transformation. Or we might more precisely call it a trope of altered succession: of contingent transformations in inherited place and sovereignty, a series of shifting representations that work to question the ground of representation itself—in the political as well as the semiotic sense.

If *The Dunciad* is a succession satire "for a kingdom that ought not to be," then *The Mask of Anarchy* is a succession satire for a commonwealth that Shelley would (ambivalently) *wish* to be. The outlines of this future are drawn in the central stanzas of the exhortation, the apostrophe to Freedom in which Shelley defines liberty in socioeconomic terms, as freedom from material want and exploitation as well as freedom to seek justice, wisdom, peace, and love, by the intellectual light of "Science, Poetry, and Thought" (l. 254). The violent "slaughter" that the poem imagines (the logical extension of the actual killings at Peterloo) is in one sense the dark accompaniment to this projection; given the established (and nonrepresentative) political order of the day and the Ministry's antipathy to anything resembling the exercise of democratic will, to imagine a crisis and potential violation of succession—as I have argued the poem does—is perforce to imagine at least the possibility of bloodshed. In terms of the crises of English history, to "purchase" the succession, to go outside the established line, is by definition to rebel.

The French Revolution was in its time usually figured as a "sequence" or "progression" which was connected with a shift in the paradigm for conceiving of "revolution," the "conflict between the strictly astronomical sense of repetition, a full circle, and the sense of a single *revolution* as an overthrow, a half-circle, a disruption, and so an irreversible change."[53] In England, revolution in the latter sense would most frequently have been associated with the excesses of the French and with the English idea of "rebellion." The Glorious Revolution was commonly figured as a "revolution" in the former sense, a natural cycle, like the seasonal or the diurnal, of one basically legitimate power gaining precedence over another in a peaceful revolving action.[54] Especially during and just after the counter-revolutionary wars with France, many English radicals preferred the term "reform" for their program; Shelley was no exception. When viewed against the backdrop of the question of succession, especially, the appeal to "the Laws of England" reveals *The Mask of Anarchy* to be more reformist than revolutionary, in the modern sense.

Elsewhere Shelley applies the figure of succession to natural and political change, actively attempting to avoid the taint of rebellion. On the inside cover of one of his rough draft notebooks, he wrote: "the spring rebels not against winter but it succeeds it—the dawn rebels not against night but it disperses it."[55] The blatant organicism here is potentially "conservative," as we now understand Burke's or Coleridge's theories to be. It implies the gradual slowness of change, its locus outside of human control, and its cyclical reversibility; but the note is actually more complexly allusive than this single reading allows. It suggests a sense of the old and the new as dialectically opposed contraries: the reign of winter gives way, and the fabric of night is dissolved or dispersed. The overall effect in the end is total change. From the perspective of night, this dispersal—a conventional image of the Enlightenment—looks relatively "revolutionary," just as the possibility of spring in the "Ode to the West Wind" can be read as less a comforting sign of pastoral continuity than a disturbing harbinger of stormy, overwhelming change.

It comes as no surprise that the imagery of *The Mask of Anarchy* is grounded in the organic, in Nature—this is typical of Enlightenment appeals to a universal standard (as in "natural rights") outside of the existing human order. As we have seen, the poem's oracular exhortation is made to emanate from the primal forces of the earth, and the Shape partakes of the turbulent weather. The great assembly is called on "some spot of English ground/Where the plains stretch wide around" (ll. 264–65), and the "blue sky" and "green earth" are invoked as witnesses; the poem declares that this is in order to ground the meeting in "All that must eternal be" (ll. 266–69). Given Shelley's participation in the Enlightenment discourse of natural process, his avoidance in this satire of the imagery of cyclical history (which he employs in works from *Prometheus Unbound* to *Hellas*), and his focus instead on the moment of shifting succession, can be read as a gesture toward the revolutionary possibilities opened up by reform, possibilities of the intervention by the people in processes of change.

As is true of so much of Shelley's work, one of the primary facts of *The Mask of Anarchy* is that it was not published in 1819, as he intended. Had it been published, the poem might in some measure have succeeded in its aim of actively intervening in the descent of power. It attempts to represent reform and to legislate change by encouraging its audience—particularly the reformers—to redraw the line of succession, to enact a purchase of the political inheritance outside the established line through the agency of the oppressed and unrepresented. The process was to begin with acts of passive resistance, but might well have led to confrontations with state violence. This is to represent political history as potentially discontinuous because it is at least in part contingent upon the public will. As Aristotle said, deliberative or political rhetoric must employ exhortation (or dehortation) in seeking its goal of "establishing the expediency or harmfulness of a course of action."[56] And the political matters to which deliberative exhortation can address itself, therefore, are the matters "that ultimately depend on ourselves, and which we have it in our power to set going" (p. 35).

The Mask of Anarchy is directed to those members of the "popular" audience, sympathetic to reform, who were willing to intervene and "set going" events, who were ready to take action to instigate a "great and free development of the national will" (*Defence of Poetry*, p. 508). But the poem cannot conceal its ambivalences about the power it attempts to negotiate or the process of change it urges. Yet this in no way diminishes the status of its (intended) publication as an action. It is a pivotal poem in Shelley's career, like *The Cenci*, a deliberate bid for a representative popular voice, despite his misgivings. Significantly, this most fully realized of Shelley's satires takes the form of a generic medley, perhaps a sign of his inability to trust the satiric mode on its own but also a measure of his willingness finally to deploy the mode at a moment of historical crisis in order to address the vital question of the national struggle between hope and despair.

6 "Rough Festivals" and Charisma in *Oedipus Tyrannus; or, Swellfoot the Tyrant*

ENGLAND IN 1820 was captivated by a single public spectacle: the Queen Caroline affair. On 29 January, George III died, making way at last for the Regent to take the throne.[1] The Regency itself had been a kind of preparation for this eventuality, and the only obstacle to the orderly accession of George IV was the threat that his estranged wife would now return from the Continent to claim her throne. Caroline arrived in Dover on 6 June, just as her husband was sending the lawyer's briefcase (green bag) containing secret evidence against her to a committee of fifteen lords for examination. His immediate goal was divorce, but among the possible outcomes against his wife was the ultimate charge of high treason. Nothing of the sort happened; instead, the bill was dropped. But the opposition and the radicals found in Caroline a highly visible rallying point, a cause with popular appeal, and a way to attack the King and the Ministry without falling under the sanctions of the Six Acts.

Historians continue to debate whether political change was forestalled or was given a kind of push (by being given a central symbol of cultural aspirations) by the affair.[2] But the fact of the Queen's popularity, her charisma, is not in question. The Bill of Pains and Penalties against her was dropped in November; by the end of the year her public appearances became increasingly less volatile and arguably less significant. The Ministry could begin looking toward the coronation of her husband on 19 July 1821. On Coronation Day, Caroline was turned away from the closed doors of Westminster Abbey, an exclusion that was also a symbolic gesture marking the approaching end to her brief attempt to force her way inside the circle of power, a sign of the limits of her charisma.[3]

This chapter will examine Shelley's Aristophanic satire on the Queen Caroline affair, *Oedipus Tyrannus; or, Swellfoot the Tyrant*, not as a literary oddity ("Shelley's bawdy") but as a satire meant to be published and read (though it was ultimately suppressed), meant to be popular, which nonetheless remains deeply ambivalent about what "popular" might mean in the context of the diverse forces of opposition responding to and using Queen Caroline as a symbol. In his letters, Shelley mentioned Caroline only with patronizing contempt, but this may have served in part to mask an uncomfortable realization that he shared something with the whole affair: Shelley, too, was in exile and the focus of marital scandal, accused of mistreating *his* wife Harriet (as the correspondence with Southey during that summer of 1820 painfully emphasized). As a poet who would be a "legislator," he was outside looking in, hoping to move those within the circle of power. Writing *Swellfoot*, Shelley is in a position analogous to Caroline's. Or more precisely, he is like her diverse supporters in his sincere desire to tap into the forces of opposition she came to represent. But his play also betrays an uneasiness with the interclass pageantry and spectacle of the affair, and the unstable forces this crisis over the succession could unleash. In these terms, Shelley's satiric burlesque enacts poetic charisma as an ambivalent parody of the Queen's political charisma.

• • •

The marriage of the Prince of Wales to Caroline of Brunswick in 1795 had been a farce from the beginning, a cynical expedient for getting the Prince's debts paid. The two separated almost immediately, the estranged wife spending most of her time after 1814 out of the country. By 1818, the government organized the Milan Commission under Sir John Leach, which employed domestic servants, mostly, as spies to gather evidence of her misconduct abroad. The Ministry's anxiety over the uncertain but impending succession was the main reason for the intense attention to the absent Princess. The "trial" made it clear that the real threat posed by Caroline was not to her husband's peace of mind but to the peace and stability of the realm. In one telling speech, the Queen's Solicitor-General, Thomas Denman, asked rhetorically if the Bill of Pains and Penalties, should it be passed against her, might not "one of these days perhaps be provocative of the greatest calamity which can befall a nation—I would say of a civil war resulting from a dispute as to the succession of the Crown?"[4] The image of civil war, with all its associations in English history, or of an anarchic frenzy around a disputed succession, lurked behind these debates and must have fed back into the series of popular demonstrations in support of the Queen after her return in the summer of 1820.

One year after Peterloo and only months after the execution of the Cato Street conspirators, the government was faced with the repeated display of thousands cheering the outcast Queen, often while hissing her husband and his supporters. Her entry into London in June (in a deliberately improper open carriage, with the reformer Alderman Wood riding with her) and her later appearances and daily processions to the trial had all the pomp of state triumphs and all the volatility of popular carnivals.[5] There were riots in London, and the streets leading to the Houses of Parliament were barricaded, lined with troops to control the crowds. It is not necessary to read the activity of the crowd—part popular demonstration, part organized opposition—as a manifestation of working-class consciousness in order to see that it posed a threat to the status quo. The spectacle was in the end "followed" by everyone—whether through the streets or in the press; it involved a layered cross section of English social classes, as in the public sphere of an urban festival or carnival, where masking, mummery, and temporary license work to mix social groups (though not to blend them). In this it was like the traditional universal tour or state progress, as established by the time of Elizabeth, but less orderly and more demotic, and with the difference that Caroline was fighting for her crown, not celebrating her accession. This attached to her public appearances a sense of imminent danger, even the threat of revolution.

The symbolism and pageantry of traditional royal processions has been much discussed, especially in the form they reached during the Renaissance.[6] But it is important to realize that related ritual processions and parades—and their burlesque or parodic versions—were still practiced everywhere in Shelley's England. To name only one immediate and less familiar example: while at Eton he would have experienced, and may have participated in, the famous procession *ad montem*, in which the boys wore a medley of type costumes, representing everything from military ranks to civil professions and servants, and marched to a nearby hill, brandishing poles and flags.[7] This display was regularly attended by important persons—including royalty—and it included a range of carnival activities, among them mock violence and the playful extortion of money from passersby.

The carnivalesque license of such rituals, their allegory, and—in the case of the state progress—their movement over territory to represent power have made them favored subjects for New Historicists and others interested in the semiotics of culture, beginning with Clifford Geertz. In a 1977 essay, Geertz takes as his point of departure Weber's concept of charisma (as mediated in Edward Shils) and sketches three case studies— from Elizabethan England, fourteenth-century Java, and nineteenth-century Morocco—in which charisma is exercised through royal processions.[8] Charisma, as Geertz summarizes the concept, is not so much a personal quality or essence as it is a relational event, a matter of "the connection between the symbolic value individuals possess and their relation to the active centers of the social order . . ." (p. 122). A center in this sense is not fixed; it is a nexus of combustible social energy,

> the point or points in a society where its leading ideas come together with its leading institutions to create an arena in which the events that most vitally affect its members' lives take place. It is involvement, even oppositional involvement, with such arenas and with the momentous events that occur in them that confers charisma. It is a sign, not of popular appeal or inventive craziness, but of being near the heart of things.

> (pp. 122–23)

The social construction of charisma is most evident in "the ceremonial forms by which kings take symbolic possession of their realm," particularly royal progresses (p. 153).

Caroline's progresses and public appearances qualify as charismatic in just this sense, as a challenging parody of her husband's assumed legitimacy. This is reinforced by the fact that she was in effect competing for her place, fighting for possession of the center. In fact, the "most flamboyant expressions" of charisma "tend to appear among people at some distance from the center, indeed often enough at a rather enormous distance, who want very much to be closer" (Geertz, p. 144). The most dramatic example of her doomed charisma was displayed in the counterpageantry accompanying her funeral procession—as even her corpse became the focus of competing municipal, royal, and radical interests, in a series of bizarre parades, demonstrations, roadblocks, riots, and skirmishes along the route of her final "progress."[9]

• • •

"There is no decisive news yet from London about the Queen," Shelley wrote to Claire Clairmont from Bagni di San Giuliano on 15 November 1820, "it is expected this day, and all the papers of the trial have been kept for you" (*Letters*, II, 597). Once again it is made clear just how far Shelley in Italy was cut off from the center of English politics, how much he was forced to depend on gossip and the "newspaper erudition" he later referred to as a necessity of his exile (in the preface to *Hellas*). Most of his news from England at the time came through the letters of friends like Hunt and Peacock, or thirdhand, through the Paris newspaper, *Galignani's Messenger*, which (as Shelley notes) often repeated parts of stories printed in *The Examiner* (12 July 1820, p. 213). His letters about the affair reveal an almost wistful sense of distance from the center of events, as he repeats gossip and engages in political analysis.

On 30 June 1820, Shelley comments to the Gisbornes on "public affairs in England":

> How can the English endure the mountains of cant which are cast upon them about this vulgar cook-maid they call a Queen? It is scarcely less disgusting than the tyranny of her husband, who, on his side, uses a battery of the same cant. It is really time for the English to wean themselves from this nonsense, for really their situation is too momentous to justify them in attending to Punch and his Wife. Let the nation stand aside, and suffer them to beat till, like most combatants that are left to themselves, they would kiss and be friends. And Peers and Peeresses to stalk along the streets in ermine! It is really time to give over this mummery. Whilst 'that two-handed engine', &c.
>
> The National Debt is indeed a two-edged sword.
>
> (*Letters*, II, 207)

Here we have the germ of *Swellfoot the Tyrant*, including all the salient topics—the perceived financial crisis, the carnivalesque violence, the display of the royal domestic dispute ("Punch and his Wife," "this mummery"), and the seriousness of the people's plight (with hints of violence)—incongruously mixed in with the ridiculous events.

Behind the disgust lies Shelley's real fear (mixed with hope) that the government might fall as a result of the trial. He depicted such a fall, nervously and ambivalently, as potentially fortunate for the people, as opening up the possibility of a governmental succession. On 17 September 1820, he hopes that "the mistake into which the ministers have fallen will precipitate them into ruin; whoever may be their successors in power, it is impossible that they should exercise it worse" (*Letters*, II, 235). In an earlier letter (20 July), he had joked that perhaps the Queen, like Pasiphae, had been consorting with a bull, and that Parliament should therefore consider "a bill to exclude all Minotaurs from the succession" (*Letters*, II, 220). In *Swellfoot*, Shelley makes the Minotaur a potent symbol of the people in the collective act of seizing the succession. More often he refers to "successors" as the parliamentary legislators who might take over, should the present government fall.

In a letter to Byron (17 September), Shelley says that he has heard rumors that the exiled Lord may have carried dispatches from Italy to the Queen.

> Do you take no part in the important nothings which the most powerful assembly in the world is now engaged in weighing with such ridiculous deliberation? At least, if Ministers fail in their object, shall you or not return as a candidate for any part of the power they will lose? Their successors I hope, & you if you will be one of them, will exert that power to other purposes than their's.—As to me, I remain in Italy for the present.

> (*Letters*, II, 236)

Facetiousness aside, Shelley may have expected that Byron would play a role in a new Whig ministry, and his pained envy of Byron's closeness to the center of power—his charisma—can be read in the last sentence. The prominence of the words "power" and "powerful" in this and the previous letter, along with the idea that Byron might soon be acknowledged as a "legislator" of some sort, suggests the arguments Shelley was soon to construct in *A Defence of Poetry* for the existence of an alternative power, wielded even by those poets who would, like the nightingale, remain unseen.

By the time the letter to Byron had been written, Shelley had begun his own attempt to participate in events—an attempt that would eventually fail when the work was suppressed under threat of prosecution[10]— *Oedipus Tyrannus; or, Swellfoot the Tyrant*. It, too, focuses on a possible succession, brought about by the financial pressures and the catalyst of the royal dispute. "Cobbett's euthanasia seems approaching," Shelley had written to Peacock, "and I suppose you will have some rough festivals at the apotheosis of the Debt" (*Letters*, II, 212–13). "Cobbett's euthanasia" probably refers to the "killing" of the country's economy—or to the literal killing of the poor—by a financial crash brought about by the ascension and ultimate ceremonial "apotheosis" of the country's true deity, the national debt.[11] The references to "Punch and his Wife" and "rough festivals" are telling: they suggest that Shelley saw the Queen Caroline affair in the topsy-turvy context of English folk customs, including "rough music" and popular fairs (where puppet plays were seen alongside other grotesque spectacles), and the dangerous license they gave to the lower orders.

The immediate occasion for composing the drama, as Mary Shelley later told it, was an Italian festival.[12] At the baths outside of Pisa, Shelley was inspired on St. Bartholomew's Day, 24 August 1820, by the noises of the celebration taking place outside his windows: while reading aloud one of his very serious odes (either the "Ode to Liberty," as Mary said, or perhaps the "Ode to Naples"),[13] he was interrupted by the grunting of hogs being brought to the fair. The hogs suggested Aristophanes' chorus of frogs, and the idea arose to write an Aristophanic satire around a chorus from the "swinish multitude."

But the festival day itself would probably have carried significant associations with England. Until it was abolished in 1855, Bartholomew Fair was one of the more riotous "rough festivals" on the calendar. Begun in the twelfth century (significantly, by a former royal jester), it involved livestock markets, menageries, and various revelries and theatricals. St. Bartholomew celebrations included in some regions pagan survivals like "burning Bartle"—an effigy of mysterious origin representing, according to one legend, a pig thief.[14] In 1818, the popular fair competed with a London reform meeting, helping to keep attendance at the latter low.[15] In 1822 thousands rioted when the authorities threatened to shut down the related festival at Smithfield.[16] In a famous satiric passage of *The Prelude*, Wordsworth disapprovingly describes "that ancient festival" and its chaotic "anarchy and din,/Barbarian and infernal" (ll. 686–87) as a grotesque image of "blank confusion!" (l. 722), made up of popular and vulgar entertainments, including "The Horse of knowledge, and the learned Pig" (l. 708).

> . . . Wild Beasts, Puppet-shows,
> All out-o'-the-way, far-fetched, perverted things,
> All freaks of nature, all Promethean thoughts
> Of man, his dullness, madness, and their feats

All jumbled up together, to compose
A Parliament of Monsters.

(ll. 713–18)[17]

As early as Ben Jonson, Bartholomew Fair had been associated with the most extreme kind of popular raucousness ("yearly enormities").[18] His comedy of the same title incorporates disguises, satire on the legal system and Puritanism, whoring in the pig stalls, and a concluding knockabout puppet play, a fair that sounds a great deal like Shelley's depiction of England in 1820.

Shelley's satire on the royal puppet farce contains not only the swinish chorus but also "the public sty" (the House of Commons), bawdy jokes, the transformation of pigs into bulls, and a monstrous Minotaur ("John Bull") that the Queen ("Iona Taurina") rides in her hunt of the verminous ministers during a violent, ritualistic feast. The satirical mix has many sources, of course, but the English "ancient festival" taking place at the moment Shelley conceived of the drama—and its fortuitous appropriateness to the Queen's charismatic engagement of the boisterous crowd—is surely important. Besides providing part of the context for the play, it reveals Shelley's position of remoteness—his exile—highlighted in this case by the distance between the rural Italian fair and the festivities in London.

As Mikhail Bakhtin has argued, the literary genres of parody, satyr play, and satire are rooted in the collective rituals of carnival, its heteroglossic mix of "high" and "low" languages, violations and inversions, and tropes of transformation.[19] Discussing the novel (and its ancestor, Menippean satire), he suggests that the satirical masks of the fool or clown "grant the right . . . to parody others,"

> the right to act life as a comedy and to treat others as actors, the right to rip off masks, the right to rage at others with a primeval (almost cultic) rage—and finally, the right to betray to the public a personal life, down to its most private and prurient little secrets.

(p. 163)

Shelley's Aristophanic satire is carnivalesque in precisely this way. It draws upon a popular tradition—a set of conventions, "masks," and "licenses"—within which (as Bakhtin indicates) Aristophanes also belongs (pp. 218–20).

The Old Comedy was originally performed at the festival of Dionysus, and most critics agree with Aristotle that it has generic roots in the "protosatiric" tradition of iambic poetry as practiced, for example, by Archilochus and Hipponax.[20] This does not mean that Aristophanes himself was primarily a political poet. The scabrous quality of his comedy is a sign of its "institutionalized and culturally sanctioned exemption from" normative standards, its situation in the delimited public space of the festival.[21] For Shelley, Aristophanes' texts would have been the property of privilege and learning; festivals, on the other hand, were clearly associated with plebeian culture (though open to other groups). His recombination of these modes in *Swellfoot* forcefully brings together learned comedy and "learned pigs," classical allusions and popular forms.

This is precisely the kind of generic mixture, and the accompanying interaction of social classes, that Shelley would naturally have associated with English festivals. At London's Bartholomew Fair, for example, an eighteenth-century spectator could witness ballad opera, pantomime-ballet, and a wide diversity of entr'acte and afterpiece performances— all alongside ropedancers, tumblers, freak shows, and puppet farces.[22] As these diversions suggest, the fairs were predominantly plebeian territory. But as one ephemeral poem on Bartholomew Fair makes clear, class diversity—whatever the statistical realities—was part of the lore surrounding festival audiences.

> Each wooden house then groans to bear
> The populace that croud the Fair. . . .
> The chambermaid and Countess sit
> Alike admirers of the wit:
> The Earl and footman *tête-à-tête*
> Sit down contented in one Seat.
> The Musick plays, the Curtain draws
> The Peer and 'prentice clap applause.
> The house is filled with roaring laughter
> From lowest pit, to highest rafter.[23]

It is a fact that royalty visited the stalls at Bartholomew Fair on more than one occasion, and entrepreneurs were known to improve and clean up their facilities in order to entice the higher orders to mix with the crowd.[24] But these are pointed examples of deliberate mixing (or slumming) rather than proof of a harmonious blending of classes.

Shelley's term "rough festivals" would also have carried connotations of a more exclusively lower-order—and violent—tradition, that of charivari or rough music, ritual processions to the tune of satirical songs and raucous noise, which were part of English popular culture during the eighteenth century and into the nineteenth century.[25] These impromptu pageants of public ridicule and violence, protean in their forms and political applications, present the crowd as a deliberative body and a punitive mob. They draw on a repertoire of theatrical symbols to create a deliberate "countertheater," including mock triumphs, effigy burnings, and—most significantly for *Swellfoot*—mock hunts, in which the victim of community hostility is figured as a stag to be chased down by dogs and killed.[26] Rough music could be directed against political targets: it occasionally had Jacobite and (later) Jacobin overtones. But what is most interesting in the present context is that the practice was commonly aimed at sexual offenders, including the perpetrators of marital misconduct and, particularly, adulterous or dominating women (and/or their submissive husbands). Thus it might naturally have been associated with the sordid situations of the Queen Caroline affair.[27]

As a customary practice, rough music is characteristically ambivalent toward the structures of power.[28] Viewed from one perspective, at least, such rituals are normative and punitive; and in their mockery, they at least partly underwrite the authority of the forms they satirize. Actual occurrences of rough music seem more often than not to have been culturally "conservative," directed against the deviant, the outsider, or the violator of the status quo. Sometimes these targets happen to have included those in power. *Swellfoot* is not rough music per se but is (among other things) an appropriation of and commentary upon such practices. It is a critical response to the dangerously unstable element in the people's ambivalent support for the Queen, and it evinces ambivalences of its own—toward the people.

Shelley's two-act burlesque concludes with a rough-music mock hunt of the King by the Queen (with the people).[29] The titular monarch who rules the "Swinish multitude"—a conventional play on Burke's famous phrase[30]—is confronted with an oracle that echoes Denman's speech on behalf of the Queen, offering only two options: "reform or civil war." The oracle sees a time when the Queen will hunt the King through the streets with hogs for hounds. Like that other Oedipus, Swellfoot persists in his tyranny until the oracle is fulfilled. In the climactic allegorical scene, the goddess Famine is addressed by Liberty, and the Queen is transformed into a huntress, riding the monstrous "Ionian Minotaur" (John Bull) and scattering the King and his ministers as they are metamorphosed into vermin. Throughout, the play works by incongruities, by treating "Sophocles' matter in the spirit of Aristophanes."[31]

In this it resembles cartoons like those of Gillray and Cruikshank.[32] It is doubtful that Shelley could have seen any of the flood of Caroline prints in Italy, but, as I have argued in the preceding chapters, Shelley's satire in general drew from a mixture of common cultural sources (in the broad sense of "popular"). He did not need to see actual prints in order to write a satire sharing much of their iconography and rhetorical devices; such things were in the air, carried by the banter of Leigh Hunt's columns in *The Examiner*, for example, and other written satires, as well as by the previous decades of pamphlets Shelley may have seen.[33] Many of these satirical materials were drawn from or, in turn, influenced unlicensed theatricals and school performances, which in turn had strong ties to the substrata of popular practices that included fairs and rough music. These were the sorts of performances with which Shelley—growing up in Sussex, attending Eton and Oxford, and living for a time in London—was surely familiar. Most important, Shelley's use of the idiom of such materials seems to indicate a desire to *make* his satire popular in the sense that the pantomime, for example, or other fair theatricals were popular: not that it was intended for an exclusively plebeian or demotic reception, but that it is set in an imagined public arena of discourse that envisioned the possibility of a mixed-class response, where genres and groups could interact in that *virtual* (or generic) space Bakhtin called "the public square where the folk gather."[34]

One of the specifics of this popular idiom is its multilayered referential allusiveness. We see this in satiric prints, in particular, which often combine "texts" of different sorts and on many levels, layering emblematic pictures, direct labels, mottoes from literature or the Bible, sonnets, ballads, and epigrams. Unlike *The Mask of Anarchy*, however, *Swellfoot* openly adopts the convention of *satirizing* such satiric allusiveness—a convention which is perhaps most evident in a loyalist parody such as THE DORCHESTER GUIDE, OR, A HOUSE THAT JACK BUILT. This takes aim at the most famous Hone satire of all, *The Political House That Jack Built*, turning the original's anticlericalism on its head.[35] Its targeted "priest" is clearly a Dissenting preacher in a wide-brimmed hat (and having distinctly swinish features). The print has no motto; indeed, the parody satirizes in its preface the overuse of mottoes by the radical printmakers:

> Not yet sufficiently advanced in radical perfection to oppropriate [*sic*] to my own use the labours of others, I abstain from affixing mottos to my pictures: I have, indeed, taken a small liberty with Mr. Milton; but, as he cannot see the theft, I trust, a good-natured public will not turn Informer.

The satire here is obviously aimed at the patchwork learning of the lower-order or middling radicals, whose use of biblical, classical, and modern literary sources, and incorporation of myth, animal fable, and aphorism, were characteristic of many popular works.

Swellfoot also plays on this kind of bounding overallusiveness, siding with the radicals but apparently joining with the educated as well in mocking the pretentious methods of much lower-order radical discourse. Critics have long recognized that *Swellfoot* is too learned, with its Greek puns and allusions to Aristophanes and Sophocles, to have been appreciated by a simply defined "popular" (or plebeian) audience.[36] It may well be that "Shelley is experimenting with yet another conception of audience," drawing in the learned, upper-order reader only to place him in the position of being identified with the targets of Iona's violence in the final scene.[37] Even more likely is the possibility that Shelley has in mind an audience less "pure" in its composition, that some notion of a thickly multilayered audience (in terms of class, education, and position relative to reform) is part of the poem's complex satiric intention. Its multilayered allusive idiom could correspond to an imagined class mixture among its readers, an implied readership made up of interacting interests—a volatile social *satura*.

• • •

This conception of audience(s) may be reflected in the play's mixture of the tragic and the ludicrous. The opening scene is "A magnificent Temple, built of thigh-bones and death's-heads, and tiled with scalps. Over the Altar the statue of Famine, veiled . . ." (p. 390). Into this solemn setting enters the broadly caricatured George IV, who speaks in comically inflated language of the "supreme Goddess" Famine. References to his obesity and coiffure set the (low) tone for what is to follow:

> . . . this kingly paunch
> Swells like a sail before a favouring breeze,
> And these most sacred nether promontories
> Lie satisfied in layers of fat; and these
> Boeotian cheeks, like Egypt's pyramid,
> (Nor with less toil were their foundations laid),
> Sustain the cone of my untroubled brain,
> That point, the emblem of a pointless nothing!

(I.3–10)

The relentless jokes on the King's corporeal body, starting with the title, play off his gout and love of rich food, partly with the intention of baiting the censors. As Shelley was well aware, Leigh Hunt had been imprisoned for writing a similar libel (the year Shelley published *The Devil's Walk*), calling the Regent "this *Adonis in loveliness*," a "corpulent gentleman of fifty!"[38]

But Shelley is deadly serious about the exploitation the corpulence represents at a time of widespread poverty. Mary Shelley's somewhat apologetic note to the poem first made this point, calling it a "mere plaything of the imagination," clearly full of "the ridiculous," but also noting that it reveals a "deep sympathy for the sorrows of humanity, and indignation against its oppressors" (p. 410). The absurdity has a serious purpose: to target perversions of social relations—down to their material details— that were dramatized in the Queen Caroline affair. Particularly in its characterizations of Utilitarian "Jews"—Solomon, Moses ("the sow-gelder"), and Zephaniah—the play takes a swipe at Malthusian doctrines, then controversial in reformist circles.[39] Its underlying tone of pathos is part of a "sentimental" (full of sympathetic feeling) way of challenging Malthusian heartlessness; on the other hand, many of its moments of apparent cynicism about the *prospects* of the "swine" are based in a penetrating analysis of the entrenched structures of poverty and exploitation. For Shelley, the social violence of poverty and hunger has human agents, causes more personal and specific than Malthusian numbers, but he shares the Utilitarians' bleak evaluation of the seriousness of the problem.

Swellfoot's tyrants actively plot systematic oppression. When the Pig Chorus cries "Iona for ever!—No Swellfoot!," Mammon (Liverpool) reacts:

> It had been but a point of policy

> To keep Iona and the Swine apart.
> Divide and rule! but ye have made a junction
> Between two parties who will govern you
> But for my art.

> (I.342–46)

This "junction/Between two parties"—the Queen's popular support—is based in economic distress. But we should notice that it also represents an extremely volatile social mixture with explosive possibilities. When the chorus surrounds Iona to protect her in Act II, its strophe is explicit in its pragmatism: "Hog-wash has been ta'en away:/If the Bull-Queen is divested,/We shall be in every way/Hunted, stript, exposed, molested" (II.i.137–40). The play's ominous oracle ("reform or civil war") is especially threatening when it comes to the "lean-pig faction" made dangerous by hunger, the "PIGS OUT-OF-DOORS" who break down the doors of Parliament ("The Public Sty") in Act II (p. 403). As in *The Mask of Anarchy*, here the forces of change must work outside the boundaries of legitimate representation. But here the noble mass meeting degenerates into a noisy rout.

As they plead for fairness, the pigs' squeals modulate to grunts—from "Eigh!" to "Aigh!" to "Ugh!"—a bathetic parody (after Aristophanes' famous frogs) of the cries of "Woe!" in Greek tragedy. The swine are sacrificial beasts whose slaughter not only serves the royal demand for fat but also staves off for a time a plague of famine and violence. Like Satan in *The Devil's Walk*, this monarch lives off the parasitic husbandry of his subjects. The swinish chattels appeal to feudal order in their complaints, which are reminiscent of the people's appeal to "the old laws of England" in *The Mask of Anarchy*. Here, however, the tale of traditional hereditary order is a completely transparent fiction.

> Under your mighty ancestors, we Pigs
> Were bless'd as nightingales on myrtle sprigs,
> Or grasshoppers that live on noonday dew,
> And sung, old annals tell, as sweetly too;
> But now our sties are fallen in. . . .

> (I.39–43)

(If pigs could fly.) Again, as in *The Mask of Anarchy*, this suggests that liberty is a necessary condition for the general "health" of the populace.

The present horror is that, deprived of liberty, starved, and diseased, the pigs are to be butchered and consumed anyway: their "sties are fallen in." The "unhappy nation" of swine point out that they must be fed if they are to feed; even self-interest should argue they be better cared for, and "besides, it is the law!" (l. 66).

Defiant challenges combine with an appeal to rights under the law and the imagery of butchery, bloodshed, "colons," and "bristle." We have seen in other poems and poetic fragments how Shelley deliberately represents his revulsion at cannibalistic political relationships. There is a sense of deep revulsion undermining all of *Swellfoot*'s jokes, as if they were too close to home truths about English society. But the satire's relentless attacks on Crown, Church, and taste also served the purpose of shocking the status quo. The play was deemed worthy of suppression, despite its esoteric allusiveness.

The Chorus of Swine complains about "Boeotia's" (a proverbial site of stupid citizens) excesses of wealth and poverty, and the violence that protects this arrangement—the bellicose "Boeotian League," the play's version of the Holy Alliance. The Chorus of Priests praises the same arrangement as they hail their patron goddess: "We call thee FAMINE!/ Goddess of fasts and feasts, starving and cramming!" (II.ii.5–6). Their mock prayers belong generically to the parodies of solemn religious rituals in Aristophanes.[40]

In Act II (scene ii), the ghastly goddess at her feast confronts the graceful female figure of Liberty, "rises," and then abruptly disappears "though a chasm of the earth" (as if through a mechanical stage trap in a pantomime trick or transformation scene), and Queen Iona is transformed into a huntress. No Artemis, she *is* terrible in the pursuit of her enemies. This brief Liberty-Famine scene is the climax of the piece. Against the manipulative or coercive rhetoric of the rest of the skit, Shelley juxtaposes a short and relatively simple exhortative speech by the goddess Liberty, introduced by this stage direction:

> [A graceful figure in a semi-transparent veil passes unnoticed through the Temple; the word LIBERTY is seen through the veil, as if it were written in fire upon its forehead. Its words are almost drowned in the furious grunting of the PIGS, and the business of the trial. She kneels on the steps of the Altar, and speaks in tones at first faint and low, but which ever become louder and louder.

(p. 408)

Analogous to Shelley's reading voice being drowned out by the pigs at the baths of San Giuliano, Liberty's speech goes almost unnoticed among the raucous "business of the trial." In the ensuing slapstick ending, she is summarily forgotten by the play itself: she never speaks again, and it is not clear from the stage directions whether she is to disappear or remain, mute, at center stage.

This forgotten exit is emblematic of Shelley's fear that the cause of reform was being drowned out by the uproar over the Queen (even as the Whig opposition was being advanced). Before disappearing, Liberty, too, addresses the goddess Famine—the current head of the realm.

> I charge thee! when thou wake the multitude,
> Thou lead them not upon the paths of blood.
> The earth did never mean her foison
> For those who crown life's cup with poison
> Of fanatic rage and meaningless revenge—
>   But for those radiant spirits, who are still
> The standard-bearers in the van of Change.
>   Be they th' appointed stewards, to fill
> The lap of Pain, and Toil, and Age!—
> Remit, O Queen! thy accustom'd rage!
> Be what thou art not! In voice faint and low
> FREEDOM calls *Famine*,—her eternal foe,
> To brief alliance, hollow truce.—Rise now!

(II.ii.90–102)

The incantatory language and rhythms of this passage should be familiar to readers of Shelley's other satires, but this is not the kind of curse we have seen elsewhere. Even that destructive rhetorical power would seem out of place on *Swellfoot*'s farcical stage. True, the imperative to Famine— "Be what thou art not"—is a call for a transformation in fundamental social relations, both an exhortation to Famine and an implied *de*hortation to the people (warning them away from revenge). But the speech is not addressed directly to the people, nor to the real "Queen" herself, the charismatic focus of the action. Given the dark overtones of the conclusion, and these structural indirections, it is worth considering the question, Who, precisely, *is* being addressed by the satire as a whole?

Aristophanic comedy commonly included the sometimes satirical device of the parabasis, in which a character would break the frame of the play at a key moment in order to address the audience directly, often speaking on behalf of the playwright. Topical and political references—as well as passionate exhortation—are common in parabases, expressed in a mixed "admonitory/abusive/didactic" mode.[41] Like a parabasis, the speech to Famine is addressed directly to Shelley's audience. Of his planned volume of "*popular songs* wholly political," Shelley said that the purpose was to "awaken & direct the imagination of the reformers" (1 May 1820, *Letters*, II, 191). For him, "the reformers" would most likely have included an elite element, those relatively educated leaders who might identify themselves as potential "standard-bearers in the van of Change," and poets and political orators were clearly foremost among this imagined leadership.

Shelley's own tendency to set apart as his primary audience "the more select classes of poetical readers"[42] can mislead us into assuming that a too narrowly defined demotic audience is implied for the "popular songs." In the Romantic and modern eras, at least, "popular" often means "middling," not "select," precisely because it *is* broader (not only "lower"), less unitary in level of understanding and taste. When it comes to *The Mask of Anarchy* or *Swellfoot the Tyrant*, Shelley's notion of writing for a "popular" readership probably involves a dynamic concept: the negotiation of working relationships or transfers of power among the various constituent elements in his composite audience. In this he might well have agreed with a later (and very different) satirist, Bertolt Brecht:

> *Popular* means: to be understandable to the broad masses, taking up their forms of expression, and enriching them . . . representing the most progressive section of the people in such a way that it can take over leadership . . . transmitting the achievements of the section now in leadership to the sections striving for leadership.[43]

The sophisticated intertextual allusions of the Liberty-Famine scene can be explained by recognizing that Shelley intended to address the major poets of the age as a key group among the "leadership" in his audience. As Kenneth Neill Cameron first pointed out, the scene is clearly indebted to the young Coleridge's "LETTER from LIBERTY to Her Dear Friend FAMINE" and the other essays in the collection *Conciones ad Populum* (1795).[44] Once more in this final satire, as he had in *The Devil's Walk*, Shelley turns to Coleridge as a model for political writing, as a source of political energy and hope that he obviously associated with the 1790s more than with his own postwar era.

Coleridge's "LETTER from LIBERTY" depicts in a highly traditional alle-gorical mode the usurpation of true religion by "The Dry-nurse of that detested Imp, Despotism," a harlot with "MYSTERY" on her forehead.[45] Shelley inverts the values, making the mysteriously veiled figure inscribed "LIBERTY" his displaced deity, and FAMINE the usurper. In Coleridge, Lib-erty addresses Famine:

> O FAMINE, most eloquent Goddess! plead thou my cause. I meantime will pray fervently that Heaven may unseal the ears of its vicegerents, so that they may listen to your first pleadings, while yet your voice is faint and distant, and your counsels peaceable. —
>
> ("LETTER from LIBERTY," p. 31)

Shelley, too, is in the somewhat desperate position of pleading with and petitioning power while hoping for the best. But his parody of the "plea" makes it into an explicit question of the *rhetorical* leadership of the "multi-tude" ("lead them not"). The "vicegerents" (or "stewards") are not tyrants but the poets, demagogues, and orators of the reform movement.

In this collection Shelley found much to imitate, including the ambiv-alent stance of arguing against revenge while promoting reciprocal in-dignation. He obviously took from it specific iconography (of skeleton temples and sacrifices), frank talk of blood, and the analysis of revolution-ary resentment ("the Ancients fatted their Victims for the Altar, we pre-pare ours for sacrifice by leanness" ["On the Present War," *Conciones*, p. 68]). But the result is more than mere "imitation": it amounts to a kind of provocative intergenerational intertext. What is most significant is the choice of model and what it says about—and does to—Shelley's own situation. As in his relation to Wordsworth, here Shelley seems to be trying to place himself in the lineage of Coleridge the poet while distanc-ing himself from the negative example of his ideology, to learn the snares that he must escape on the way to a just poetic authority.

His swerves away from the *Conciones*, therefore, his attempts to rewrite his model, are as significant as his appropriations of it. Coleridge repre-sents Famine and Liberty as closely related, sisters pleading cooperatively. Shelley manipulates and complicates the relationship between the two (who are now "foes"). In *Swellfoot*, Famine is in control of the people, and Liberty's imprecation can only limit her power. The two are "eternal" enemies—it is only for the purposes of the present crisis that they have come together in their "brief alliance" or "hollow truce." The word "hollow" may ironically suggest that the truce is empty, a show for expediency's sake, of no real substance. Or it may imply the quality of "emptiness," in the sense of hunger, that must characterize any truce with Famine. But more positively, "hollow" may suggest that the truce is made on a limited, historical scale of time: that it takes place in the midst or center of events (as in the "hollow" of the night or winter), not at some end point of their resolution. In this sense, the alliance between Liberty and Famine is only temporary, a provisional response to contingent circumstances or a truce in the eye of the storm. At best, it may limit the extent of the "tragedy" sure to accompany the rising of the "hollow" goddess. At least, as a result of the alliance, something good may come out of the inevitable turmoil.

In the satire, Famine's rising initiates a transformation scene, in which the pigs "who EAT the loaves are turned into BULLS," while "The image of FAMINE sinks through a chasm in. the earth, and a MINOTAUR rises" (p. 409). In place of the falsely promised transfiguration of the Queen (whether into a monster or an angel), the pigs themselves are changed into free-born English "Bulls," while the conniving ministers are revealed as "vermin." The Ionian Minotaur is "JOHN BULL," a hunter who "can leap any gate in all Boeotia,/Even the palings of the royal park" (II.ii.109–11). The Queen is decked out as a huntress, in an allusion to the convention of flattering the monarch (as a type of Diana) and a joke on *this* monarch's vulgar taste in clothes.

Instead of reform, the conclusion would seem to portend civil war—the oracle's second option.

> "Boeotia, choose Reform or civil war!
> When through the streets, instead of hare with dogs,
> A Consort Queen shall hunt a King with Hogs,
> Riding on the Ionian Minotaur."

(I.113–16)

But the implied time frame is vague: when, exactly, is "When"? The suggestion seems to be that the nation must "choose" its future *at the signal of* the Queen's hunt. That is, the conclusion of the Queen Caroline affair—even if it ends in rioting or rebellion—will only mark a fork in the road toward either *greater* violence (civil war) or substantial reform.

Shelley was uncertain about the revolutionary nature of the Queen's affair, skeptical and yet convinced that *some* far-reaching change was impending.[46] The question for him was not whether political instability of some sort could (or should) be avoided, but what form it would take and how quickly it would pass. The ominous oracle of *Swellfoot* is also printed as the play's epigraph—but with the space for the word "Boeotia" left blank, thus seeming to call on the play's readers, the *English* nation, to "choose reform or civil war." But this is not quite the same thing as a direct dehortation from violence addressed to the people. *Swellfoot* is less clearly a poem of nonviolence even than *The Mask of Anarchy* is. It offers only an admonition against excess and escalation while, on the figurative level, concluding with the image of the huntress chasing down the verminous ministry—presumably to the death. "Give them no law (are they not beasts of blood?)," she calls out to the pigs, "But such as they gave you. Tallyho! ho!" (II.ii.125–26). This is a far cry from the "old laws of England" that (in 1819) were to protect the "sons of England" from the yeomanry.

As a literary figure, the Queen's violent ride can be read as parodic of *The Mask of Anarchy* and the numerous other scenes of transformation and succession throughout Shelley's poetry. Politically, it suggests that any deeper and more extensive change is yet far in the future. This structural self-parody should be read along with the famous closing chorus of *Hellas* (written in 1821) and Shelley's accompanying note on the certainty of ongoing violence, when compared with more hopeful visions. In *Swellfoot* any prophecy beyond the oracle's fatal choice is out of the question, or at least outside the frame of satire.

This limitation is conditioned by the facts of class and collective identity. The "Consort Queen's" vengeful ride on the Minotaur parodies her own class confusion, her behavior (consorting with Italian commoners and servants, and consulting with Alderman Wood), and her stirring up of public support. The concluding hunt is a ride in which the déclassé "vulgar cook-maid," as Shelley called her, proves her mettle at the patrician sport (and her husband, his ministers, and peers become the beasts). "Hey for a whipper-in!" Iona shouts—that is, for someone to control the *hounds;* but the final words of the farce are simply her "Tallyho! tallyho!" (II.ii.119, 138). The ludicrous hunt was already a conventional satirical motif, on the level of theater and literature as well as in popular expressions of rough music in the community.

One famous pantomime, for example, *Harlequin and the Red Dwarf*

(1812), employed live animals, as well as costumed actors as "nonesuch" monsters, onstage in its spectacular burlesque hunting scene. The humor consisted largely of incongruities of decorum and violations of the carefully maintained code of the best-known aristocratic sport.[47] This pantomime could possibly have been a source for *Swellfoot*—which, in the same popular idiom, similarly makes a sexual and political joke of "riding" and being "ridden." But my real point is what it demonstrates about Shelley's popular imagery. The pantomime was already a parody of a real-life stag hunt, part of an annual Easter event at Epping Forest, the license for a kind of mumming in which "merchants and tradesmen from the City played at being country gentlemen."[48] Simply to stage a mock hunt in 1820 was to invoke social anxieties about class boundaries, mobility— and the potential for violence, as embodied in the satirical stag hunts of rough music.

Both Percy and Mary Shelley had difficulty seeing the "vulgar" Caroline as a "heroine." In one letter, Mary remarked, "—to be sure, she is injured, but it is too great a stretch of imagination to make a God of a *Beef-eater*, or a heroine of Queen Caroline.—but I wish with all my heart downfall to her enemies. . . . "[49] In this she echoes Shelley: "And Peers and Peeresses to stalk along the streets in ermine! It is really time to give over this mummery." Ermine is emblematic of purity and the honor of judges, an appropriate "mask" for the patrician (and middling) "mummers" playing at judgmental power, participating in the chaotic traveling festival destined to end either in Caroline's "uglification" or in her apotheosis.[50]

In Shelley's satire, the green bag of incriminating evidence is to be falsely represented to the pigs (the people) as a magical "test" of the Queen's purity. Mammon, the Arch-Priest of Famine (Prime Minister Liverpool), says that the pigs are to be told (in a propaganda campaign of disinformation) that the contents of the bag will make the Queen's guilt visible, as her "manifest deformity." In reality, the bag is full of black magic for perversion, distortion, and sophistry—a way to "Turn innocence to guilt, and gentlest looks/To savage, foul, and fierce deformity" (I.363–64). Accused of adultery and other sins, those baptized in the poison will be publicly destroyed: "Wither they to a ghastly caricature/Of what was human!" (I.372–73). In recent years we have witnessed the continued concern of the British monarchy over sexual scandal, the choice of wives for princes, and the effect of these on public relations *and* the problem of the succession.

In 1820, Caroline's vilification would have resonated with Shelley's own experiences with calumny, especially the feud with Southey over—significantly, given the target of *Swellfoot*—Shelley's bad treatment of his wife, Harriet. The rancorous correspondence with Southey, which hinted at dueling and may have sparked "A Satire upon Satire," was taking place during the summer months of 1820—at the same time that Shelley was beginning to read about and respond to the Queen Caroline affair. And it is surely significant that, only months later, the Shelleys were snubbed by their friends the Gisbornes as the result of gossip spread in London (the kind of "calumny" Shelley attributed to Southey). In one telling letter Mary openly compared their own awkward situation to Queen Caroline's, suggesting that spies might well be preparing to present a green bag of "scandal" against *them* (*Letters of MWS*, I, 159); in another letter she says with obvious bitterness they had become "Pariahs" (161). The fact is that the Shelleys' social position in 1820 was uncomfortably close to the outcast Queen's, which may help to explain something of their mixed feelings about her and her vulgar "friends."

Swellfoot remains to the end unsure when it comes to the "swinish multitude" it would ostensibly champion. It is surely significant that the people's finest hour in the play comes when they metamorphose into something *else*—into bulls or the hybrid "man-bull," the Minotaur, John Bull. This monstrous beast of the people can be read as a parody of another Shelleyan figure for revolutionary change, Demogorgon ("people monster") in *Prometheus Unbound*. The satire, however, very carefully emphasizes that the people are to be *led* on the proper "path"—are even to be driven by the Queen—and that the "standard bearers in the van of Change" (poets and others) are to serve as an elite leadership for the populace. *Swellfoot* refuses to treat the people's choice as a *real* heroine, using her only as a secondary or transitional figure beneath the idealized feminine figure of Liberty (and even beneath the "Queen," Famine). The pigs ignore Liberty in their scramble for bread and revenge. The skit depicts what must have been for Shelley a political nightmare: Iona/Caroline displaces true Liberty at center stage.

At the climax Iona empties the bag of transformative poison (meant for her) over the heads of the King and his court. They are thus metamorphosed into vermin or—a resonant phrase for the genre of satire itself—"a ghastly caricature/Of what was human." But the play has already suggested that the bag was a diabolical tool of deception, not really a "true test of guilt or innocence" (as the swine are to be told). As the Queen's accusers are turned into subhuman caricatures, it is hard not to see this bit of business as a case of Shelley's keeping his distance from his own machinery. Implicitly, broad satire is itself reflexively satirized in the passage.[51] Of the coming transformation of the Queen, Mammon acidly remarks, "This, trust a priest, is just the sort of thing/Swine will believe" (I.397–98).

Throughout the play, Shelley's attempts at sublimity seem undermined by the inherent satire of events, just as his poetry reading was drowned out by the Italian festival. This is why in *Swellfoot* the typical figure of the Shelleyan sublime—the goddess of Liberty—is given only a walk-on part and then ignored. The outrageous representations in the press of Queen Caroline as a kind of goddess, which the satire incorporates, are bound by chance to reflect back upon Shelley's own allegorical images of apotheosis, from *Queen Mab*, to "Hope" and her cooperating "Shape" in *The Mask of Anarchy*, to the numerous incarnations of Liberty throughout his work, including *Swellfoot*. Are these "idealisms" (so the subtext of the play seems to ask) really "the sort of thing/Swine will believe"?

• • •

In the Queen Caroline affair Shelley had a ready-made example from the noisy arena of politics of the actual workings of charisma—a social effect analogous to that which he desired for his own poetry. But the nature of Caroline's charismatic effect was too close to the deceptions and masks of "mummery" (and too close to the rough music of the mob) to provide a comfortable model. Just months later (February–March 1821) Shelley would draft *A Defence of Poetry*, an earnest exploration of poetry's effect and influence, written as a *counter*satiric response to Peacock—one of the eminent satirists of the age. It is against the background of *Swellfoot* and its frantic satire, I would suggest, that we should reread the essay's well-known statements on "the awakening of a great people to work a beneficial change in opinion or institution," of "a great and free development of the national will," and the poet as a "nightingale" who sings for himself but whose "auditors . . . feel that they are moved and softened, yet know not whence or why."[52]

In a discussion of Restoration literature, the essay says that in such historical periods,

> Comedy loses its ideal universality: wit succeeds to humour; we laugh from
> self-complacency and triumph instead of pleasure; malignity, sarcasm and

contempt, succeed to sympathetic merriment; we hardly laugh, but we smile. Obscenity, which is ever blasphemy against the divine beauty in life, becomes, from the very veil which it assumes, more active if less disgusting: it is a monster for which the corruption of society for ever brings forth new food, which it devours in secret.

(p. 491)

With only a slight adjustment of perspective, this can be read as an inversion of Shelley's earlier description of the effect of true poetry, its "replenishing" of the imagination, and its "new intervals and interstices whose void for ever craves fresh food" (p. 488). And, although this was surely not part of Shelley's conscious intention, it is difficult from our vantage *not* to read the denunciation of comedy as potentially applicable to *Swellfoot*'s burlesque—with its humorous monster, the Minotaur, and its contemptible, obscene occasion—whether or not Shelley himself would have approved such an application. The point is that *Swellfoot* is deeply ambivalent, not simply confused, about both its genre and its audience. Although it reflects at times a real glee in its puns and off-color jokes, this seems subsumed in the end in a darker sense of historical absurdity, a sense of how contingent was the political future on the vagaries of the public.

In the advertisement, Shelley promises the rest of his trilogy: *Swellfoot in Angaria* (or in feudal servitude, perhaps under the dominance of Iona and the Minotaur?) and the final play, *Charité* (which could mean either "charity" to the swine—or "forgiveness" of the oppressors). These plays will be made available to "the reading Public," however, only if they can be "found" (p. 390), an implicit challenge to the audience's imagination and propensity to change the future. Shelley's last satire, like *A Defence of Poetry*, addresses the problem of influencing a "reading Public" that, in the end, was never given the chance to read *Swellfoot*.

For Shelley, the successful reception of poetry depends on the influence of a kind of charisma. Poetic effect is a socially constructed, relational event in which the "symbolic value" of imagination meets society's "leading ideas," in conjunction with (or in opposition to) its "leading institutions," in a public arena of exchange (Geertz, *Centers, Kings, and Charisma*, p. 122). Poetry, as Shelley argues in the famous words of the *Defence*, was "The most unfailing herald, companion, and follower" of social change, a power "at once the center and circumference" (pp. 508, 503). Like Queen Caroline, Shelley is at a distance from the center of his society and wants very much to be closer. His anxieties about the social class and intellectual abilities of his audience, however, and about the effects his writing might stimulate, about what the people might believe or be moved by, and where his responsibilities lay, make *Swellfoot* deeply ambivalent. The satire seems intent to tap into the "rough," demotic social forces Caroline represented, but without relinquishing its elite right to "awaken and direct" those forces.

And in the end (not unlike the Whig leadership at the time), the satire seems to want to have a popular effect without merely making a spectacle of itself, without engaging in the charisma of mere "mummery," with all the indulgence—and the threatening mixture of classes—that the term suggests. As the burlesque runs through its rapid succession of scenes, it satirizes nearly everything and everyone involved, including the prophetic authority of Shelley himself. Its final raucous business seems to steal the show from *any* attempt to control or direct plebeian festivals, including the quiet attempt (in the Liberty-Famine scene) that Shelley has carefully folded into this most saturnalian of his poems. As a satire, *Swellfoot* sees history as, potentially, a farce. This situates it as a transitional work in Shelley's career, as he moves away from the confident, exhortative energies of *The Mask of Anarchy* and toward the darker, more deeply ironic vision of *The Triumph of Life*.

7 Beyond Satire

Genre and the Problem of Moral Authority

SATIRE, IT IS OFTEN SAID, is the most protean of genres—if it is a genre at all.[1] Formalist descriptions usually do not apply beyond the strict examples of Roman *satura*, the last kind of satire with a clearly codified structure; or they are limited to making simple generalizations and observations about, say, the bipartite division that is common to many verse satires. Apart from such limited explications, "satire" simply becomes a hopelessly vague term for any writing that is tendentiously ironic or denigrating. As I suggested at the outset of this study, these difficulties indicate an important fact about satire: its useful resistance to essentialist or formalist definitions of genre. It should be clear that there can be no satire apart from some particular social context, just as there can be no significant social gesture without a shared network of relational meanings. The necessity for context may be clearest at the borderlines of our critically constructed categories and genres, where distinctions overlap and blur. The very act of probing the boundaries between one genre and another often reveals those boundaries to be socially constructed and thus shifting—a heuristic situation of the text or authorial persona within a field of contingent circumstances, rather than any timeless set of features or forms.

In this chapter I will raise questions about the boundaries of satire by pursuing the "satiric" to the point where it is no longer self-identical but can be construed as something else altogether: the dream vision or *kataplous* of "The Triumph of Life." I intend thus to demonstrate what "the satiric" can teach us about the rest of Shelley's poetic corpus and, at the same time, to end this book with a gesture that has itself become a generic convention within Shelley studies—by turning the particular perspective gained by reading Shelley's satire on his last, most complex, and most problematic poetic work.

• • •

Shelley's best-known poetic fragment is not a satire, but it shares its central figure, the triumphal procession, with *The Devil's Walk*, *The Mask of Anarchy*, and *Swellfoot the Tyrant*. More important, it shares with these satires a particular kind of rhetorical orientation—an ironic claim to criticize the quotidian world from a moral position beyond the world, a position traditionally associated with the satire of Juvenal, the moral sublime of the *genus grande*. My point of departure for discussing this orientation—perhaps surprisingly—derives from Northrop Frye's *Anatomy of Criticism*, with its protostructuralist scheme of modes and related mythoi, those "narrative categories of literature broader than, or logically prior to, the ordinary literary genres."[2]

Frye's structure of universal literary mythoi is based on the cycle of four seasons and makes a closed circle, which also (fortuitously for my purposes) makes it possible to figure the circulation from one mythos to another, at the boundaries where two meet. For example, as comedy ("the Mythos of Spring") becomes more and more ironic and realistic, it shifts to approach the side of the chart Frye reserves for satire and irony—that is, "Spring" falls back to "Winter." On the other side of the circle, satire grows less and less ironic along his spectrum until it eventually gives way to tragedy ("Winter" yields to "Autumn"). I have deliberately imagined examples moving in the reverse of the normal seasonal progression in order to emphasize the basic fact (and theoretical limitation) of this scheme: its declared independence from material and cultural determinants, its static, spatialized, timeless, and totalizing form. As Terry Eagleton has observed, these mythoi are finally "transhistorical" because Frye's autonomous archetypal scheme necessarily "finds in literature a *substitute* history, with all the global span and collective structures of history itself."[3]

But I think that we can extract something of value from Frye's model, namely, its suggestion of the potential *circulation* of generic energy and the permeability (and indeterminacy) of generic categories. One such revision of the scheme, by Michael G. Cooke, has stressed the joint "rootedness" of apparently different modes (such as elegy, prophecy, and satire), the way these "intrinsic possibilities of any situation . . . *will normally* be 'simultaneously present' in a text, and be given certain relative values."[4] Prophecy, for example, usually establishes itself in relation to—through the containment or exploitation of—the connected mode of satire. What Cooke comes close to suggesting is that Frye's modal circle can be deliberately reconstrued as dynamic; that is, it can be kept turning.

But even such a dynamic, relational model must be opened up to the recognition of broader cultural and historical contingencies rather than merely timeless literary (or, as in Cooke, affective) structures. Frye himself opens the door to this appropriation of his scheme, in the midst of a comparison of romance with mock romance, when he suggests that the use of a particular generic option may be *class*-determined. A parodic form, he says, might be preferred by the rising classes for ideological reasons, as a challenge to the established values of aristocratic romance (Frye, p. 233). This seems to me to underscore a very important point— that generic variations are actually realized, shift, or circulate according to the orientation of the individual work or authorial persona in relation to particular and always changing cultural contexts.

Once this is understood, it becomes possible to reconstruct Frye's kind of structural model in order to explore the ways in which satire blends into comedy on the one hand and into tragedy on the other, to place individual works along a spectrum of relational characteristics—rather than in categorical pigeonholes—while at the same time avoiding the assumption that this reveals anything transhistorical about the essential "spirit of satire." On the contrary, this blending of genres can be taken to indicate quite a different thesis: that genres are relationally defined, that they are ever-shifting precisely because they are socially constructed—and social contexts are ever-shifting. Generic kinship along a continuum of possible identities is a function of changing social context. In this light I want to examine "Juvenalian" satire as a mode with shifting borders, one of which is shared with Dantesque dream vision. On that border, somewhere between the Juvenalian and the Dantesque, I will locate Shelley's "The Triumph of Life."

The Romantic period found the satire of Juvenal especially congenial, though his poetry was paradoxically viewed as sublime and scurrilous at the same time.[5] In the early nineteenth-century era of political reaction, however, Juvenal was most often made over to represent an elusive public ideal: the independent rather than co-opted poetic voice, the artist free to attack corruption and to challenge the dominant structures of power. Within this fiction, Juvenal was made an oppositional power fueled by the righteous indignation of his exile (according to legend, he had been cast out of Rome because of his satire).[6] This constructed authorial identity was a perfect mirror of the Romantics' own problems with exile, and their desire to speak to and for the larger community. In this way, Romantic poets exploited Juvenal for his *prophetic* currency, which made perfect sense, generically, because it played upon an age-old kinship between satire and prophecy. In the era of intense partisanship and "apostasy," of Edmund Burke and the independent Whigs, the Romantics idealized the Juvenalian as a transcendently ironic gadfly's voice in the wilderness.

The vogue for Juvenal was widespread during the Romantic period. In 1838, Wordsworth wrote an answer to a letter of inquiry in which he denied ever having produced "certain fierce Poems of the hour" in his youth. All he would admit to producing was one conventional imitation of Juvenal's "Satire on Nobility," but (he added) "How far the choice of a subject might be influenced by the run at that time against the Aristocracy, I am unable to say . . . ."[7] The conjunction of the antiaristocratic feeling of the 1790s with Juvenalian satire is significant, and historically includes the later turning away from such feeling. At the time of his equivocating letter—when Wordsworth was only five years away from the Laureateship—he responded to the inquiry with an understandable lack of relish. Southey's *Wat Tyler* episode and Coleridge's "Apologetic Preface" had shown just how unpleasant public accusations of youthful Jacobinical fierceness could be, and Wordsworth's impatience reflects the fact that he had long endured similar accusations. In this case, however, the early poetry in question (which is easy enough to confuse with a classical academic exercise) was never of much *public* consequence. But his disingenuous denial suggests that the imitation was at least worth denying.

Wordsworth's imitation was more than a schoolboy's exercise. Its incipient fierceness did not add up to powerful poetry, whether due to Wordsworth's discomfort in the mode or to the awkwardness of the epistolary collaboration,[8] but it added up to over one hundred lines of verse based directly on Juvenal's eighth satire. These were produced in collaboration (mostly through correspondence) with the Reverend Francis Wrangham, between 1795 and 1797 (significantly, the same years when Coleridge and Southey were writing their newspaper satires).[9] That such exercises were common does not diminish their significance. On the contrary, it reinforces the popularity of Juvenal during this era of revolution abroad and Jacobinism at home.

Horace and Juvenal had long been made into generic bookends, a set of complementary satiric models. Dr. Johnson's imitations of the latter remained the standards against which all others were measured (as Wordsworth's letter makes clear), in the same way that Pope's Horatian writings set the standard for the *sermo*, urbane kind of satire. But since Casaubon and Dryden the two satirists had also traditionally been distinguished as very different—even opposite—models. Juvenal's stock may have risen during the Romantic period, since "early nineteenth-century Englishmen, because of the defiance of law and morality by wealthy aristocrats and even royalty, felt greater affinity with the debauched imperial city under Nero and Domitian."[10] Or it could be that the perceived threat of being absorbed into a hegemonic system of counterrevolution made the idealized, "moral" Juvenal (rather than the temporizing Horace) particularly attractive to self-styled friends of liberty.

It is no accident that William Gifford, later editor of *The Anti-Jacobin* and always associated with polemical journalism as much as with literary satire, was chief among the Juvenalians. It is therefore significant that the introduction to his highly influential translation of 1802 incorporates the work of a French Revolutionary translator, Jean Dusaulx, who had held up Juvenal as exemplary precisely because the Roman had remained "independent" of established power.[11] This adoption of a distinctly *Girondist* ideal of disinterestedness is of course highly ironic, coming from Gifford, the Tory satirist whom William Hazlitt excoriated as "the invisible link, that connects literature with the police"—who had sacrificed the claims of "independence" for those of "respectability."[12] Dryden had used the same language to praise Persius: "He sticks to his one Philosophy; he shifts not sides, like Horace . . . ."[13] But Gifford makes it clear that in his own era Juvenal has taken over this political integrity, generating a kind of aura that could be shared by textual incorporation and appropriation.[14]

Wordsworth's imitation of Juvenal is only one ephemeral instance of this widespread interest in the Juvenalian, but it has the distinct advantage of coming from the Romantic poet (besides Shelley) from whom we least expect satire. This makes it a fascinating and instructive document of the unromantic within the Romantic. Looking like retrograde Augustanism, it actually is perfectly in tune with the republican and Jacobinical spirit of its age (the 1790s). In its attacks on the aristocracy, it differs subtly from many ideological uses of Juvenal in subsequent decades, when reaction and apostasy offered other political targets as visible and tempting to satirists as the English aristocracy—prominent turncoats like Wordsworth himself. The young Wordsworth modernizes Juvenal by substituting topics and persons for the original targets or by adding his own parallel (but not always directly imitative) lines, with the result that the standard exercise of classical imitation is turned into a species of fiery radical poetry for which all three of the older Romantic poets later felt compelled to defend themselves. The young Southey ("a friend of Coleridge") even provided some lines for the project. According to Wordsworth, he wrote this punning (and wholly unexceptional) couplet: "Heavens! who sees majesty in George's face?/Or looks at Norfolk and can dream of grace?" (Wordsworth, *Letters*, I, 158).

Although the older Wordsworth told the truth in claiming that he never took very seriously "the Juvenal scheme" (which he called a mere "snack of satire"), as a public "scheme" it did possess a personal significance for him at the time. One reason was that it enabled him to work on other writing—including *Guilt and Sorrow*, of which he says in one of the series of letters to Wrangham, "Its object is partly to expose the vices of the penal law and the calamities of war as they affect individuals" (Wordsworth, *Letters*, I, 167–68, 159). In other words, *Guilt and Sorrow* was written to carry out the traditional moral mission of satire—the exposing of vice—and, as Wordsworth said, writing *satire* enabled such moral poetry (and implicitly set its standards) as well as sharpening his poetic abilities on the things of the world.

> As to writing it is out of the question. Not however entirely to forget the world, I season my recollection of some of its objects with a little ill-nature, I attempt to write satires! and in all satires whatever the authors may say there will be found a spice of malignity. Neither Juvenal or Horace were without it, and what shall we say of Boileau and Pope or the more redoubted Peter [Pindar].
>
> (Wordsworth, *Letters*, I, 169)

Despite the declared moral mission, Wordsworth (like Shelley) finds that satire always contains the "spice of malignity," the violence that fuels invective (and perhaps makes the "snack" enticing); this seems to be one of the reasons he cannot fully take it seriously as "writing." Nevertheless, at this time in his career, he admits that this kind of writing is of practical use: at the very least it engages him in "worldly" subjects.

As some critics have noted, satire never fully disappears from Wordsworth's later poetry.[15] In the preface of 1815, he includes in his list of the "moulds" or "forms" of poetry "philosophical satire, like that of Horace and Juvenal."[16] He distinguishes this from "personal and occasional satire," which he thinks is rarely "general" or universal enough to be true poetry (p. 433). The mixed-genre, "composite order" of *The Prelude* clearly includes satire—and not always without topicality, if usually free from "personality." Most significantly, Coleridge remarked that in *The Recluse*, Wordsworth was to have assumed "something of the Juvenalian spirit as he approached the high civilization of cities and towns, and opening a melancholy picture of the present state of degeneracy and vice . . . ."[17]

Such a melancholy satiric voice is arguably the primary rhetorical force in Book VII of *The Prelude*. In one key passage Wordsworth's peripatetic speaker reports on urban folly and vice in the busy public way, residents and architecture alike becoming the garbled signs of corruption or ridiculousness:

> Here, there, and everywhere, a weary throng,
> The comers and the goers face to face—
> Face after face—the string of dazzling wares,
> Shop after shop, with symbols, blazoned names,
> And all the tradesman's honors overhead:
> Here, fronts of houses, like a title-page
> With letters huge inscribed from top to toe;
> Stationed above the door like guardian saints,
> There, allegoric shapes, female or male,
> Or physiognomies of real men,
> Land-warriors, kings, or admirals of the sea,
> Boyle, Shakespear, Newton, or the attractive head
> Of some quack-doctor, famous in his day.

> (VII. 171–83)[18]

In this procession of the damned the faces are mostly anonymous, but the imagery also contains specific satiric barbs. The general examples fall bathetically into the "quack-doctor" (which is Dorothy Wordsworth's correction of "Scotch doctor"), the ludicrous and real-life John Graham, founder of the Temple of Health, who was one of the original targets of Wordsworth's imitation of Juvenal.[19] These lines are Juvenalian—in the sense that the Romantics would understand—because the speaker expresses a distanced, independent disgust with the general tendency to confusion, a stance apart from or above the "throng."

Later in Book VII the topical strain resumes in several places. For example, the early image of "The endless stream of men and moving things" (l. 158) has a pendant near the end of the book, in which the psychic effects of such near-miss human encounters are expressed with a darker pathos, in antiurban imagery, as recalling "A second-sight procession, such as glides/Over still mountains, or appears in dreams (ll. 602–03).

Book VII's satiric pictures of the hubbub of London are overwhelmed by the final frightening experience of "blank confusion" at St. Bartholomew's Fair (part of the context of *Swellfoot the Tyrant* in Chapter 6): "What a hell/For eyes and ears, what anarchy and din/Barbarian and infernal—'tis a dream/Monstrous in colour, motion, shape, sight, sound" (ll. 659–62). This chaos is the epitome of the city, and the descriptive lines on the "procession" take on more than a visionary dreariness, a kind of sensory horror that has its full meaning only in the context of the poem as a whole. A vision of failed healing and lonely crowds, the procession of London takes on the dreamlike, emblematic quality of Dante's vision of the otherworld.

• • •

In Shelley's work, it is clear, Dantesque dream vision and the related *kataplous* or journey to the underworld and procession of the dead play crucial roles, from the "Ode to the West Wind" to *The Mask of Anarchy*, from *Peter Bell the Third* to "The Triumph of Life." Indeed, the latter two works—disparate as the styles of the satire and the vision are—have been compared by more than one critic. Richard Holmes has noted the connection in a discussion of *Peter Bell the Third*: "The very last long poem of Shelley's life, 'The Triumph of Life,' still shows a continuity of theme with this section of *Peter Bell the Third*, developing especially the idea of a grotesque ceaseless procession of vain human activity. The ultimate classical model for such writing is Juvenal."[20]

The links to *Peter Bell the Third*, and (by way of it) to Wordsworth, are only logical. Both the passages in *The Prelude* and in Shelley's satire thematize the man-made urban Hell in a conventional way, in a direct line with Juvenal's third satire. And even though Dante seemed to know Juvenal only at second hand, his work shows remarkable affinities with these features of the pagan satirist's work when it comes to his vision of the Inferno.[21] What both kinds of poetry share on the fundamental level of rhetorical intent is the purpose of high moral criticism of the community's failed social order. This is why Juvenal could be represented by later Christian apologists as a useful moral scourge.

Frye's cycle of genres, once it is recontextualized, offers a way to picture this generic kinship as more than simply an inherited tradition. Any satire ("militant irony") is potentially related to visions of the dead because both forms imply a similarly judgmental, moral stance on society: "The *danse macabre* and the *kataplous* are ironic reversals of the kind of romanticism that we have in the serious vision of the other world. In Dante, for instance, the judgements of the next world usually confirm the standards of this one . . ." (Frye, p. 233). This observation actually works against the grain of Frye's preference for timeless structures, pointing to the way in which Dante and Lucian (or, say, Juvenal) assume specific positions—in relation to their particular societies—from which to offer moral critiques of society. In this sense they play prophetic (as well as satiric) roles. They employ an ironic perspective and grotesque distortions to effect their critiques, features of both poets' work that are culturally bound, anything but timeless, even verging on the ephemeral and topical. Dante's prophecy, like history, requires footnotes.

Dante is widely recognized as a source for "The Triumph of Life," and I am suggesting simply that Juvenal is the common denominator, helping to form the differential boundary of the generic range that includes Shelley and Dante. The Juvenalian stance of social authority is thus the key to understanding Shelley's problematic attempts in "The Triumph of Life" to produce a prophetic, moral rhetoric. It is not my intention to add to the list of sources for Shelley's fragment. Instead, I want to suggest that the poem's powerful and complex effects are bound up with more than one genre—are in fact the result of a relational generic medley that includes serious satire as one important component. Institutional practices of literary taxonomy can serve to conceal the presence of such generic relations, so it is helpful to begin by locating specific affinities between "The Triumph of Life" and conventional satires. First, Roman verse satires often share a conventional setting, a "background" against which the satiric dialogue takes place: "Not infrequently it is a moving panoramic background . . . some setting wherein people pass by and thus provide a steady stream of type-figures on whom the Satirist can comment to the Adversarius."[22]

The vantage from "beside a public way" and the triumphal procession in Shelley's poem work in the same way: the van of Life's progress, with those who follow and are followed by it, is a vision of dead souls, a kind of darkly satiric Lucianic *kataplous*. But the poem also provides a historical and allegorical panorama of representative "type-figures" that are the focus of the dialogue between the poet and Rousseau. In fact, the grotesque caricature with which the Enlightenment thinker is himself first presented, the metamorphosed "grim Feature," a gnarled root in the hillside, can be seen as setting a darkly satiric tone for the dialogue. The speaker and Rousseau are not Satirist and Adversarius—neither of Shelley's figures fully possesses the ironic perspective necessary to the role of Satirist. Still, the comparison of the "Triumph"'s setting with the locus of classical satire serves to define the character of the poem's high irony and how it informs its critique of the world.

As in *The Inferno*, in "The Triumph of Life" the "otherworld" is in one sense a way of figuring the reality of this world. Its vision is emphatically not that of an *after*life. The figures in the procession are more than allegorical—they are historically referential or topical, including persons of recent concern to Shelley and his contemporaries, as well as history's actors, a gallery of those who have been conquered by "empire" in one form or another that amounts to a figure standing for "historical figures" as a general category: "All those whose fame or infamy must grow/Till the great winter lay the form and name/Of their own name with them forever low—" (ll. 125–27).[23] These lines occur in a famous but highly vexed passage of the poem seeming to differentiate the general mass of the conquered from

> the sacred few who could not tame
> Their spirits to the Conqueror, but as soon
> As they had touched the world with living flame
>
> Fled back like eagles to their native noon . . .
>
> (ll. 119–22)

The destroying winter comes to all—and to their names—with the possible exceptions suggested in circumlocution: Socrates and Jesus, two of the "sacred few" representing two related cultural perspectives.

> for they of Athens and Jerusalem
> Were neither mid the mighty captives seen

> Nor mid the ribald crowd that followed them
>
> Or fled before. . . .

> (ll. 134–37)

The ambiguities of this passage begin with the radical uncertainties of the manuscript text; precisely how its apparent opposition is to be taken, or even how we are to regard the "sacred few," is open to question.[24] Are we to see them as having successfully transcended the world and "Life"? Where is the realm of "noon" to which they flee, and what sets them apart from the fate of the many—the "crowd"? That general fate seems in keeping with the mythos of winter: darkly ironic and grimly "ribald" (to use the poem's term).

What is surprising is that a poem of such radical linguistic and philosophical skepticism, a work seemingly so concerned with universal problems of ontology and epistemology, should bother to make so many topical, historical references; and this may offer a clue for reading the passage. Historical commentary and authoritative judgment are conventional parts of the Dantesque generic mix with which Shelley is working. Dante, as Shelley says, employed "words of hate and awe" to speak with urgency to and about historical, earthly persons and events in medieval Florence. Given the powerful deconstructive readings of "The Triumph of Life" in recent decades, it is very important to remember that even the idealized historical figures of Socrates and Jesus are to Shelley historical, contextualized figures representing Athenian democracy and Jewish and Christian cultures—and that their refusal of power is as much a matter of ideology as of metaphysics. Seen in this way, they also appear as the antithesis of the central problem for Shelley's generation, "apostasy." Both Jesus and his prototype, Socrates, escape—in Shelley's view, through self-possession or purity of purpose, and ultimately through self-sacrifice—the kind of collusion that Shelley's satires so relentlessly attack.

A passage in Byron's "The Prophecy of Dante," which Shelley read with pleasure in late 1821 (just before he composed "The Triumph of Life"), reinforces the sociopolitical reading of these figures. Shelley describes "the sacred few" who "Fled back like eagles to their native noon" (ll. 128–31); Byron employs the eagle's height—the region of "native noon"—to signify the ideal against which to measure poetic apostates.[25] The third canto (in the voice of Dante) refers prophetically to poets to come:

> But few shall soar upon that eagle's wing,
>   And look in the sun's face, with eagle's gaze,
>   All free and fearless as the feather'd king,
> But fly more near the earth; how many a phrase
>   Sublime shall lavish'd be on some small prince
>   In all the prodigality of praise!
> And language, eloquently false, evince
>   The harlotry of Genius, which, like beauty,
>   Too oft forgets its own self-reverence,
> And looks on prostitution as a duty.

(Canto III, ll. 70–79)[26]

This is just one of numerous Juvenalian passages in "The Prophecy of Dante."[27] Throughout the poem Byron rails against corruption, often through imagery of deviant sexuality and disgust that would easily have been associated with Juvenal, who was traditionally seen as the most ribald and at the same time the most sublimely moral satirist (especially in his fifth and seventh satires).

What Byron's "Prophecy" makes explicit, its idealization of those who escape co-optation, is also part of Shelley's "The Triumph of Life." The contrast between the poets and the "anarchs" serves to demonstrate the historical fact of the relentless dominance of institutional power. Once we begin to look beyond the purely formal or linguistic readings of this text, it is remarkable how much the "Triumph of Life" thematizes pragmatic problems of political tyranny and authority.

Some of the most fantastic, dreamlike elements of the poem gesture toward traditional satiric representations of this theme of power. Near the end of the fragment, Rousseau explicitly invokes Dante to give his imprimatur to an infernal vision of unmasking, the scene in which numerous simulacra fall away but take on an uncanny, hyperreal life of their own, a mockery of reality. Some of these "phantoms" are said to have danced "in a thousand unimagined shapes . . . ."

> "And others sate chattering like restless apes
>   On vulgar paws and voluble like fire.
> Some made a cradle of the ermined capes
>
> "Of kingly mantles, some upon the tiar
> Of pontiffs sate like vultures, others played
>   Within the crown which girt with empire

"A baby's or an idiot's brow, and made
　　Their nests in it; the old anatomies
　Sate hatching their bare brood under the shade

"Of demon wings, and laughed from their dead eyes
　To reassume the delegated power
　　Arrayed in which these worms did monarchize

"Who make this earth their charnel."

(ll. 493–505)

Satire would be an accurate generic classification for this violent and diabolical beast fable. It is as if the various figures from Shelley's satires— *The Devil's Walk*, *Peter Bell the Third*, *The Mask of Anarchy*, *Swellfoot the Tyrant*, and the notebook fragments—all come together in a parliament of skeletons, demons, shades, masks, and imperial pomp. Satiric degeneration is the dominant theme, and the imagery and tone recall Spenser's allegory, Swift's absurdity, and Pope's Universal Darkness. The passage is a topical satire on empire, though tending toward a universal vision. Then, in a kind of nightmare figure of succession-as-negation, mask gives way to mask, shadow to shadow, until almost all have withered and fallen "by the way side." This resting place marks with significant inertia the "public way" beside which the poet began. At this lowest point—in the wake of a patently satiric vision—the fragment makes a final turn and then breaks off for good just after the question "Then, what is Life?"

• • •

Whether or not this fragment should be read as a palinode to Shelley's entire career (and, based on the textual as well as biographical evidence, such a reading seems far too simple and too final), it is clearly a deeply ambivalent and skeptical document—one with an inexorable violence at its center. In light of what I have been arguing throughout this book, it would seem obvious that, like *The Prelude*, "The Triumph of Life" contains in its generic blend a kind of satire. But—and this is crucial—it could not have been written merely as a satire because it could never fully trust the "militant irony" of satiric weapons as the ground of its authority. Tilottama Rajan has argued that the poem hovers uncertainly between condemning and rehabilitating Rousseau (pp. 344–49). This suggests an intriguing parallel to Shelley's satiric attempt (in *Peter Bell the Third*) to "rehabilitate" Wordsworth. The earlier satire, we recall, ends with the whole community's "ghastly life without a sound," a grotesque state of empty, unimaginative sleep; and the last line of *Peter Bell the Third* could serve as a motto for Shelley's final dream vision of "Life" as well: "How should it ever pass away?"

Even the 1819 satire contains a marked ambivalence about the sufficiency of the satiric mode. In "The Triumph of Life," Shelley's judgment again seems suspended, caught between satirizing and reenvisioning "what was once Rousseau." As a dream vision the poem moves in a surreal generic space where imaginative transformations—or nightmarish metamorphoses—remain open alternatives. Dante deploys dialectal modes, the violent satire of *The Inferno* depicting the eternal punishments of his enemies in the temporal realm, but always in relation to divine, beatific vision. Shelley alludes in "The Triumph of Life" to this very dialectic: the Florentine's "words of hate *and* awe" (my italics). Shelley may well have recognized that Dante had in effect pressed satire into the service of authoritative prophecy.

This is something like what Shelley attempts in "The Triumph of Life," except that he remains radically unsure that the satiric part of the equation—even in a dialectical medley including exhortation—can contribute to a positive moral effect, or even whether such an effect is possible. He seems finally uncertain about the generic borders of "hate" and "awe," satiric judgment and prophetic projection. In "The Triumph of Life" exhortation would seem to come too late, succession to be too endlessly cyclical, for satire—or any other mode that would claim a clear moral ground—to function as a sufficient cure. Through an identification with Rousseau, the poet identifies himself as a social outsider, a kind of pariah, as he had in the curse against Lord Eldon. But here the precise place of the outsider is questioned rather than defiantly celebrated, used as a weapon, or fatalistically embraced as a final refuge from society.

Dante and Juvenal claim very different but comparable authorities. "The Triumph of Life," at least as Shelley left it, seems to me to call into question the poet's ability to return to the world and speak with any such authority, to find a place "beside the public way" and apart from the "serious folly" of "the ribald crowd," from which to offer a critique. Shelley envisions just such a respite elsewhere, in a notebook fragment that echoes "The Triumph of Life": a seemingly personal, autobiographical draft, "The Boat on the Serchio."[28] There, Shelley's protagonists are social outcasts, a little band of exiles who escape the general crush.

> And many rose
> Whose woe was such that fear became desire;—
> Melchior and Lionel were not among those;
> They from the throng of men had stepped aside . . .

(ll. 34–37)

The contrast in tone and image with "The Triumph of Life" is highly instructive. It is at the very least an interesting coincidence that Lionel is Shelley's name for *both* the autobiographical, reclusive poet here and also for the autobiographical activist poet in *Rosalind and Helen*—who, significantly, writes public satires.

It is equally instructive that Rousseau in "The Triumph" is first swept up in the pageantry of the "throng" and then falls "by the way side." It is not clear what might have happened to him or to the poet he guides had the poem continued, nor is it clear that their vantage on the passing car ("which now had rolled/Onward") counts as an escape, or exempts them from its terrible power. What does seem clear is that the possibility of distance, of ethical judgment—on which satire *and* serious prophecy have traditionally depended—is severely constrained in the poem, because the poet seems likely to be implicated one way or another in the inexorable violence of Life's triumph. Stepping aside will not suffice. The kind of Juvenalian (or Dantesque) "independence" I have been outlining as an ideal in Shelley's day—the authoritative position outside society and its polemics from which to rail against society with the insider's passionate interest—seems finally a remote possibility in the context of the manuscript fragment's vision and its uncertain, truncated ending.

"The Triumph of Life" is a wintry dream, not a satire per se. But by recognizing Shelley's bending of conventional generic limits, we can see the poem's kinship with satire and, more important, can see that its mixed descent from Dante and Juvenal is more a function of the moral and social stance it adopts within history—especially on the contemporary problems of poetry, apostasy, and power—than of any essential generic content *or* linguistic imperative.[29] This is why I have placed Shelley's poem in the vicinity of Wordsworth's satiric rhetoric, along the broader categorical spectrum that includes the Dantesque and the Juvenalian, in order to cast it in a different light, to reemphasize the moral design of Shelley's work, and then to situate satire within that design. Generic taxonomy is usually too crude an instrument to measure the ways Shelley uses satire in composite rhetorical blends whose ultimate aims were social and ethical.

What Shelley's final fragment emphasizes, however, especially when placed in the context of the body of satiric works I have been discussing, is the problematic nature of those aims, the degree to which he (and his contemporaries) desired the satiric voice to be what, it would seem, it can never easily or finally be: the voice of moral authority.

Notes

INTRODUCTION

1. I discuss Brecht's and Leavis's interest in *The Mask of Anarchy* in Chapter 5 below. The one full-length treatment of Shelley's satire that I am aware of is Victor Ewart Lindsey's doctoral dissertation, "Satire in the Poetry of Percy Bysshe Shelley" (University of Arkansas, 1982), which applies useful sources to the problem and contains some helpful observations and readings, as cited below. Though I refer to the evidence of Shelley's prose where it is necessary to my arguments, I have mostly restricted this study to his satirical *poetry*—partly because of considerations of genre, and partly because of the poor state of available texts (a situation that should be remedied in the forthcoming Clarendon Press edition of *The Prose Works,* edited by E. B. Murray and Timothy Webb).

2. The term "self-fashioning" has by now become conventional, but I use it intentionally to invoke the "cultural poetics" of Stephen Greenblatt—as articulated, for example, in his *Renaissance Self-Fashioning from More to Shakespeare* (Chicago and London: University of Chicago Press, 1984), p. 9.

3. The issue of individual agency versus ideological hegemony has a long and complex history in Marxism and critical theory. But on the pragmatic problems of agency and structure in historicist criticism and cultural studies, see Stephen Greenblatt, "Towards a Poetics of Culture," in his *Learning to Curse: Essays in Early Modern Culture* (New York and London: Routledge, 1990), pp. 146–60, and various essays in the collection *The New Historicism,* ed. H. Aram Veeser (New York and London: Routledge, 1989), particularly Louis A. Montrose, "Professing the Renaissance: The Poetics and Politics of Culture," pp. 15–36.

CHAPTER 1: SHELLEY'S SATIRES IN ROMANTIC CONTEXT

1. For example, Edmund Blunden, in defending *Swellfoot the Tyrant,* feels compelled to address "the rumour that Shelley cannot make a joke," in his *Shelley: A Life Story* (London: Collins, 1946), pp. 274–75. Thirty years later Timothy Webb, in *The Violet in the Crucible: Shelley and Translation* (Oxford: Clarendon Press, 1976), was still saying that "it was against Shelley's nature to be funny as Aristophanes (or Byron) is funny," but also admitted that "the real Shelley's sense of humour was idiosyncratic but well developed" (p. 137). My point is that the idiosyncrasies can in part be explained when we recognize that Shelley's "humor" is often satirical.

In this observation I follow Victor Ewart Lindsey's dissertation, "Satire in the Poetry of Percy Bysshe Shelley" (University of Arkansas, 1982).

2. A significant early source on both Shelley's earnestness (his "grave disposition") *and* his prankishness ("a certain sly relish for the practical joke")—though one always to be treated skeptically—is Thomas Jefferson Hogg, *The Life of Percy Bysshe Shelley*, 2 vols. (London and Toronto: J. M. Dent & Sons, 1933), I, 160. Hogg also tells of the young Shelley's surprising delight at the "bitter, wrathful satire" of Byron's *English Bards and Scotch Reviewers* (179–80). In general, Hogg's sometimes contradictory stories reveal a deeper psychological truth: that Shelley's satiric sense of humor was bound up with, and even represented the other side of, his moral earnestness and the tendency to express it as revulsion. For examples of Shelley's hysterical or "diabolical" laughter, see Newman Ivey White, *Shelley*, 2 vols. (London: Secker & Warburg, 1947), I, 159; II, 155.

3. Letter of John Grove, February 1857, quoted in Hogg, *Life*, I, 196–97.

4. "To Laughter," in *The Poems of Shelley*, ed. Geoffrey Matthews and Kelvin Everest (London and New York: Longman, 1989), I, 520.

5. "A Cat in Distress," in *Shelley and His Circle*, vol. IV, ed. Kenneth Neill Cameron (Cambridge, MA: Harvard University Press, 1970), pp. 813–19, (p. 818).

6. Nora Crook, "Shelley's Earliest Poem?" *Notes & Queries* (continuous series) 232.4 (December 1987), 486–90. The speculations on the poem's date are Crook's.

7. Clifford Geertz, "Thick Description: Toward an Interpretive Theory of Culture," in his *The Interpretation of Cultures* (New York: Harper Collins/Basic Books, 1973), pp. 3–30.

8. On this and the other problems I refer to in this paragraph, see David Perkins, *Is Literary History Possible?* (Baltimore and London: Johns Hopkins University Press, 1992), pp. 121–52.

9. Girard's theory is most succinctly outlined in his *Violence and the Sacred*, trans. Patrick Gregory (Baltimore and London: Johns Hopkins University Press, 1972). The limitations of the theory are demarcated by its twin obsessions with origins and ends. On the one hand, Girard reduces everything to a founding act (and thus has recourse to some outdated notions of the "primitive," to name just one consequence). On the other hand, he has increasingly focused on biblical revelation as a kind of end to history and its sacrifices. Another problem lies with the consequences of such a theory: when it is so unequivocally focused on victimage as *the* center of social existence, it may help to perpetuate the very process

it would unmask. Although Girard desires to expose this mechanism, his focus may privilege the violence it deplores, perpetuating a vision of culture that excludes more hopeful, liberating possibilities. For these reasons, my use of Girardian theory is partial and skeptical, applied at times against itself, and always with qualifications.

10. The most thorough and convincing critical treatment of the role of genre in this period is Stuart Curran's *Poetic Form and British Romanticism* (New York and Oxford: Oxford University Press, 1986). Curran notes in the first chapter that satire is "an extremely vital mode in British Romanticism, one whose full dimensions have never been addressed in criticism" (pp. 12–13). He omits it from his study only for practical reasons, based on its special problems of topicality and ephemerality.

11. M. H. Abrams, *Natural Supernaturalism: Tradition and Revolution in Romantic Literature* (New York: W. W. Norton, 1971), p. 13.

12. Jerome J. McGann, *Towards a Literature of Knowledge* (Oxford: Clarendon Press, 1989), p. 39.

13. Jerome J. McGann, "Literary Pragmatics and the Editorial Horizon," in *Devils and Angels: Textual Editing and Literary Theory,* ed. Philip Cohen (Charlottesville and London: University Press of Virginia, 1991), pp. 1–21 (p. 13). McGann's forthcoming anthology, *The New Oxford Book of Romantic Poetry,* will, he says, include a focus on satirical poetry, especially from the 1790s (pp. 12–13). See as well the anthology *Romantic Parodies 1797–1831,* ed. David A. Kent and D. R. Ewen (London and Toronto: Associated University Presses, 1992), with an important introduction by Linda Hutcheon and including parodic works by little-known authors as well as canonical Romantics. It would seem that satiric and parodic poetry of the period may soon receive a great deal more attention from critics, which may contribute to ongoing reconsiderations of the unity of Romanticism as a "movement." This, at any rate, is my suggestion in Steven E. Jones, "Reconstructing Romantic Satire," *American Notes & Queries* 6.2,3 (April–July, 1993), 131–36. (Special issue: *Romantic Studies.*)

14. This commonly understood history of the genre can be found in Thomas Lockwood, *Post-Augustan Satire: Charles Churchill and Satirical Poetry, 1750–1800* (Seattle and London: University of Washington Press, 1979). Lockwood frankly admits from the start that he views his study as "something in the way of an autopsy" (p. 3).

15. Wordsworth's phrase occurs in "Resolution and Independence." Robert Southey defended Chatterton's mother and sisters against the exploitation of the biographer Herbert Croft in the 1790s, and was

responsible (in collaboration with Joseph Cottle) for bringing out the first collected edition of the poet's works in 1803. See the useful summary of events in the otherwise somewhat reductive psychological study by Louise J. Kaplan, *The Family Romance of the Impostor Poet Thomas Chatterton* (New York: Atheneum, 1988), pp. 252–57.

16. Letter to Theodore Watts quoted in T. Hall Caine, *Recollections of Dante Gabriel Rossetti* (London: Elliott Stock, 1882), p. 185. Rossetti also suggestively observes: "Read him carefully, and you will find his acknowledged work essentially as powerful as his antiquities, though less evenly successful—the Rowley work having been produced in Bristol leisure, however indigent, and the modern poetry in the very fangs of London struggle."

17. "Monody on the Death of Chatterton," in *The Poems of Samuel Taylor Coleridge,* ed. Ernest Hartley Coleridge (London: Humphrey Milford, Oxford University Press, 1931), pp. 13–15.

18. Marjorie Levinson, in *Keats' Life of Allegory: The Origins of a Style* (Oxford: Basil Blackwell, 1988), refers to "the anomaly of a writer who would seem to have preferred the inferior reputation of translator-editor to the glory of proper poetic genius: that is, originality." However, she says, he was actually pursuing "the bad originality of the counterfeiter" (p. 11). My focus is on the slightly different but related contrast between "originality" and *satire,* and my argument is that Chatterton illustrates how individual, original genius is only *apparently* in contradiction with the "insincere" modes of public satire.

19. *Apostate Will,* in *The Complete Works of Thomas Chatterton,* 2 vols., ed. Donald S. Taylor (Oxford: Clarendon Press, 1971), I, 1–2.

20. *Kew Gardens,* in *The Complete Works,* I, 512–42 (ll. 1087–94, p. 542).

21. On the ideal of an independent opposition and the Burkean Whigs, see Alan Liu, *Wordsworth: The Sense of History* (Stanford: Stanford University Press, 1989), pp. 411–13.

22. Quoted in Alvar Ellegard, *Who Was Junius?* (Stockholm, Goteborg, Uppsala: Almquist & Wiksell, 1962), pp. 25, 23.

23. See George Rudé, *Wilkes and Liberty* (Oxford: Oxford University Press, 1962), pp. 173, 181.

24. *Adonais,* in *Shelley's Poetry and Prose,* ed. Donald H. Reiman and Sharon B. Powers (New York and London: W. W. Norton, 1977), pp. 390–406 (p. 399, l. 271; p. 403, ll. 399–401). (This edition is hereafter cited as *Shelley's Poetry and Prose.*)

25. Hogg, *Life,* I, 159.

26. Not surprisingly, this context is common in Byron studies— but Shelley's admiration for (and emulation of) Byron in this regard often goes unnoticed. On Byron's roots among the classical and journalistic sources I have mentioned, including especially William Gifford, see Frederick L. Beaty, *Byron the Satirist* (DeKalb: Northern Illinois University Press, 1985).

27. Donald S. Taylor, *Thomas Chatterton's Art: Experiments in Imagined History* (Princeton: Princeton University Press, 1978), pp. 182–84.

CHAPTER 2: LEARNING TO SATIRIZE

1. Thomas Jefferson Hogg, *Life of Shelley* (London and Toronto: J. M. Dent, 1933), I, 92. The account is quoted by P. M. S. Dawson in relation to *Prometheus Unbound*, in his *The Unacknowledged Legislator: Shelley and Politics* (Oxford: Clarendon Press, 1980), p. 11. It is always possible that the hearty laughter in the story is partly the function of Hogg's remembrance, but it is probably not Hogg's fault that, as with other such anecdotes about Shelley's sense of humor, we are left with a basic uncertainty about his tone and intentions.

2. Robert C. Elliott, *The Power of Satire: Magic, Ritual, Art* (Princeton: Princeton University Press, 1960). Victor Ewart Lindsey first connected this sort of theorizing of satire with Shelley's satires in his dissertation, "Satire in the Poetry of . . . Shelley" (University of Arkansas, 1982).

3. Elliott, *Power of Satire*, pp. 6–8. Lycambes was the father of Archilochus's betrothed. Some versions of the story say that he and his daughter hanged themselves, suggesting that the satiric curse was a social-psychological effect of public shame.

4. On the rhetorical versus the strictly "magical" power of satire, see Ronald Paulson, ed., *The Fictions of Satire* (Baltimore: Johns Hopkins University Press, 1967), p. 79.

5. Aristotle was the first to connect Old Comedy with iambic poetry. On the stylistic links between the two forms, see Ralph M. Rosen, *Old Comedy and the Iambographic Tradition* (Atlanta: Scholars Press, 1988).

6. Tobin Siebers, *The Mirror of Medusa* (Berkeley: University of California Press, 1983); and René Girard, especially *Violence and the Sacred*, trans. Patrick Gregory (Baltimore and London: Johns Hopkins University Press, 1972).

7. Robert Southey, *The Curse of Kehama*, in *Poems of Robert Southey*, ed. Maurice H. Fitzgerald (London, New York, Toronto, Melbourne: Oxford

University Press, 1909), pp. 117–207. (Hereafter cited by section and line number.)

8. *Paradise Lost,* ed. Frank Allen Patterson, in *The Works of John Milton,* 18 vols. (New York: Columbia University Press, 1931), II (Part I).

9. Timothy Webb, in his edition of *Shelley: Selected Poems* (London: Everyman's Library, 1977), p. 193n, suggests that Shelley's curse might be indebted to another famous example, Byron's *Manfred.*

10. *Prometheus Unbound,* in *Shelley's Poetry and Prose,* ed. Donald H. Reiman and Sharon B. Powers (New York and London: W. W. Norton, 1977), pp. 130–210.

11. Alan Bewell, *Wordsworth and the Enlightenment: Nature, Man, and Society in the Experimental Poetry* (New Haven and London: Yale University Press, 1989), pp. 154–57.

12. Preface to *Lyrical Ballads,* in *The Poetical Works of William Wordsworth,* ed. Ernest de Selincourt and Helen Darbishire, 5 vols. (Oxford: Clarendon Press, 1940–49), II, 401.

13. Quoted in Bewell, *Wordsworth and the Enlightenment,* p. 156.

14. *Biographia Literaria* (part II), ed. James Engell and W. Jackson Bate, in *The Collected Works of Samuel Taylor Coleridge,* Bollingen ser. (London: Routledge & Kegan Paul; Princeton: Princeton University Press, 1983), VII, 6. (This edition cited hereafter as Coleridge, *Collected Works.*)

15. For "The Rime of the Ancient Mariner," I cite the text as it appeared in *Sibylline Leaves* (London, 1817; facs. repr. Oxford and New York: Woodstock Books, 1990), pp. 1–39 (p. 19).

16. My summary of the Chancery proceedings is based on Newman Ivey White, *Shelley,* vol. II (London: Secker & Warburg, 1947); and on *Shelley and His Circle,* vol. V, ed. Donald H. Reiman (Cambridge, MA: Harvard University Press, 1973), pp. 82–89, 96–99, 103–17. White reprints in an appendix portions of legal documents for the proceedings (II, 508–17).

17. "To the Lord Chancellor," in *Shelley: Poetical Works,* ed. Thomas Hutchinson, corr. G. M. Matthews (London: Oxford University Press, 1970), pp. 542–44. (This edition is hereafter cited as *Poetical Works.*) Shelley seems to have revised the work as he recopied it in 1820; for the date, text, and tone of the poem, see Donald H. Reiman, *Manuscripts of the Younger Romantics,* vol. V, *The Harvard Shelley Manuscripts,* ed. Donald H. Reiman (New York: Garland, 1991), pp. 41, 145, 190n, 202.

18. Figure 1 shows the title page of a William Hone satire, THE POLITICAL SHOWMAN—AT HOME! (British Museum 14148 [1821]), in which a Hydra-headed monster represents the collaborative reaction of the Euro-

pean crowns. In the background, a threatening volcano (Vesuvius) of revolution erupts.

19. This is the charter of Chancery as explained by William Blackstone, *Commentaries on the Laws of England,* 4 vols. (Oxford: Clarendon Press, 1773), III, 47.

20. *King Lear,* in *The Riverside Shakespeare,* ed. G. Blakemore Evans et al. (Boston: Houghton Mifflin, 1974), pp. 1249–1305.

21. Robert C. Elliott, *The Power of Satire* (Princeton: Princeton University Press, 1960), p. 288.

22. J. L. Austin, *How to Do Things with Words* (Cambridge, MA: Harvard University Press, 1962), p. 14.

23. See headnote, *Poetical Works,* p. 542; and Donald H. Reiman's notes on the text in *The Harvard Shelley Manuscripts,* V, pp. xxvii–xxviii.

24. Elliott, *Power of Satire,* p. 289.

25. Southey, *The Curse of Kehama,* p. 117. This epigraph comes back to haunt Shelley in 1820, when he quotes it in the bitter correspondence with Southey on (among other issues) Shelley's alleged mistreatment of Harriet Shelley and his consequent responsibility for her suicide. (See Chapter 4.)

26. On the convention of "the satirist satirized," see Elliott, *Power of Satire,* p. 259; Paulson, *The Fictions of Satire,* pp. 75–79; and Michael Seidel, *Satiric Inheritance, Rabelais to Sterne* (Princeton: Princeton University Press, 1979), p. 4. So far as I know, Seidel was the first to apply Girardian theory to satire, and he has influenced my thinking on satire as "sacrificial"—with the satirist playing the role of his own *pharmakos* or scapegoat.

27. Jerrold E. Hogle, *Shelley's Process: Radical Transference and the Development of His Major Works* (New York and Oxford: Oxford University Press, 1988), pp. 138–47. Girard is only one of a number of theoretical sources for Hogle's formidable study, used to explain the reflection of the Other in "A Satire upon Satire," for example (p. 147), or the escalation of violence in *The Mask of Anarchy* (pp. 130–47).

28. The draft of "A Satire upon Satire" now exists in two portions, in two separate manuscripts: Huntington MS. HM 2176 (pp. 14r, 15v, 16r) and Bodleian MS. Shelley adds. e. 20 (fol. 44r–v). The text of the fragment I quote here and in later chapters is from Steven E. Jones, "Shelley's Fragment of 'A Satire upon Satire': A Complete Transcription of the Text with Commentary," *Keats-Shelley Journal* 37 (1988), 136–63.

29. *Metamorphoses* (IV:774–86), trans. Frank Justus Miller, 2 vols.

(Cambridge, MA: Harvard University Press, 1971), I, 233, as discussed by Siebers, *Mirror of Medusa,* pp. 2–4.

30. Shelley, "On the Medusa of Leonardo da Vinci in the Florentine Gallery," in *Poetical Works,* pp. 582–83.

31. This curse of Nemesis was an invention of the Alexandrian poets, which Ovid adopts, according to Siebers, *Mirror of Medusa,* p. 80.

32. "Lines to a Reviewer," in *Poetical Works,* p. 625.

33. "Lines to a Critic," in *Poetical Works,* p. 550.

34. *Metamorphoses* (III:396–99), I, 153.

35. Huntington MS. HM 2177, p. *27V. My text of the "Proteus Wordsworth" fragment is from Steven E. Jones, "Apostasy and Exhortation: Shelley's Satiric Fragments in the Huntington Notebooks," *Huntington Library Quarterly* 53.1 (Winter 1990), 41–66.

36. John Lemprière, *Bibliotheca Classica; or, A Classical Dictionary* (London: T. Cadell, 1788; facs. repr. New York: Garland, 1984).

37. Thomas Love Peacock, "Sir Proteus: A Satirical Ballad," in *The Halliford Edition of the Works of Thomas Love Peacock,* 10 vols. (New York: AMS Press, 1967), VI, 277–313.

38. A. Bartlett Giamatti, "Proteus Unbound: Some Versions of the Sea God in the Renaissance," in *The Disciplines of Criticism: Essays in Literary Theory, Interpretation, and History,* ed. Peter Demetz, Thomas Greene, and Lowry Nelson, Jr. (New Haven: Yale University Press, 1968), pp. 437–76. Theresa M. Kelley, "Proteus and Romantic Allegory," *ELH* 49 (1982), 623–52, treats the figure in light of Paul de Man's theories on the rhetoric of Romanticism.

39. *The Letters of Percy Bysshe Shelley,* ed. Frederick L. Jones, 2 vols. (Oxford: Clarendon Press, 1964), II, 195 (8 May 1820). (Hereafter this edition will be cited as *Letters,* followed by volume and page numbers.) According to Jones, Shelley actually wrote: "a kind of an excuse for Wordsworth & [word canceled]." The other "chameleon" was probably either Coleridge or Southey.

40. Giamatti, "Proteus Unbound," p. 439.

41. "An Exhortation," in *Poetical Works,* p. 579.

CHAPTER 3: "FOND OF THE DEVIL"

1. The narrative that follows is based on the accounts in Newman Ivey White, *Shelley* (London: Secker & Warburg, 1947), I, 245–52; and William Michael Rossetti, "Shelley in 1812–13," *The Fortnightly Review* 15 (January 1871), 68–69.

2. "Sonnet on Launching Some Bottles Filled with *Knowledge* into the Bristol Channel," from "The Esdaile Notebook," in *Shelley and His Circle*, vol. IV, ed. Kenneth N. Cameron (Cambridge, MA: Harvard University Press, 1970), p. 977.

3. *A Letter to Lord Ellenborough*, in *The Complete Works of Percy Bysshe Shelley*, ed. Roger Ingpen and Walter E. Peck, 10 vols. (New York: Charles Scribner's Sons, 1930), V, 291. (This edition is hereafter cited as *The Complete Works*.)

4. White, *Shelley*, II, 250–51, argues convincingly that if Sidmouth *had* received and read a copy of the tract, the persecution against Shelley would likely have been more serious than mere surveillance.

5. *Shelley and His Circle, 1773–1822*, vol. VII, ed. Donald H. Reiman (Cambridge, MA: Harvard University Press, 1986), pp. 1–12.

6. Linda Hutcheon, *A Theory of Parody: The Teachings of Twentieth-Century Art Forms* (New York and London: Methuen, 1985), p. 6

7. *The Devil's Walk*, in *Poetical Works*, pp. 878–80.

8. In the *Morning Post* version of "The Devil's Thoughts" (6 September 1799), the 's' in "stable" (in the line "On this dunghill beside his stable") is very faintly printed (or so it appears in microfilm), though E. H. Coleridge gives "stable" for all versions in his list of variants. Shelley's legal viper could have been suggested to him by the accidentally ambiguous typography ("stable"/"table"); this would support the hypothesis that he saw the poem in a newspaper clipping at Southey's.

9. Ronald Paulson, ed., *The Fictions of Satire* (Baltimore: Johns Hopkins University Press, 1967), p. 115.

10. *Peter Bell the Third*, in *Shelley's Poetry and Prose*, pp. 328–29.

11. See Jeffrey Burton Russell, *Mephistopheles, the Devil in the Modern World* (Ithaca, NY, and London: Cornell University Press, 1986), pp. 158–59.

12. British Museum 12593. The iconography alludes to an earlier satire by Gillray, in which Fox is the Devil (British Museum 6012), and was adapted again during the Queen Caroline affair (1821), with the outcast Queen in the Devil's position (British Museum 14191). Cruikshank's version satirizes an actual letter from Napoleon to the Regent; in the print, the sunbeams contain the names of the allied enemies of Bonaparte—but most prominently, Wellington. For a discussion of this print's place in Cruikshank's ongoing satiric war against Napoleon and in the context of his artistic practice, see Robert L. Patten, *George Cruikshank's Life, Times, and Art*, vol. I, 1792–1835 (London: Lutterworth Press, 1992), p. 115.

13. Ibid., p. 117.

14. George Speaight, *Punch and Judy: A History* (London: Studio Vista, 1970), p. 68; and Robert Leach, *The Punch and Judy Show: History, Tradition and Meaning* (London: Batsford Academic and Educational, 1985).

15. Romantic satanism was first systematically expounded by Mario Praz, *The Romantic Agony*, trans. Angus Davidson (London: Oxford University Press, 1954). The insights of this important study, especially on the role of violence in Romanticism, need to be updated in light of recent theory and criticism of the Romantics.

16. "On the Devil, and Devils," in *The Complete Works*, VII, 87–104 (87).

17. J. C. D. Clark, *English Society 1688–1832: Ideology, Social Structure and Political Practice during the Ancien Regime* (Cambridge: Cambridge University Press, 1985), p. 381; see also Newman Ivey White, "Literature and the Law of Libel: Shelley and the Radicals of 1840–42," *Studies in Philology* 22 (January 1925), 34–47.

18. Iain McCalman, *Radical Underworld: Prophets, Revolutionaries and Pornographers in London, 1795–1840* (Cambridge: Cambridge University Press, 1988), p. 147. See in addition the introduction and primary texts in Iain McCalman, ed., *The Horrors of Slavery and Other Writings by Robert Wedderburn* (New York and Princeton: Markus Wiener, 1991), especially the reprint of a burlesque tract, "The Holy Liturgy, or Divine Service, upon the Principle of Pure Christian Diabolism . . . " (pp. 153–54).

19. McCalman, *Radical Underworld*, p. 150.

20. Vincent Carretta, *George III and the Satirists from Hogarth to Byron* (Athens and London: University of Georgia Press, 1990), p. 271.

21. Jerome J. McGann, *The Romantic Ideology: A Critical Investigation* (Chicago and London: University of Chicago Press, 1983), pp. 118–23.

22. Dedication to *Peter Bell*, in *The Poetical Works of William Wordsworth*, ed. Ernest de Selincourt and Helen Darbishire, 5 vols. (Oxford: Clarendon Press, 1940–49), II, 331.

23. John Hamilton Reynolds's "Peter Bell" is helpfully reprinted in David A. Kent and D. R. Ewen's anthology, *Romantic Parodies 1797–1831* (London and Toronto: Associated University Presses, 1992), pp. 173–84. As the editors point out, Reynolds was accidentally able to prefigure Wordsworth's rhyme scheme by choosing to imitate that of "The Idiot Boy" (p. 173). For the timing of both parodies and the question of whether Shelley knew *Peter Bell*, see *The Bodleian Shelley Manuscripts*, vol. I, *Peter Bell the Third and "The Triumph of Life,"* ed. Donald H. Reiman (New York: Garland, 1986), p. 8.

24. On the cultural nexus of *Peter Bell*, Methodist enthusiasm, and superstition, see Alan Bewell, *Wordsworth and the Enlightenment* (New Haven and London: Yale University Press, 1989), pp. 109–41.

25. For "The Witch of Atlas" as a response to *Peter Bell*, see John E. Jordan, "Wordsworth and *The Witch of Atlas*," *ELH* 9 (1942), 320–25; and Richard Cronin, "Shelley's Witch of Atlas," *Keats-Shelley Journal* 26 (1977), 88–100.

26. See especially Halévy's *England in 1815* (London: Ernest Benn, 1949), pp. 410–40.

27. One of the more influential of the revisionists is J. C. D. Clark (see note 17 above). Essentially the same complaint is lodged by A. D. Harvey, *Britain in the Early Nineteenth Century* (New York: St. Martin's Press, 1978), who argues that "Historians' concentration on Methodism has diverted attention from major alterations in the structure of Old Dissent in the period, from certain crucial developments within the Church of England, and from the steady progress of free-thinking" (p. 64).

28. McCalman, *The Horrors of Slavery*, p. 10.

29. J. C. D. Clark, *English Society*, p. 258.

30. Shelley, *Letters*, I, 216.

31. Intermittently serialized in seven articles in *The Examiner*, ed. Leigh Hunt, 8 May–25 December 1808.

32. *The Revolt of Islam* (8:22), 11. 3387–92, in *Poetical Works*, p. 120. I quote the lines as they were printed in *The Quarterly Review*, 21 April 1819, p. 464.

33. Shelley, *Letters*, II, 135.

34. "The Vision of Judgment," in *Lord Byron: The Complete Poetical Works*, ed. Jerome J. McGann and Barry Weller, 7 vols. (Oxford: Clarendon Press, 1980–92), VI, 309–45 (316).

35. "Apologetic Preface" to "Fire, Famine, and Slaughter," in *Sibylline Leaves* (1817; facs. repr. Oxford and New York: Woodstock Books, 1990), pp. 89–109. (The poem is on pp. 111–16.)

36. "On the Devil, and Devils," p. 93.

37. F. R. Leavis, *Revaluation: Tradition and Development in English Poetry* (New York: George W. Stewart, 1947), p. 145; William Keach, *Shelley's Style* (New York and London: Methuen, 1984), pp. 94–97. As Kent and Ewen point out (in their note to *Peter Bell the Third* in *Romantic Parodies*, p. 385), one minor index of Shelley's closeness to his target is the joking signature, "Miching Mallecho"—"M.M." being a visual inversion of "W.W."

38. *A Defence of Poetry*, in *Shelley's Poetry and Prose*, p. 503.

39. Keach, *Shelley's Style,* p. 91.

40. Wordsworth, *The Excursion* (IV:325–27), in *The Poetical Works of William Wordsworth,* V, 118–19.

41. For a reading of *Peter Bell the Third* (along with Byron's satire) in relation to Augustan tradition, see Claude Rawson's "Byron Augustan: Mutations of the Mock-Heroic in *Don Juan* and Shelley's *Peter Bell the Third,*" in *Byron: Augustan and Romantic,* ed. Andrew Rutherford (New York: St. Martin's Press, 1990), pp. 82–116. Rawson notes that Shelley reduces Dulness from Pope's sublime darkness to "chatty drawing-room proportions" (p. 87), but observes that the poem "can be thought of in some ways as a low-key *Dunciad*" (p. 86). However, I think he underestimates the importance of his own observation, the significance of that ("low-") "key." Although he clarifies the satire's High-literary sources, he predictably fails to discover polished Augustan-style wit in Shelley's rougher, more deliberately demotic, generic mixture.

42. "Ode: The Morning of the Day Appointed for a General Thanksgiving. January 18, 1816," in *The Poetical Works of William Wordsworth,* III, 155–63. After 1845, part of the poem was separated off, with some variants, as "Ode: 1815" (151–55).

43. Huntington Manuscript HM 2177, p. *51v; text in Mary A. Quinn, ed., *The Mask of Anarchy Draft Notebook,* vol. IV in *The Manuscripts of the Younger Romantics* (New York: Garland, 1985), pp. 280–81. See also the discussion in Steven E. Jones, "Apostasy and Exhortation: Shelley's Satiric Fragments . . . ," *Huntington Library Quarterly* 53.1 (Winter 1990), 41–66.

44. Huntington Manuscript HM 2177, p. *52v; see text in Quinn, *Draft Notebook,* pp. 274–77; and Steven E. Jones, "Apostasy and Exhortation," pp. 54–55, 57.

45. It helps to remember that Shelley's vision of cannibalistic heavenly carnage in the "Feast" fragment is the angry product of an ideologically committed vegetarian.

46. For a useful assessment of criticism's interest in the violence of language and of culture, see Tobin Siebers, *The Ethics of Criticism* (Ithaca, NY: Cornell University Press, 1988).

CHAPTER 4: "PAPER WARFARE" AND SINGLE COMBAT

1. V. G. Kiernan, *The Duel in European History: Honour and the Reign of Aristocracy* (Oxford: Oxford University Press, 1989), p. 102. The statistics in this paragraph are taken from Kiernan; unless otherwise noted,

facts will subsequently be drawn, as cited, from Kiernan or from Robert Baldick, *The Duel: A History of Duelling* (London: Chapman & Hall, 1965).

2. Baldick, *The Duel*, p. 113.

3. William Hazlitt, *The Spirit of the Age* (London: Colburn, 1825; facs. repr. Oxford: Woodstock Books, 1989), p. 305.

4. David V. Erdman,, "Coleridge and 'The Review Business,' " *The Wordsworth Circle* 6.1 (1975), 3–50.

5. Baldick, *The Duel*, pp. 74–76.

6. "The Duellist," in *The Poetical Works of Charles Churchill*, ed. W. Tooke, 2 vols. (London: Bell & Daldy, 1866), II, 154–91.

7. Wendy Hinde, *George Canning* (New York: St. Martin's Press, 1973), pp. 226–28.

8. *Collected Letters of Samuel Taylor Coleridge*, ed. E. L. Briggs, 6 vols. (Oxford: Clarendon Press, 1956–71), III; Coleridge essentiallly repeats his opinions on this subject to various correspondents, e.g., pp. 227, 233, 235, 241.

9. Robert Isaac Wilberforce and Samuel Wilberforce, *The Life of William Wilberforce*, 5 vols. (London: J. Murray, 1838), I, 193, 355.

10. *The Letters of Thomas Moore*, ed. Wilfred S. Dowden, 2 vols. (Oxford: Clarendon Press, 1964), I, 102–07.

11. Quoted in ibid., I, 102.

12. *English Bards and Scotch Reviewers*, in *The Complete Poetical Works*, I, 227–64.

13. *The Letters of Thomas Moore*, I, 135–36, 161–62, 165–68.

14. *Don Juan*, in *The Complete Poetical Works*, V, 216.

15. Laurence S. Lockridge, *The Ethics of Romanticism* (Cambridge: Cambridge University Press, 1989), p. 448.

16. Kiernan, *Duel in European History*, p. 21.

17. *The Friend* (part I), in Coleridge, *Collected Works*, vol. IV, ed. Barbara E. Rooke (Princeton: Princeton University Press, 1969), pp. 425–26.

18. *The Watchman*, in Coleridge, *Collected Works*, vol. II, ed. Lewis Patton (1970), p. 251.

19. *Lectures 1808–1819 on Literature* (part I), in Coleridge, *Collected Works*, vol. V, ed. R. A. Foakes (1987), p. 46.

20. Quoted in Kiernan, *Duel in European History*, p. 228.

21. As documented in the context of the earlier history of dueling by Frederick Robertson Bryson, *The Sixteenth-Century Italian Duel: A Study in Renaissance Social History* (Chicago: University of Chicago Press, 1938), pp. xi–xii, xxiv.

22. On Byron and Southey, see Leslie Marchand, *Byron: A Biography,* 3 vols. (New York: Knopf, 1957), II, 752–53, 933–34; III, 967–68. On Shelley's dispute with his erstwhile mentor, see Kenneth Neill Cameron, "Shelley vs. Southey: New Light on an Old Quarrel," *PMLA* 57 (1942), 489–512.

23. *Byron's Letters and Journals,* ed. Leslie Marchand, vol. VI (Cambridge, MA: Belknap Press of Harvard University Press, 1976), p. 83. (Hereafter cited parenthetically in the text as *BLJ,* followed by volume and page numbers.) Byron also referred in November 1819 to a planned duel with Brougham (*BLJ,* VI, 242n).

24. Most recently, Jerrold E. Hogle, in *Shelley's Process* (New York and Oxford: Oxford University Press, 1988), has said that in the fragment Shelley "abandons satire for good, indeed quite firmly and explicitly . . . " (p. 147). As should be clear, I disagree about both the firmness and the explicitness of what the fragment reveals. Another reading of the fragment as rejecting "negative" satire can be found in Ann Thompson's "Shelley and 'Satire's Scourge,' " in *Literature of the Romantic Period 1750–1850,* ed. R. T. Davies and B. G. Beatty (Liverpool: Liverpool University Press, 1976), pp. 135–50.

25. The text of this fragment is from Steven E. Jones, "Shelley's 'A Satire upon Satire,' " *Keats-Shelley Journal* 37 (1988), 136–63.

26. "Epilogue to the Satires, Dialogue 2," in *Poetry and Prose of Alexander Pope,* Twickenham Edition, vol. IV, (London: Methuen; New Haven: Yale University Press, 1969), 324–25.

27. Alan Liu, *Wordsworth: The Sense of History* (Stanford: Stanford University Press, 1989), pp. 298–99, interprets this sensibility in the context of Michel Foucault's work on the eighteenth century's displacement of public punishment by incarceration, *Discipline and Punish: The Birth of the Prison,* trans. Alan Sheridan (New York: Vintage Books, 1979).

28. This is essentially the way Victor Ewart Lindsey reads the fragment in his dissertation, "Satire in the Poetry of . . . Shelley" (University of Arkansas, 1982), pp. 65–72: as rhetorically and morally equivocal, a way for Shelley to have "the pleasure of using a literary weapon he rejects" (p. 72).

29. "Letter to Maria Gisborne," in *Shelley's Poetry and Prose,* pp. 313–21. This poem could, of course, be read as a satire. It is interesting (and pleasant) in its own right, a kind of lighthearted, *sermo,* Horatian epistle. But because of its essentially private and comic nature, and the frank bias of my study toward what I see as Shelley's primary satiric concerns (vio-

lence, exhortation, and authority), I have not included it in the list of satires to be examined.

30. Cameron, "Shelley vs. Southey," pp. 492–95.

31. Southey's letter is reprinted in Shelley, *Letters,* II, 204n.

32. Reprinted in ibid., 205n.

33. Baldick, *The Duel,* pp. 35–38, explains that seconds functioned in effect as diplomats, whose carefully equivocal approaches to one another beforehand might avert a fight.

34. William Godwin, *Enquiry Concerning Political Justice and Its Influence on Modern Morals and Happiness* (New York and Harmondsworth, U.K.: Penguin Books, 1985), pp. 179–81.

35. Donald H. Reiman, "Shelley as Agrarian Reactionary," in his *Romantic Texts and Contexts* (Columbia: University of Missouri Press, 1987), pp. 260–74 (p. 270).

36. See Thomas Jefferson Hogg, *Life of Shelley* (London and Toronto: J. M. Dent, 1933), I, 60–61, for accounts of Shelley's shooting expeditions around Oxford. Shelley's interest in target shooting—a stereotypically masculine, competitive sport—was revived years later under the influence of the unregenerate duelist Lord Byron. During one period of frequent shooting with Byron (in 1822, probably just after the "Satire upon Satire" fragment), Shelley provoked a mock challenge to a duel by his friend Edward Williams. A note from Willliams implies a shared joke about Shelley's affections for Williams's wife, Jane: " . . . I feel that I must parade you at 10 paces if you go on thus—If you will call yourself or send your second we will point out the ground." MS. Shelley adds c. 12, fol. 24 (r), transcribed and discussed in B. C. Barker-Benfield, *Shelley's Guitar: A Bicentenary Exhibition of Manuscripts, First Editions and Relics of Percy Bysshe Shelley* (Oxford: Bodleian Library, Oxford University, 1992), p. 178.

37. Newman Ivey White, *Shelley* (London: Secker & Warburg, 1947), II, 351–54.

38. Kiernan, *Duel in European History,* p. 203; Baldick, *The Duel,* pp. 169–78.

39. Samuel Stanton, *The Principles of Duelling: With Rules to Be Observed in Every Particular Respecting It* (London: T. Hookham, 1790), p. 35.

40. Although Napoleon was strongly opposed to dueling, it was extremely popular during the Empire. Baldick, *The Duel,* pp. 89–91.

41. Kiernan, *Duel in European History,* p. 97.

42. *Boswell's Life of Johnson,* ed. George Birkbeck Hill, rev. L. F. Powell, 6 vols. (Oxford: Clarendon Press, 1934), II, 180.

43. *Political Jusice,* p. 179.

44. The scapegoat schema that follows is based on Girard's *Violence and the Sacred,* as well as his *The Scapegoat,* trans. Yvonne Freccero (Baltimore: Johns Hopkins University Press, 1986).

45. There are several useful examples of such caution in the intriguing conversations collected in Robert G. Hammerton-Kelly, ed., *Violent Origins: Walter Burkert, René Girard, and Jonathan Z. Smith on Ritual Killing and Cultural Formation* (Stanford: Stanford University Press, 1987).

46. Baldick, *The Duel,* pp. 42–44; Bryson, *Italian Duel,* pp. 33–34.

47. Quoted in Baldick, *The Duel,* p. i.

48. Walter Benjamin, "Theses on the Philosophy of History," in his *Illuminations,* ed. Hannah Arendt, trans. Harry Zohn (New York: Schocken Books, 1969), p. 256.

49. On politics as macroethics—in both Godwin and Shelley—see Lockridge, *Ethics of Romanticism,* pp. 138, 327–28.

50. "A Discourse on the Manners of the Ancients Relative to the Subject of Love," in *The Complete Works,* VII, 223–29 (225). And compare the text of and commentary on Shelley's draft (Bodleian MS. Shelley adds. e. 11) in *The Bodleian Shelley Manuscripts,* vol. XV, *The 'Julian and Maddalo' Draft Notebook,* ed. Steven E. Jones (New York: Garland, 1990), pp. 19–43.

51. The overall transition from the rationalism of moral-sense thinkers to theories of imagination by the Romantics is summarized in Lockridge, *Ethics of Romanticism,* pp. 53–57.

52. *Political Justice,* pp. 638–39. Significantly for my purposes, Godwin goes on to add that "The argument against political coercion is equally strong against the infliction of private penalties, between master and slave, and between parent and child. There was, in reality, not only more gallantry, but more of reason in the Gothic system of trial by duel than in these" (p. 641).

53. "Speculations on Morals," in *The Complete Works,* VII, 80.

54. Preface to *The Cenci,* in *Shelley's Poetry and Prose,* p. 240.

Chapter 5: Satire of Succession

1. *Manchester Observer,* 31 July 1819, quoted in Donald Read, *Peterloo: The 'Massacre' and Its Background* (Manchester: Manchester University Press, 1958), p. 113.

2. E. P. Thompson, *The Making of the English Working Class* (New York: Vintage, 1966), pp. 682–84. For an opposing view, see Donald Read, *Peterloo,* pp. 113–22.

3. My use of the term "succession satire" follows Michael Seidel, *Satiric Inheritance* (Princeton: Princeton University Press, 1979), p. 234.

4. P. M. S. Dawson, in *The Unacknowledged Legislator,* (Oxford: Clarendon Press, 1980), pp. 221–22, rightly suggests that Shelley's famous term from the peroration of *A Defence of Poetry,* "unacknowledged legislators," can best be understood in the context of the practical politics of the reform movement. Shelley simply globalizes the claim to include "the World" (*Poetry and Prose,* p. 508).

5. Philip Lawson has pointed to the unique role Peterloo has played, as a kind of test case for historiographic method, in "Reassessing Peterloo," *History Today* 38 (March 1988), 24–29. The narrative that follows is based on Lawson's overview, in comparison with the accounts of Read and Thompson.

6. Ibid., 25–29.

7. See, for example, Robert Walmsley, *Peterloo: The Case Reopened* (Manchester: Manchester University Press, 1969), e.g., p. 540; but Read also fits the category of revisionist, as, to a lesser extent, does Lawson.

8. Michael Henry Scrivener usefully adjudicates Walmsley's dispute with Thompson in *Radical Shelley: The Philosophical Anarchism and Utopian Thought of Percy Bysshe Shelley* (Princeton: Princeton University Press, 1982), arguing that Walmsley's narrative can actually be interpreted as *supporting* the theory of Peterloo as "class conflict" (like Thompson's) rather than as "police riot" (p. 198). For a useful summary/critique of Thompson, especially his use of the slippery category of "experience," see William H. Sewell, Jr., "How Classes Are Made: Critical Reflections on E. P. Thompson's Theory of Working-Class Formation," in *E. P. Thompson: Critical Perspectives,* ed. Harvey J. Kaye and Keity McClelland (Philadelphia: Temple University Press, 1990), pp. 50–77.

9. Edmund Burke, *Reflections on the Revolution in France,* ed. Conor Cruise O'Brien (Harmondsworth, U.K.: Penguin Books, 1986), e.g., pp. 169–70, 173.

10. Jacob Epstein, "Understanding the Cap of Liberty: Symbolic Practice and Social Conflict in Early Nineteenth-Century England," *Past and Present* 122 (February 1989), 75–118.

11. *The Clerical Magistrate* (*The Political House That Jack Built*), British Museum 13303; *The Radical Pulpit,* British Museum 13689. For both, see the indispensable work by M. Dorothy George, *Catalogue of Political and Personal Satires in the British Museum,* 11 vols. (London: Trustees of the British Museum, 1870–1954), IX and X. British Museum 13689 is part of a larger PARODY ON THE POLITICAL HOUSE THAT JACK BUILT (British Mu-

seum 13678–90); as George indicates, both prints are probably connected to George Cruikshank's 1819 print, *Preachee & Floggy Too!* (British Museum 13281). (Other prints—including Figures 1 and 2 in previous chapters—are cited in the text by British Museum catalog number, as found in George's *Catalogue*.)

12. I. J. Prothero, *Artisans and Politics in Early Nineteenth-Century London: John Gast and His Times* (Baton Rouge: Louisiana State University Press, 1979), sums up the importance of this tactic: "Behind all the publications, declarations of rights, refusal to petition, and organisation, lay the ultimate aim of radical Reform through a national convention, when the unfranchised, now enlightened and united, should elect their own representatives who would go to Parliament and claim their rightful place" (p. 103).

13. *A Proposal for Putting Reform to the Vote Throughout the Kingdom,* in *The Complete Works,* VI, 63.

14. The remark on representation is in the fragment "on the Game Laws" (in Mary Shelley's hand) in a Library of Congress Shelley notebook, as cited by Dawson, *The Unacknowledged Legislator,* p. 46. In "A Philosophical View of Reform," Shelley refers to the "unrepresented multitude" (*The Complete Works,* VII, 23).

15. David Groves, "Francis Jeffrey and the 'Peterloo' Massacre of 1819," *Notes & Queries* 37 (December 1990), 418. The speech was made at a "Celebration of Mr. Fox's Birth Day," and ended with the conventional toasts "to Parliamentary Reform."

16. *The Mask of Anarchy,* in *Shelley's Poetry and Prose,* pp. 301–10.

17. Scrivener offers one reading of political cartoons and their psychosexual symbolism in relation to *The Mask* (*Radical Shelley,* pp. 196–210). Earlier, connections between the two modes were made in Stuart Curran, *Shelley's Annus Mirabilis: The Maturing of an Epic Vision* (San Marino, CA: Huntington Library, 1975), p. 238 n. 3; Curran in turn credits Karl Kroeber with pointing out at least one important cartoon source or analogue—one which I discuss below. The general methods for using this sort of popular material were pioneered by Carl Woodring in *Politics in English Romantic Poetry* (Cambridge, MA: Harvard University Press, 1970). In this rare case, however, I think Woodring exactly misses the point of Shelley's mixture of genres in *The Mask* when he remarks, "Political it certainly is, but less satiric than prophetic" (p. 265).

18. Richard Cronin, *Shelley's Poetic Thoughts* (New York: St. Martin's Press, 1981), p. 42.

19. Curran, *Shelley's Annus Mirabilis,* pp. 190–91. Later, Shelley

composed his own masque and antimasque for the unfinished drama *Charles I.* See Nora Crook's facsimile edition of Bodleian MS. Shelley adds. e. 17, *The Bodleian Shelley Manuscripts,* vol. XII, *The "Charles the First" Draft Notebook* (New York: Garland, 1991); and the discussion of the issues of "power and art" in the masque/antimasque in Scrivener, *Radical Shelley,* pp. 299–302.

20. Morton D. Paley, in "Apocapolitics: Allusion and Structure in Shelley's *Mask of Anarchy,*" *Huntington Library Quarterly* 54.2 (Spring 1991), 91–109, reads the "skewed" and "strangely disparate lengths" of the poem's "structural units" as significant (p. 93), especially given the symmetry *within* the final part (and lacking in the first part)—a mark of the *Mask*'s juxtaposition of "apocalypse and millennium" (p. 91). While this is an interesting observation, I read Shelley's "apocalyptic" imagery in this satire as only one part of his intentionally artificial and conventional language, part of the repertoire of reform discourse he appropriated for very pragmatic political ends. As I see it, Shelley is in the end closer to radical or opposition politicians than to the chiliastic or millenarian orators whose discourse he might tap into on occasion.

21. "The Anachronistic Procession or Freedom and Democracy," in *Bertolt Brecht, Poems 1913–1956,* ed. John Willett and Ralph Manheim (London and New York: Methuen, 1987), pp. 409–14. Among Shelley scholars, Richard Cronin first compared Brecht's poem with Shelley's (*Shelley's Poetic Thoughts,* pp. 39–55).

22. "Weite und Vielfalt der realistichen Schreibweise," *Schriften zur Literatur und Kunst* (2), in his *Gesammelte Werke* (Frankfurt am Main: Suhrkamp Verlag, 1967), XIX, 340–49.

23. Walter Benjamin, "Theses on The Philosophy of History" in his *Illuminations,* ed. Hannah Arendt, trans. Harry Zohn (New York: Schocken Books, 1969), p. 256.

24. Walter Benjamin, "Brecht's Threepenny Novel" in his *Reflections,* ed. Peter Demetz, trans. Edmund Jephcott (New York: Schocken Books, 1986). In a section of the essay entitled "Satire and Marx," Benjamin writes, "Marx, who was the first to undertake to bring back the relations between people from their debasement and obfuscation in capitalist economics into the light of criticism, became in so doing a teacher of satire who was not far from being a master of it. Brecht was his pupil. Satire, which was always a materialistic art, has in him now become a dialectical one, too" (p. 202). Interest in Shelley's satires by Brecht and Benjamin represents a significant, little noticed feature of their reception history. The two seem to have known *Peter Bell the Third,* for example; Brecht

refers to it in a satirical poem of his own on Los Angeles as Hell, and Benjamin quotes Brecht's German translation of the famous lines on London as Hell in his fragmentary work (published as) *Charles Baudelaire: A Lyric Poet in the Era of High Capitalism,* trans. Harry Zohn (London and New York: Verso, 1983), p. 59.

25. "Über experimentelles Theater," *Schriften zum Theater* (1), in his *Gesammelte Werke* (Frankfurt am Main: Suhrkamp Verlag, 1967), XV, 285–305 (302).

26. "Volkstümlichkeit und Realismus," *Schriften zur Literatur und Kunst* (2), pp. 322–31 (p. 326). For a brief argumentative summary of Brecht's famous debate with Lukács and others over socialist realism, see Terry Eagleton, *Marxism and Literary Criticism* (Berkeley: University of California Press, 1976), pp. 63–76.

27. Mary Claire Randolph, "The Structural Design of Formal Verse Satire," in *Satire: Modern Essays in Criticism,* ed. Ronald Paulson (Englewood Cliffs, NJ: Prentice-Hall, 1971), pp. 171–89.

28. *Don Juan,* in *The Complete Poetical Works,* V, 506.

29. *The Correspondence of Alexander Pope,* ed. George Sherburn, 5 vols. (Oxford: Clarendon Press, 1956), III, 419.

30. "Essay on Christianity," in *The Complete Works,* VI, 227–52. This "essay," like much of Shelley's prose, is actually a fragmentary draft in one of his notebooks, as noted by Scrivener, who treats it at length but judiciously refers to it simply as Shelley's "theological fragment" (*Radical Shelley,* pp. 87–107).

31. Cicero, *De Oratore,* Book II, trans. E. W. Sutton, 2 vols. (Cambridge, MA: Harvard University Press, 1967), I, 453–54.

32. Edwin Black, *Rhetorical Criticism: A Study in Method* (Madison: University of Wisconsin Press, 1978), pp. 138–47.

33. For examples and a discussion of some of the chiliastic and emotional forms of this rhetoric, see Thompson, *The Making,* pp. 380–88.

34. "Song: To the Men of England" in *Poetical Works,* pp. 572–73. On the influence of this and other of Shelley's popular songs on later radicals, see Carl Woodring, *Politics,* p. 353 n. 31; and Donald H. Reiman, *Percy Bysshe Shelley* (New York: St. Martin's Press, 1968), p. 96. As Reiman points out, the "Song" had the distinction of being parodied as "Beasts of England" in George Orwell's *Animal Farm.*

35. Jerrold E. Hogle, *Shelley's Process* (New York and Oxford: Oxford University Press, 1988), pp. 134–38, offers a useful reading of the poem from a Girardian perspective, arguing that Shelley anticipates Girard in his nonviolence. I would caution that—not unlike Girard's own theory—

Shelley's purported critique of violence in the satire remains profoundly ambiguous in its representations.

36. See Quinn's text in *The Mask of Anarchy Draft Notebook* (New York: Garland, 1985), pp. 38–39. Because of what it reveals about the composition of the poem, I quote from this text of the draft (cited as Quinn) below. It is crucial to remember, however, that Shelley's revisions moved away from (or sublimated) these cruder images of violence.

37. Epstein, "Understanding the Cap of Liberty," pp. 101–04.

38. The contested use of feminine allegory is analyzed by Anna Clark in "Queen Caroline and the Sexual Politics of Popular Culture in London, 1820," *Representations* 31 (Summer 1990), 47–68 (49).

39. Light plays a central role in much Shelleyan imagery, producing imagined effects analogous to the sublime visual effects of paintings by William Turner, for example, as explained by Karl Kroeber in "Romantic Historicism: The Temporal Sublime," in *Images of Romanticism,* ed. Karl Kroeber and William Walling (New Haven: Yale University Press, 1978), pp. 149–65.

40. M. Dorothy George, *English Political Caricature to 1792: A Study of Opinion and Propaganda,* 2 vols. (Oxford: Clarendon Press, 1959), I, 123.

41. Ibid. Other forms also referred to as a "transparency" include the simpler painting of an image on glass, the transfer of a print image to glass, and the creation of a semitransparent print on paper, to be used as a hearth screen or lampshade, for example. On 18 July 1817, Claire Clairmont reports that she accompanied Peacock to see an exhibition of such pictures in London. *The Journals of Claire Clairmont,* ed. Marion Kingston Stocking (Cambridge, MA: Harvard University Press, 1968), p. 84 (and see n. 25). On a less expensive version, one that could be created in the homes of middling types, see the illustrated how-to book by Edward Orme, *An Essay on Transparent Prints, and on Transparencies in General* (London: Printed for the author, 1807). This is the kind of transparency described by Jane Austen in *Mansfield Park,* ed. Tony Tanner (New York: Penguin Books, 1966), p. 174, as among Fanny's dowdy "comforts" and ornaments in the East Room: "three transparencies made in a rage for transparencies, for the lower panes of one window, where Tintern Abbey held its station between a cave in Italy, and a moonlight lake in Cumberland . . . ." Orme's transparencies are cited by Barbara Maria Stafford in her interesting (if sweeping) survey of eighteenth-century cultural formation, *Body Criticism: Imaging the Unseen in Enlightenment Art and Medicine* (Cambridge, MA, and London: MIT Press, 1991), pp. 377–78. Stafford is surely right that such technology is about the displacement of reality by

various forms of illusion or imagination (p. 342). I would add that it is one place where such interests meet the *satiric* milieu of the period. I wish to thank Anselmo Carini of the Art Institute of Chicago for his information on transparencies.

42. See, for example, the satirical *Political Medley* (1740), reproduced in Carretta's *George the Third and the Satirists* (Athens and London: University of Georgia Press, 1990), p. 13, which calls itself "a Curious Print, or Deceptio Visus."

43. *The Examiner,* 26 January 1817, p. 57. This issue, immediately following the one in which Shelley's "Hymn to Intellectual Beauty" first appeared, was one the young poet was especially likely to have seen.

44. For 1809, see *The Diary of Harriet Grove,* in *Shelley and His Circle,* vol. II, ed. Kenneth Neill Cameron (Cambridge, MA: Harvard University Press, 1961), p. 517nn, where Harriet reports that her party went to Covent Garden to see both *Richard III* and Thomas Dibdin's famous pantomime, *Harlequin and Mother Goose; or The Golden Egg* (17 April). On 19 April they saw Dibdin's comic opera *The Cabinet,* along with a comedy and a farce. For 1818, see *The Journals of Claire Clairmont,* p. 84, which records that on 16 February, Shelley's party—including Thomas Love Peacock—attended a tragedy followed by the pantomime *Harlequin Gulliver; or, The Flying Island.* In fact Claire's entries for these days (just over a year before Shelley wrote *The Mask of Anarchy*) document a total immersion in the cultural milieu of London, with its ongoing medley of "high" and "low" forms: Shakespearean tragedy, pantomime, and ballet-pantomime; opera, opera buffa, and a famous musical machine (the "Apollonicon"); the Elgin Marbles at the British Museum; and an exhibition of transparencies painted on glass. Interestingly, the social ringmaster of all this entertainment was Shelley's mentor in satire, Peacock—on occasion joined by the witty parodist Horace Smith. In 1809, Shelley had enjoyed similarly mixed theatrical, musical, and special-effect entertainments in London, including visits to the popular Panorama of Grand Cairo. My point is simply that it would be surprising if this heteroglossia did *not* come to mind when Shelley attempted in 1819 to write popular satirical poetry for a reception by London audiences.

45. David Mayer, *Harlequin in His Element: The English Pantomime, 1806–1836* (Cambridge, MA: Harvard University Press, 1969).

46. Quoted in ibid., p. 13.

47. *An Address to the People on the Death of Princess Charlotte,* in *The Complete Works,* VI, 73–82.

48. Mayer, *Harlequin,* p. 54.

49. See Seidel, *Satiric Inheritance,* p. 234.

50. *Absalom and Achitophel. A Poem,* ed. Edward Niles Hooke and H. T. Swedenberg, Jr., in *The Works of John Dryden,* Vinton A. Dearing, textual ed., 20 vols. (Berkeley: University of California Press, 1956–89, II, 3–36; 62–96.

51. Blackstone, *Commentaries on the Laws of England* (Oxford: Clarendon Press, 1773), I, 194–95.

52. "Fragment: 'What Men Gain Fairly,' " in *Poetical Works,* p. 574. For a text and discussion of the draft, see Quinn, *Mask Notebook,* pp. 246–47, who suggests that the fragment may have been begun as a separate "popular song" (p. 179).

53. Ronald Paulson, *Representations of Revolution (1789–1820)* (New Haven and London: Yale University Press, 1983), p. 50.

54. On the way in which even the American Revolution, for example, could exploit this concept to argue that it followed in the "natural" tradition of the English Revolution, see Gary Wills, *Inventing America: Jefferson's Declaration of Independence* (New York: Vintage Books, 1979), pp. 49–64.

55. Bodleian MS. Shelley adds e. 18.

56. Aristotle, *Rhetoric* I:4, in *The Rhetoric and the Poetics of Aristotle,* trans. W. Rhys Roberts (New York: Modern Library, 1954; repr. 1984), p. 35.

CHAPTER 6: "ROUGH FESTIVALS" AND CHARISMA

1. The narrative on the following pages is based on Elie Halévy, *The Liberal Awakening 1815–1830,* trans. E. I. Watkin (New York: Peter Smith, 1949), pp. 80–106; Lloyd Paul Stryker, *For the Defense: Thomas Erskine* (Garden City, NY: Doubleday, 1947), pp. 526–78; Thea Holme, *Caroline: A Biography of Caroline of Brunswick* (New York: Atheneum, 1980); and I. J. Prothero, *Artisans and Politics* (Baton Rouge: Louisiana State University Press, 1979), pp. 132–55.

2. E. P. Thompson (*The Making of the English Working Class* [New York: Vintage Books, 1966], pp. 708–09) speaks of "the humbug of the Queen's case," suggests that the revolutionary qualities of the movement "had been lost, somewhere on the way between Peterloo and Cato Street," and argues that the Queen's affair marked a shift to a middle-class and Whig leadership of reform. For the ongoing debate over the effects of the affair on the reform movement, see Thomas W. Laqueur, "The Queen Caroline Affair: Politics as Art in the Reign of George IV," *Journal of*

Modern History 54 (September 1982), 417–66; and Anna Clark, "Queen Caroline and the Sexual Politics of Popular Culture in London, 1820," *Representations* 31 (Summer 1990), 47–68. We should keep in mind, as Prothero points out (*Artisans and Politics,* p. 141), that "the fact of agitation" may be "more important than its ostensible aim," and that the popular support for Caroline was never completely controlled by the reform leaders—especially not after December 1820.

3. Holme, *Caroline,* pp. 224–25, points out that the pageantry of the coronation itself was in direct competition with Caroline's counterpageantry, and notes the very interesting fact that the outcast Queen, locked out of Westminster Abbey on Coronation Day, went that evening to the theater—where she saw a performance imitating the very ceremonies from which she had been excluded (p. 226).

4. Quoted in Stryker, *For the Defense,* p. 541.

5. Roger Sales, *English Literature in History 1780–1830: Pastoral and Politics* (New York: St. Martin's Press, 1983), points to the carnivalesque, theatrical qualities of both the Queen's affair (pp. 166–86) and Shelley's poem (pp. 187–203); he also notes the connection to popular prints by Hone and others (pp. 188–91), saying that the observable "similarities may have been the result of the fact that both Shelley and the ideographic satirists were operating from within the same alternative grammar of politics. . . . they both present politics as a ghastly farce" (p. 191). These observations, along with his earlier mention of pantomime and politics (in another context), have been suggestive for my own approach to *Swellfoot.*

6. A standard account can be found in Roy Strong, *Splendour at Court: Renaissance Spectacle and Illusion* (London: Weidenfeld & Nicolson, 1973); see also D. M. Bergeron, *English Civic Pageantry 1558–1642* (Columbia: University of South Carolina Press, 1971). Alan Liu provides a theoretical critique of New Historicism's uses of pageantry and spectacle, as paradigmatic figures in its own discourse, in "The Power of Formalism: The New Historicism," *ELH* 56 (Winter 1989), 721–71.

7. Recounted in T. A. J. Burnett, *The Rise & Fall of a Regency Dandy: The Life and Times of Scrope Berdmore Davies* (Boston and Toronto: Little, Brown, 1981), p. 24.

8. Clifford Geertz, "Centers, Kings, and Charisma: Reflections on the Symbolics of Power," in his *Local Knowledge: Further Essays in Interpretive Anthropology* (New York: Harper Collins/Basic Books, 1983), pp. 121–46. The essay was first published in 1977, its primary focus "the inherent sacredness of sovereign power" (p. 123).

9. Prothero, *Artisans and Politics,* pp. 147–55, prints a useful map of

the procession (pp. 134–35) and narrates in detail the complicated maneuverings of those involved. In a final testimony to her power, the radicals attempted one last time to "transfer" the Queen's charisma to the funeral of two men who had been killed during demonstrations at *her* funeral procession (pp. 152–53).

10. A few copies were sold before the publisher (J. Johnson, Cheapside) agreed to suppress the satire, apparently under pressure from the Society for the Suppression of Vice, according to H. Buxton Forman, *The Shelley Library* (London: Reeves and Turner, 1886), pp. 98–99.

11. Kenneth Neill Cameron, "Shelley, Cobbett, and the National Debt," *Journal of English and Germanic Philology* 42 (1943), 197–209.

12. Mary Shelley's note, reprinted in *Poetical Works,* p. 410. Shelley was of course familiar with the elaborate Italian carnival in several of its manifestations (and before 1820), and this must also be seen as part of *Swellfoot's* context. But "carnival," like "triumph," became for him a negative poetic figure. A little over a year after he wrote the satire, he produced the personal lyric "The Serpent Is Shut out from Paradise" (January 1822), which includes lines on being forced to wear "the idle mask/Of author, great or mean,/In the world's carnival" (ll. 29–31; *Shelley's Poetry and Prose,* p. 448).

13. Carlos Baker suggests that, based on the dates of composition, Shelley was more likely to have been reading the "Ode to Naples." *Shelley's Major Poetry: The Fabric of a Vision* (Princeton: Princeton University Press, 1948), p. 176 n. 35.

14. "Burning Bartle" was especially common in parts of Yorkshire, according to Christina Hole, *British Folk Customs* (London: Hutchinson, 1976), p. 35. The name may have been given to a pagan figure after it became associated with the established rituals of St. Bartholomew's Day.

15. Prothero, *Artisans and Politics,* p. 104.

16. Howard V. Harper, *Days and Customs of All Faiths* (New York: Fleet, 1957), pp. 217–19.

17. *The Prelude: 1799, 1805, 1850,* ed. Jonathan Wordsworth, M. H. Abrams, and Stephen Gill (New York and London: W. W. Norton, 1979), pp. 263–65. Quotations here are from the 1850 text.

18. *Bartholomew Fair,* II.i.42, in *The Complete Plays of Ben Jonson,* ed. G. A. Wilkes, 4 vols. (Oxford: Clarendon Press, 1982), IV, 5–122.

19. M. M. Bakhtin, *The Dialogic Imagination,* ed. Michael Holquist, trans. Caryl Emerson and Michael Holquist (Austin: University of Texas Press, 1981), pp. 158–224. An important theoretical extension of the Bakhtinian carnivalesque is provided by Peter Stallybrass and Allon White

in *The Politics and Poetics of Transgression* (Ithaca, NY: Cornell University Press, 1986), which deals with the relation of "high" and "low" discourses at the site of the fair, including complex political ambiguities and the emergence of modern authorship—and the symbol of the pig—a cluster of topics obviously central to the arguments of the present chapter.

20. Ralph Rosen, *Old Comedy and the Iambographic Tradition* (Atlanta: Scholars Press, 1988); but for a cautionary reminder, see Stephen Halliwell, "Aristophanic Satire," in *English Satire and the Satiric Tradition,* ed. Claude Rawson (New York: Basil Blackwell, 1984), pp. 6–20, on the limited extent to which this drama can be thought of as "topical" or "popular" in the modern sense.

21. Halliwell, "Aristophanic Satire," p. 19.

22. Sybil Rosenfeld, *The Theatre of the London Fairs in the 18th Century* (Cambridge: Cambridge University Press, 1960).

23. Published in *Farrago or Miscellanies in Verse and Prose* (1739), quoted in Rosenfeld, *Theatre of the London Fairs,* p. 46.

24. Rosenfeld, *Theatre of the London Fairs,* pp. 46–47, 150–51.

25. E. P. Thompson, *Customs in Common: Studies in Traditional Popular Culture* (New York: New Press, 1991), pp. 467–538. Douglas Gray suggests a link between one form of satire and such social practices, in "Rough Music: Some Early Invectives and Flytings," in *English Satire and the Satiric Tradition,* ed. Claude Rawson (New York: Basil Blackwell, 1984), pp. 21–43 (p. 25).

26. Thompson refers to a "ritual hunt with diabolic undertones" (*Customs,* p. 471), the Devon stag hunt in which a surrogate victim played the part of the hunted: "The 'stag' was run to earth on the door-step of the victim, and a bladder of bullock's blood which he carried on his breast was pierced by a hunter's knife and spilled upon the stones outside the victim's house" (pp. 470–71). For my purposes, this suggests the sacrificial quality of such rituals and, by implication, of the "satiric" practices of which they are composed.

27. Shelley aims his music more against the husband than the wife, of course, and some have suggested that there was an overall increase in the number of male targets of rough music in the nineteenth century. See Thompson, *Customs,* p. 505; and Anna Clark, "Queen Caroline," p. 66 n. 60, who notes the apparent statistic (as found in Thompson's earlier work), thus implying its potential relevance to the Queen Caroline affair.

28. Thompson, *Customs,* p. 478.

29. I cite the text of *Oedipus Tyrannus; or, Swellfoot the Tyrant* as found in *Poetical Works,* pp. 389–410.

30. On Shelley's allusion to Burke's phrase and other satirical and polemical responses (including Daniel Isaac Eaton's), see Roland Bartel, "Shelley and Burke's Swinish Multitude," *Keats-Shelley Journal* 18 (1969), 4–8.

31. Carl Woodring, *Politics and English Romantic Poetry* (Cambridge, MA: Harvard University Press, 1970), p. 270.

32. Newman Ivey White, "Shelley's Swell-foot the Tyrant in Relation to Contemporary Political Satires," *PMLA* 36 (1921), 332–46. White establishes the identities of many of Shelley's characters by finding analogues in satirical prints. Carlos Baker, *Shelley's Major Poetry,* pp. 173–81, adds to these identifications and explains Shelley's transliterative puns. For example, Purganax ("Castle-king") is Castlereagh, Laoktonos ("People-slayer") is Wellington, Dakry ("Teary") is Eldon (who was commonly mocked for his public displays of false emotion). Mammon, as the "Arch-Priest" (or Prime Minister) is probably Liverpool. Leech is Vice Chancellor Leach, who organized the special Milan Commission to spy on Caroline, and therefore Gadfly and Rat are likely to be other members of the Commission (White proposes Cooke and Browne).

33. One written satire in the popular idiom that we know Shelley read—and which clearly became a source for *Peter Bell the Third* and *Swellfoot*—is Thomas Moore's *The Fudge Family in Paris* (London: Longman, Hurst, Rees, Orme, and Brown, 1818). Shelley thought enough of Moore's satire to dedicate *Peter Bell the Third* to the author, the pseudonymous Thomas Brown. Like *Swellfoot,* Moore's *The Fudge Family* contains Greek puns, jokes on royal gout and corpulence, a comparison between the Regent and a "man-milliner" (cf. *Swellfoot* I:412, p. 401), references to "Rat," parodies of Castlereagh's oratory, and a satire on literary apostasy.

34. *The Dialogic Imagination,* pp. 159–60.

35. DORCHESTER GUIDE (December 1819), British Museum 13318–30. See M. Dorothy George, *Catalogue of Political and Personal Satires,* vol. IX (London: Trustees of the British Museum, 1949).

36. Thomas Medwin, *The Life of Percy Bysshe Shelley* (London: Oxford University Press, 1913), first said that *Swellfoot* should have been considered "harmless as regards the public, who could not possibly understand it" (p. 254). Michael Scrivener, *Radical Shelley* (Princeton: Princeton University Press, 1982), agrees that the play's classicisms are obscure, and even finds the play's anti-Malthusianism to run counter to much reform discourse (p. 262).

37. Stephen C. Behrendt, *Shelley and His Audiences* (Lincoln and London: University of Nebraska Press, 1989), pp. 204–05.

38. *The Examiner,* 22 March 1812, pp. 177–80 (p. 179). Hunt was responding with satirical polemic to exorbitant praise of the Regent in the Loyalist press.

39. Stallybrass and White, *The Politics and Poetics of Transgression,* p. 64, point to the conventional hatred and demonization at carnival time of the "Lenten Jew" (who will not eat the fair's main dish and central symbol, the pig). It is not clear whether Shelley's "Jews" refers to specific persons, but they are clearly anti-Semitic stereotypes of economically self-interested Utilitarians. John Todhunter, *A Study of Shelley* (London: C. Kegan Paul, 1880), pp. 207–08, suggests Rothschild as one target; Milton Millhauser, "Shelley: A Reference to Ricardo in *Swellfoot the Tyrant,*" *Notes & Queries* 176 (14 January 1939), 25–26, points to another; Kenneth Neill Cameron, *Shelley: The Golden Years* (Cambridge, MA: Harvard University Press, 1974), p. 629 n. 9, most convincingly proposes that Moses is Malthus. On Shelley's attitude toward the great Utilitarian, see C. E. Pulos, "Shelley and Malthus," *PMLA* 67 (March 1952), 113–24. On Mathus as a point of contention within the reform movement, see Halévy, *The Liberal Awakening,* pp. 40–46.

40. See, for example, *Lysistrata,* in *Four Plays by Aristophanes,* trans. William Arrowsmith (New York: New American Library, 1984), pp. 335–468 (pp. 365–71), in which an oath for peace is sworn (and drunk) by the women early on, at once a parody and a symbol of their deadly serious purpose. In fact, apart from the most obvious source for the chorus of hogs, *The Frogs, Lysistrata* (which we know Shelley read in 1818) is the play by Aristophanes that is arguably closest to *Swellfoot,* though I am not aware that anyone has ever pointed this out. Like Shelley's skit, Aristophanes' play is about marital relations and sexuality, an oracle, a "masculine" woman, the vulgarity of the mob, the virtues of peace, and the senselessness of violence. It mixes the sacred with the profane, double entendres with high allegory, and at its climax, a semiveiled nude female figure appears at a central altar. At the conclusion, the powerful huntress Artemis is invoked. Most of all, it is a play about a tentative emergency coalition among diverse social groups, forged to bring about the needed peace. Yet another intriguing parallel can be found in *The Eumenides,* in *Aeschylus I,* trans. Richmond Lattimore (Chicago: University of Chicago Press, 1953), p. 169, in which a chorus prays for peace and to ward off revenge—and civil war.

41. Rosen, *Old Comedy,* p. 21 n. 46. Halliwell, "Aristophanic Satire," pp. 16–18, argues that the parabasis is distinguished by its strongly rhetorical qualities, its imitation of an oration before a court or political body

(p. 17). The Liberty-Famine scene can be seen as Shelley's attempt to speak oratorically, through Liberty, to the reformers.

42. Preface to *Prometheus Unbound,* in *Shelley's Poetry and Prose,* p. 135.

43. "Volkstümlichkeit und Realismus," in *Gesammelte Werke* (Frankfurt am Main: Suhrkamp Verlag, 1967), XV, 325.

44. *Shelley: The Golden Years,* pp. 361–62, 629–30 n. 43. The language of Coleridge which Shelley is imitating comes from the "Introductory Address" to the series of lectures, which describes "the Temple of Despotism" as "built of human skulls, and cemented with human blood" (p. 48)—a passage later partially disclaimed by Coleridge and attributed to Robert Southey (*Conciones ad Populum. Or Addresses to the People,* in *Lectures 1795 on Politics and Religion,* in Coleridge, *Collected Works,* ed. Lewis Patton and Peter Mann, vol. I ([Princeton: Princeton University Press, 1971], pp. 21–74 [18n]). It is possible that Shelley learned of Southey's authorship of the passage at their crucial meeting at Keswick in 1811 (see Chapter 3 above). It is interesting to speculate that the sources for *Swellfoot* (Shelley's final satire) might therefore have been explicitly the same collaborative pair who influenced his first satire, *The Devil's Walk.*

45. *Conciones ad Populum,* pp. 25–74 (p. 30).

46. Shelley remarks on the relative security of property (versus monetary funds), in the event of an uprising, in *Letters,* II, 223.

47. *Harlequin and the Red Dwarf* (1812) is discussed by David Mayer, *Harlequin in His Element* (Cambridge, MA: Harvard University Press, 1969), pp. 103–04, who also reproduces an 1813 plate depicting the absurd hunting scene (p. 105). Other potentially relevant pantomimes include *Harlequin's Salutation to John Bull, Paddy Bull, Sandy Bull and Taffy Bull* (1810) and *The House That Jack Built; or, Harlequin Tattered and Torn* (1821). The last, performed after *Swellfoot* was written, nevertheless illustrates the traffic in iconography and point of view among various forms: cartoons, pamphlets, and popular theatricals.

48. Mayer, *Harlequin in His Element,* p. 103. The event was satirized (by W. Heath?) in a print of 1819, "THE EPPING HUNT OR HOBBIES IN AN UPROAR" (British Museum 13404), which caricatures Londoners chasing the stag on fashionable velocipedes.

49. *The Letters of Mary Wollstonecraft Shelley,* ed. Betty T. Bennett, 3 vols. (Baltimore and London: Johns Hopkins University Press, 1980), I, 156. (Hereafter cited in the text as *Letters of MWS.*)

50. Mumming is yet another feature of the nexus of overlapping social customs that Shelley's kind of "popular" satire inevitably invokes. In various instances it was a traveling, house-to-house form of processional

masking that involved ritual expropriation ("collecting"), rough *un*-masking, and/or the threat of mob violence, as well as the possibility of some degree of class interaction (as in Tolstoy's famous account in *War and Peace*). For all of these reasons, "mummery" seems a particularly apt metaphor for the Queen Caroline affair. See Herbert Halpert, "A Typology of Mumming," in *Christmas Mumming in Newfoundland: Essays in Anthropology, Folklore, and History*, ed. Herbert Halpert and G. M. Story (Toronto: University of Toronto Press, 1969), pp. 34–61.

51. Both Woodring, *Politics*, pp. 271–72, and William Keach, *Shelley's Style* (New York and London: Methuen, 1984), pp. 113–14, note an undeniable element of self-parody in *Swellfoot*.

52. *A Defence of Poetry*, in *Shelley's Poetry and Prose*, pp. 480–508 (pp. 508, 486).

CHAPTER 7: BEYOND SATIRE

1. David Worcester, *The Art of Satire* (New York: Russell & Russell, 1960), p. v; his scheme of various subgenres shows the strain of trying to fit the "protean" satiric "spirit" into neat classifications. Only Roman verse satire, as practiced by Horace or Juvenal, can be said to fit a conventional *form*. This is what Quintilian meant by the modest claim that satire was entirely Roman, as explained by G. L. Hendrickson, "Satura Tota Nostra Est," in *Satire: Modern Essays in Criticism*, ed. Ronald Paulson (Englewood Cliffs, NJ: Prentice-Hall, 1971), pp. 37–51.

2. Northrop Frye, *Anatomy of Criticism: Four Essays* (New York: Atheneum, 1966), p. 162.

3. Terry Eagleton, *Literary Theory: An Introduction* (Minneapolis: University of Minnesota Press, 1983), p. 92.

4. Michael G. Cooke, *Acts of Inclusion: Studies Bearing on an Elementary Theory of Romanticism* (New Haven and London: Yale University Press, 1979), pp. 53–54.

5. Gilbert Highet, *Juvenal the Satirist: A Study* (Oxford: Clarendon Press, 1954), pp. 219–21; and R. C. Whitford, "Juvenal in England, 1750–1802," *Philological Quarterly* 7 (1928), 9–16.

6. Highet, *Juvenal the Satirist*, pp. 23–27.

7. 26 January 1838, to Robert Shelton MacKenzie, in *The Letters of William and Dorothy Wordsworth*, ed. Ernest de Selincourt, rev. Alan G. Hill, 6 vols. (Oxford: Clarendon Press, 1935–39; rev. 1982), VI, 516. (Hereafter cited as Wordsworth, *Letters*, followed by volume and page numbers.)

8. Carl Woodring, *Wordsworth* (Boston: Houghton Mifflin, 1965), p. 11, says with characteristic wit that the poet was "ill at ease when imitating Juvenal really meant imitating William Gifford, the best imitator of Pope," thus pointing to the public, polemical milieu in which Juvenal would have been placed at the time.

9. For the text of the Juvenal lines, see Wordsworth, *Letters,* I, 157–58, 172–77.

10. Frederick L. Beaty, *Byron the Satirist* (DeKalb: Northern Illinois University Press, 1985), p. 34.

11. Introduction to *The Satires of Decimus Junius Juvenalis,* ed. and trans. William Gifford (London: W. Bulmer, 1802), pp. xlv–li.

12. *A Letter to William Gifford, Esq.,* in *The Complete Works of William Hazlitt,* ed. P. P. Howe, 21 vols. (London and Toronto: J. M. Dent & Sons, 1932), IX, 13; and Hazlitt's *The Spirit of the Age* (London: Colburn, 1825; facs. repr. Oxford: Woodstock Books, 1989), p. 282. Hazlitt goes on to say that Gifford "as a satirist, is violent and abrupt. . . . His satire is mere peevishness and spleen, or something worse—personal antipathy and rancour" (p. 299).

13. "Discourse Concerning the Original and Progress of Satire," in *The Works of John Dryden,* vol. IV, ed. A. B. Chambers and William Frost (Berkeley: University of California Press, 1974), pp. 3–90 (p. 56). Dryden's praise of Persius is an attempt to give him his due, but he judges him generally inferior to both Horace and Juvenal.

14. For a concentrated literary history, see Upali Amarasinghe, *Dryden and Pope in the Early Nineteenth Century: A Study of Changing Literary Taste 1800–1830* (Cambridge: Cambridge University Press, 1962), especially Part II, on the major periodicals (pp. 63–134). Like most literary historians, Amarasinghe underestimates the era's interest in satire, accepting the Romantics' own antisatiric pronouncements.

15. Witness David V. Boyd, "Wordsworth as Satirist: Book VII of *The Prelude," Studies in English Literature* 13.4 (Autumn 1973), 617–31; Ford T. Swetnam, "The Satiric Voices of *The Prelude,*" in *Bicentenary Wordsworth Studies,* ed. Jonathan Wordsworth (Ithaca, NY, and London: Cornell University Press, 1970), pp. 92–110; and Carl Woodring, "Shaping Life in *The Prelude,*" in *Nineteenth-Century Lives,* ed. Laurence S. Lockridge, John Maynard, and Donald D. Stone (Cambridge: Cambridge University Press, 1989), pp. 9–25 (esp. pp. 17–22).

16. "Preface to the Edition [*Lyrical Ballads*] of 1815," in *The Poetical Works,* II, 433.

17. *Table Talk* (Part II), ed. Carl Woodring, in *The Collected Works of*

Samuel Taylor Coleridge (Princeton: Princeton University Press, 1990), XIV, 177.

18. *The Prelude,* ed. Jonathan Wordsworth, M. H. Abrams, and Stephen Gill (New York and London: W. W. Norton, 1979). (All quotations in this chapter are from the 1805 text.)

19. Ibid., p. 34 n. 3.

20. Richard Holmes, *Shelley: The Pursuit* (London: Quartet Books, 1976), p. 554.

21. Highet, *Juvenal the Satirist,* pp. 182–83, 205.

22. Mary C. Randolph, "The Structural Design of Formal Verse Satire," in *Satire,* ed. Ronald Paulson (Englewood Cliffs, NJ: Prentice-Hall, 1971), p. 174.

23. "The Triumph of Life," in *Shelley's Poetry and Prose,* pp. 455–70.

24. That the radical uncertainties of the "text" (in the poststructuralist sense) of "The Triumph of Life" are inextricably connected to the material uncertainties of its manuscript "text" (in the textual-critical sense), has been recognized by Tilottama Rajan, *The Supplement of Reading: Figures of Understanding in Romantic Theory and Practice* (Ithaca, NY, and London: Cornell University Press, 1990), e.g., pp. 323–49.

25. As noted by Carlos Baker, *Shelley's Major Poetry* (Princeton: Princeton University Press, 1948), p. 258.

26. "The Prophecy of Dante," in *The Complete Poetical Works,* IV, 229.

27. As I argue in Steven E. Jones, "Intertextual Influences in Byron's Juvenalian Satire," *Studies in English Literature* 33.4 (Autumn 1993), 771–83.

28. Donald H. Reiman connects the passages in *Shelley's "The Triumph of Life": A Critical Study* (Urbana: University of Illinois Press, 1965), p. 23. I quote "The Boat on the Serchio" as found in *Poetical Works,* pp. 654–57; but see Nora Crook's diplomatic text, transcribed from Bodleian MS. Shelley adds. e. 17, in *The "Charles the First" Draft Notebook,* vol XII of *The Bodleian Shelley Manuscripts* (New York: Garland, 1991), pp. 370–91.

29. I allude of course to Paul de Man's "Shelley Disfigured," in *Deconstruction and Criticism* (New York: Continuum, 1986), pp. 39–73. Interestingly, it is possible to view this essay's own linguistic play as "satiric" in its deconstructive, corrosive energy, as well as in its self-consciously profound (or abysmal) skepticism and pathos, attitudes not unfamiliar in the rhetoric of conventional satire.

Bibliography

Abrams, M. H. *Natural Supernaturalism: Tradition and Revolution in Romantic Literature*. New York: W. W. Norton, 1971.

Aeschylus. *Aeschylus I*. Trans. Richmond Lattimore. Chicago: University of Chicago Press, 1953.

Amarasinghe, Upali. *Dryden and Pope in the Early Nineteenth Century: A Study of Changing Literary Taste 1800–1830*. Cambridge: Cambridge University Press, 1962.

Aristophanes. *Four Plays by Aristophanes*. Trans. William Arrowsmith. New York: New American Library, 1984.

Aristotle. *The Rhetoric and the Poetics of Aristotle*. Trans. W. Rhys Roberts. New York: Modern Library, 1954; repr. 1984.

Austin, J. L. *How to Do Things with Words*. Cambridge, MA: Harvard University Press, 1962.

Baker, Carlos. *Shelley's Major Poetry: The Fabric of a Vision*. Princeton: Princeton University Press, 1948.

Bakhtin, M. M. *The Dialogic Imagination*. Ed. Michael Holquist. Trans. Caryl Emerson and Michael Holquist. Austin: University of Texas Press, 1981.

Baldick, Robert. *The Duel: A History of Duelling*. London: Chapman & Hall, 1965.

Barker-Benfield, B. C. *Shelley's Guitar: A Bicentenary Exhibition of Manuscripts, First Editions and Relics of Percy Bysshe Shelley*. Oxford: Bodleian Library, Oxford University, 1992.

Bartel, Roland. "Shelley and Burke's Swinish Multitude." *Keats-Shelley Journal* 18 (1969), 4–8.

Beaty, Frederick L. *Byron the Satirist*. DeKalb: Northern Illinois University Press, 1985.

Behrendt, Stephen C. *Shelley and His Audiences*. Lincoln and London: University of Nebraska Press, 1989.

Benjamin, Walter. *Charles Baudelaire: A Lyric Poet in the Era of High Capitalism*. Trans. Harry Zohn. London and New York: Verso, 1983.

———. *Illuminations*. Ed. Hannah Arendt. Trans. Harry Zohn. New York: Schocken Books, 1969.

———. *Reflections*. Ed. Peter Demetz. Trans. Edmund Jephcott. New York: Schocken Books, 1986.

Bergeron, D. M. *English Civic Pageantry 1558–1642*. Columbia: University of South Carolina Press, 1971.

Bewell, Alan. *Wordsworth and the Enlightenment: Nature, Man, and Society in the Experimental Poetry*. New Haven and London: Yale University Press, 1989.

Blackstone, William. *Commentaries on the Laws of England*. 4 vols. Oxford: Clarendon Press, 1773.

Blunden, Edmund. *Shelley: A Life Story*. London: Collins, 1946.

Boswell, James. *Boswell's Life of Johnson*. Ed. George Birkbeck Hill. Rev. L. F. Powell. 6 vols. Oxford: Clarendon Press, 1934.

Boyd, David V. "Wordsworth as Satirist: Book VII of *The Prelude*." *Studies in English Literature* 13 (1973), 617–31.

Brecht, Bertolt. *Bertolt Brecht, Poems 1913–1956*. Ed. John Willett and Ralph Manheim. London and New York: Methuen, 1987.

———. *Gesammelte Werke*. 20 vols. Frankfurt am Main: Suhrkamp Verlag, 1967.

Bryson, Frederick Robertson. *The Sixteenth-Century Italian Duel: A Study in Renaissance Social History*. Chicago: University of Chicago Press, 1938.

Burke, Edmund. *Reflections on the Revolution in France*. Ed. Conor Cruise O'Brien. Harmondsworth, U.K.: Penguin Books, 1986.

Burnett, T. A. J. *The Rise & Fall of a Regency Dandy: The Life and Times of Scrope Berdmore Davies*. Boston and Toronto: Little, Brown, 1981.

Byron, George Gordon, Lord. *Byron's Letters and Journals*. Ed. Leslie Marchand. 12 vols. Cambridge, MA: Belknap Press of Harvard University Press, 1973–82.

———. *Lord Byron: The Complete Poetical Works*. Ed. Jerome J. McGann and Barry Weller. 7 vols. Oxford: Clarendon Press, 1980–92.

Caine, T. Hall. *Recollections of Dante Gabriel Rossetti*. London: Elliott Stock, 1882.

Cameron, Kenneth Neill. "Shelley, Cobbett, and the National Debt." *Journal of English and Germanic Philology* 42 (1943), 197–209.

———. *Shelley: The Golden Years*. Cambridge, MA: Harvard University Press, 1974.

———. "Shelley vs. Southey: New Light on an Old Quarrel." *PMLA* 57 (1942), 489–512.

Cameron, Kenneth Neill, and Donald H. Reiman, eds. *Shelley and His Circle, 1773–1822*. (Projected) 12 vols. Cambridge, MA: Harvard University Press, 1961–. II (ed. Cameron), 1961; IV (ed. Cameron), 1970; V (ed. Reiman), 1973; VII (ed. Reiman), 1986.

Carretta, Vincent. *George III and the Satirists from Hogarth to Byron*. Athens and London: University of Georgia Press, 1990.

Chatterton, Thomas. *The Complete Works of Thomas Chatterton*. Ed. Donald S. Taylor. 2 vols. Oxford: Clarendon Press, 1971.

Churchill, Charles. *The Poetical Works of Charles Churchill*. Ed. W. Tooke. 2 vols. London: Bell & Daldy, 1866.

Cicero. *De Oratore*. Trans. E. W. Sutton. 2 vols. Cambridge, MA: Harvard University Press, 1967.

Clairmont, Claire. *The Journals of Claire Clairmont*. Ed. Marion Kingston Stocking. Cambridge, MA: Harvard University Press, 1968.

Clark, Anna. "Queen Caroline and the Sexual Politics of Popular Culture in London, 1820." *Representations* 31 (Summer 1990), 47–68.

Clark, J. C. D. *English Society 1688–1832: Ideology, Social Structure and Political Practice during the Ancien Regime*. Cambridge: Cambridge University Press, 1985.

Coleridge, Samuel Taylor. *The Collected Letters of Samuel Taylor Coleridge*. Ed. E. L. Briggs. 6 vols. Oxford: Clarendon Press, 1956–71.

———. *The Collected Works of Samuel Taylor Coleridge*. Bollingen Series. Gen. ed. Kathleen Coburn. London: Routledge & Kegan Paul; Princeton: Princeton University Press, 1969–.

———. *The Poems of Samuel Taylor Coleridge*. Ed. Ernest Hartley Coleridge. London: Humphrey Milford, Oxford University Press, 1931.

———. *Sibylline Leaves*. London: Rest Fenner, 1817; facs. repr. Oxford and New York: Woodstock Books, 1990.

Cooke, Michael G. *Acts of Inclusion: Studies Bearing on an Elementary Theory of Romanticism*. New Haven and London: Yale University Press, 1979.

Cronin, Richard. *Shelley's Poetic Thoughts*. New York: St. Martin's Press, 1981.

———. "Shelley's Witch of Atlas." *Keats-Shelley Journal* 26 (1977), 88–100.

Crook, Nora. "Shelley's Earliest Poem?" *Notes & Queries* (continuous series) 232.4 (December 1987), 486–90.

———, ed. *The Bodleian Shelley Manuscripts*. Vol. XII, *The "Charles the First" Draft Notebook*. New York: Garland, 1991.

Curran, Stuart. *Poetic Form and British Romanticism*. New York and Oxford: Oxford University Press, 1986.

———. *Shelley's Annus Mirabilis: The Maturing of an Epic Vision*. San Marino, CA: Huntington Library, 1975.

Dawson, P. M. S. *The Unacknowledged Legislator: Shelley and Politics*. Oxford: Clarendon Press, 1980.

De Man, Paul. "Shelley Disfigured." In *Deconstruction and Criticism*. New York: Continuum, 1986. Pp. 39–73.

Dryden, John. *The Works of John Dryden*. Textual ed. Vinton A. Dearing. 20 vols. Berkeley: University of California Press, 1956–89.

Eagleton, Terry. *Literary Theory: An Introduction*. Minneapolis: University of Minnesota Press, 1983.

————. *Marxism and Literary Criticism*. Berkeley: University of California Press, 1976.

Ellegard, Alvar. *Who Was Junius?* Stockholm, Goteborg, Uppsala: Almquist & Wiksell, 1962.

Elliott, Robert C. *The Power of Satire: Magic, Ritual, Art*. Princeton: Princeton University Press, 1960.

Epstein, Jacob. "Understanding the Cap of Liberty: Symbolic Practice and Social Conflict in Early Nineteenth-Century England." *Past and Present* 122 (February 1989), 75–118.

Erdman, David V. "Coleridge and 'The Review Business.'" *The Wordsworth Circle* 6.1 (Winter 1975), 3–50.

Examiner. Ed. Leigh Hunt.

Forman, H. Buxton. *The Shelley Library*. London: Reeves and Turner, 1886.

Foucault, Michel. *Discipline and Punish: The Birth of the Prison*. Trans. Alan Sheridan. New York: Vintage Books, 1979.

Frye, Northrop. *Anatomy of Criticism: Four Essays*. New York: Atheneum, 1966.

Geertz, Clifford. "Centers, Kings, and Charisma: Reflections on the Symbolics of Power." In his *Local Knowledge: Further Essays in Interpretive Anthropology*. New York: Harper Collins/Basic Books, 1983. Pp. 121–46.

————. "Thick Description: Toward an Interpretive Theory of Culture." In his *The Interpretation of Cultures*. New York: Harper Collins/Basic Books, 1973. Pp. 3–30.

George, M. Dorothy. *Catalogue of Political and Personal Satires in the British Museum*. 11 vols. London: Trustees of the British Museum, 1870–1954.

————. *English Political Caricature to 1792: A Study of Opinion and Propaganda*. 2 vols. Oxford: Clarendon Press, 1959.

Giamatti, A. Bartlett. "Proteus Unbound: Some Versions of the Sea God in the Renaissance." In *The Disciplines of Criticism: Essays in Literary Theory, Interpretation, and History*. Ed. Peter Demetz, Thomas Greene, and Lowry Nelson, Jr. New Haven: Yale University Press, 1968. Pp. 437–76.

Girard, René. *The Scapegoat.* Trans. Yvonne Freccero. Baltimore: Johns Hopkins University Press, 1986.

————. *Violence and the Sacred.* Trans. Patrick Gregory. Baltimore and London: Johns Hopkins University Press, 1972.

Godwin, William. *Enquiry Concerning Political Justice and Its Influence on Modern Morals and Happiness.* New York and Harmondsworth, U.K.: Penguin Books, 1985.

Gray, Douglas. "Rough Music: Some Early Invectives and Flytings." In *English Satire and the Satiric Tradition.* Ed. Claude Rawson. New York: Basil Blackwell, 1984. Pp. 21–42.

Greenblatt, Stephen. *Learning to Curse: Essays in Early Modern Culture.* New York and London: Routledge, 1990.

————. *Renaissance Self-Fashioning from More to Shakespeare.* Chicago and London: University of Chicago Press, 1980; repr. 1984.

Groves, David. "Francis Jeffrey and the 'Peterloo' Massacre of 1819." *Notes & Queries* 37 (December 1990), 418.

Halévy, Elie. *England in 1815.* London: Ernest Benn, 1949.

————. *The Liberal Awakening 1815–1830.* Trans. E. I. Watkin. New York: Peter Smith, 1949.

Halliwell, Stephen, "Aristophanic Satire." In *English Satire and the Satiric Tradition.* Ed. Claude Rawson. New York: Basil Blackwell, 1984. Pp. 6–20.

Halpert, Herbert. "A Typology of Mumming." In *Christmas Mumming in Newfoundland: Essays in Anthropology, Folklore, and History.* Ed. Herbert Halpert and G. M. Story. Toronto: University of Toronto Press, 1969. Pp. 34–61.

Hammerton-Kelly, Robert G., ed. *Violent Origins: Walter Burkert, René Girard, and Jonathan Z. Smith on Ritual Killing and Cultural Formation.* Stanford: Stanford University Press, 1987.

Harper, Howard V. *Days and Customs of All Faiths.* New York: Fleet, 1957.

Harvey, A. D. *Britain in the Early Nineteenth Century.* New York: St. Martin's Press, 1978.

Hazlitt, William. *The Complete Works of William Hazlitt.* Ed. P. P. Howe. 21 vols. London and Toronto: J. M. Dent & Sons, 1932.

————. *The Spirit of the Age.* London: Colburn, 1825; facs. repr. Oxford: Woodstock Books, 1989.

Hendrickson, G. L. "Satura Tota Nostra Est." In *Satire: Modern Essays in Criticism.* Ed. Ronald Paulson. Englewood Cliffs, NJ: Prentice-Hall, 1971. Pp. 37–51.

Highet, Gilbert. *Juvenal the Satirist: A Study*. Oxford: Clarendon Press, 1954.

Hinde, Wendy. *George Canning*. New York: St. Martin's Press, 1973.

Hogg, Thomas Jefferson. *The Life of Percy Bysshe Shelley*. 2 vols. London and Toronto: J. M. Dent & Sons, 1933.

Hogle, Jerrold E. *Shelley's Process: Radical Transference and the Development of His Major Works*. New York and Oxford: Oxford University Press, 1988.

Hole, Christina. *British Folk Customs*. London: Hutchinson, 1976.

Holme, Thea. *Caroline: A Biography of Caroline of Brunswick*. New York: Atheneum, 1980.

Holmes, Richard. *Shelley: The Pursuit*. London: Quartet Books, 1976.

Hutcheon, Linda. *A Theory of Parody: The Teachings of Twentieth-Century Art Forms*. New York and London: Methuen, 1985.

Jones, Steven E. "Apostasy and Exhortation: Shelley's Satiric Fragments in the Huntington Notebooks." *Huntington Library Quarterly* 53.1 (Winter 1990), 41–66.

————. "Intertextual Influence in Byron's Juvenalian Satire." *Studies in English Literature* 33.4 (Autumn 1993), 771–83.

————. "Shelley's Fragment of 'A Satire upon Satire': A Complete Transcription of the Text with Commentary." *Keats-Shelley Journal* 37 (1988), 136–63.

————, ed. *The Bodleian Shelley Manuscripts*. Vol. XV, *The 'Julian and Maddalo' Draft Notebook*. New York: Garland, 1990.

Jonson, Ben. *The Complete Plays of Ben Jonson*. Ed. G. A. Wilkes. 4 vols. Oxford: Clarendon Press, 1982.

Jordan, John E. "Wordsworth and *The Witch of Atlas*." *ELH* 9 (1942), 320–25.

Juvenal. *The Satires of Decimus Junius Juvenalis*. Ed. and Trans. William Gifford. London: W. Bulmer, 1802.

Kaplan, Louise J. *The Family Romance of the Impostor Poet Thomas Chatterton*. New York: Atheneum, 1988.

Keach, William. *Shelley's Style*. New York and London: Methuen, 1984.

Kelley, Theresa M. "Proteus and Romantic Allegory." *ELH* 49 (1982), 623–52.

Kent, David A., and D. R. Ewen, eds. *Romantic Parodies 1797–1832*. London and Toronto: Associated University Presses, 1992.

Kiernan, V. G. *The Duel in European History: Honour and the Reign of Aristocracy*. Oxford: Oxford University Press, 1989.

Kroeber, Karl. "Romantic Historicism: The Temporal Sublime." In *Images of Romanticism.* Ed. Karl Kroeber and William Walling. New Haven: Yale University Press, 1978. Pp. 149–65.

Laqueur, Thomas W. "The Queen Caroline Affair: Politics as Art in the Reign of George IV." *Journal of Modern History* 54 (September 1982), 417–66.

Lawson, Philip. "Reassessing Peterloo." *History Today* 38 (March 1988), 24–29.

Leach, Robert. *The Punch and Judy Show: History, Tradition and Meaning.* London: Batsford Academic and Educational, 1985.

Leavis, F. R. *Revaluation: Tradition and Development in English Poetry.* New York: George W. Stewart, 1947.

Lemprière, John. *Bibliotheca Classica; or, A Classical Dictionary.* London: T. Cadell, 1788; facs. repr. New York: Garland, 1984.

Levinson, Marjorie. *Keats's Life of Allegory: The Origins of a Style.* Oxford: Basil Blackwell, 1988.

Lindsey, Victor Ewart. "Satire in the Poetry of Percy Bysshe Shelley." Dissertation, University of Arkansas, 1982.

Liu, Alan. "The Power of Formalism: The New Historicism." *ELH* 56 (Winter 1989), 721–71.

————. *Wordsworth: The Sense of History.* Stanford: Stanford University Press, 1989.

Lockridge, Laurence S. *The Ethics of Romanticism.* Cambridge: Cambridge University Press, 1989.

Lockwood, Thomas. *Post-Augustan Satire: Charles Churchill and Satirical Poetry, 1750–1800.* Seattle and London: University of Washington Press, 1979.

McCalman, Iain. *Radical Underworld: Prophets, Revolutionaries and Pornographers in London, 1795–1840.* Cambridge: Cambridge University Press, 1988.

————, ed. *The Horrors of Slavery and Other Writings by Robert Wedderburn.* New York and Princeton: Markus Wiener, 1991.

McGann, Jerome J. "Literary Pragmatics and the Editorial Horizon." In *Devils and Angels: Textual Editing and Literary Theory.* Ed. Philip Cohen. Charlottesville and London: University Press of Virginia, 1991. Pp. 1–21.

————. *The Romantic Ideology: A Critical Investigation.* Chicago and London: University of Chicago Press, 1983.

————. *Towards a Literature of Knowledge.* Oxford: Clarendon Press, 1989.

Marchand, Leslie. *Byron: A Biography.* 3 vols. New York: Knopf, 1957.

Mayer, David. *Harlequin in His Element: The English Pantomime, 1806–1836.* Cambridge, MA: Harvard University Press, 1969.

Medwin, Thomas. *The Life of Percy Bysshe Shelley.* London: Oxford University Press, 1913.

Milhauser, Milton. "Shelley: A Reference to Ricardo in *Swellfoot the Tyrant.*" *Notes & Queries* 176 (14 January 1939), 25–26.

Milton, John. *The Works of John Milton.* Ed. Frank Allen Patterson. 18 vols. New York: Columbia University Press, 1931.

Moore, Thomas. *The Fudge Family in Paris.* London: Longman, Hurst, Rees, Orme, and Brown, 1818.

———. *The Letters of Thomas Moore.* Ed. Wilfred S. Dowden. 2 vols. Oxford: Clarendon Press, 1964.

Morning Post.

Orme, Edward. *An Essay on Transparent Prints, and on Transparencies in General.* London: Printed for the author, 1807.

Ovid. *Metamorphoses.* Trans. Frank Justus Miller. 2 vols. Cambridge, MA: Harvard University Press, 1971.

Paley, D. Morton. "Apocapolitics: Allusion and Structure in Shelley's *Mask of Anarchy.*" *Huntington Library Quarterly* 54.2 (Spring 1991), 91–109.

Patten, Robert L. *George Cruikshank's Life, Times, and Art.* Vol. I, *1792–1835.* London: Butterworth Press, 1992.

Paulson, Ronald. *Representations of Revolution (1789–1820).* New Haven and London: Yale University Press, 1983.

———, ed. *The Fictions of Satire.* Baltimore: Johns Hopkins University Press, 1967.

Peacock, Thomas Love. *The Halliford Edition of the Works of Thomas Love Peacock.* 10 vols. New York: AMS Press, 1967.

Perkins, David. *Is Literary History Possible?* Baltimore and London: Johns Hopkins University Press, 1992.

Pope, Alexander. *The Correspondence of Alexander Pope.* Ed. George Sherburn. 5 vols. Oxford: Clarendon Press, 1956.

———. *Poetry and Prose of Alexander Pope.* Twickenham Edition. Gen. ed. John Butt. 11 vols. London: Methuen; New Haven: Yale University Press, 1940–69.

Praz, Mario. *The Romantic Agony.* Trans. Angus Davidson. London: Oxford University Press, 1954.

Prothero, I. J. *Artisans and Politics in Early Nineteenth-Century London: John Gast and His Times.* Baton Rouge: Louisiana State University Press, 1979.

Pulos, C. E. "Shelley and Malthus." *PMLA* 67 (March 1952), 113–24.

Quarterly Review.

Quinn, Mary A., ed. *Manuscripts of the Younger Romantics*. Vol. IV, *The Mask of Anarchy Draft Notebook*. New York: Garland, 1985.

Rajan, Tilottama. *The Supplement of Reading: Figures of Understanding in Romantic Theory and Practice*. Ithaca, NY, and London: Cornell University Press, 1990.

Randolph, Mary Claire. "The Structural Design of Formal Verse Satire." In *Satire: Modern Essays in Criticism*. Ed. Ronald Paulson. Englewood Cliffs, NJ: Prentice-Hall, 1971. Pp. 171–89.

Rawson, Claude. "Byron Augustan: Mutations of the Mock-Heroic in *Don Juan* and Shelley's *Peter Bell the Third*." In *Byron: Augustan and Romantic*. Ed. Andrew J. Rutherford. New York: St. Martin's Press, 1990. Pp. 82–116.

Read, Donald. *Peterloo: The 'Massacre' and Its Background*. Manchester: Manchester University Press, 1958.

Reiman, Donald H. *Percy Bysshe Shelley*. New York: St. Martin's Press, 1968.

———. "Shelley as Agrarian Reactionary." In his *Romantic Texts and Contexts*. Columbia: University of Missouri Press, 1987. Pp. 262–74.

———. *Shelley's "The Triumph of Life": A Critical Study*. Urbana: University of Illinois Press, 1965.

———, ed. *The Bodleian Shelley Manuscripts*. Vol. I, *Peter Bell the Third and "The Triumph of Life."* New York: Garland, 1986.

———, ed. *Manuscripts of the Younger Romantics*. Vol. V, *The Harvard Shelley Manuscripts*. New York: Garland, 1991.

Rosen, Ralph M. *Old Comedy and the Iambographic Tradition*. Atlanta: Scholars Press, 1988.

Rosenfeld, Sybil. *The Theatre of the London Fairs in the 18th Century*. Cambridge: Cambridge University Press, 1960.

Rossetti, William Michael. "Shelley in 1812–13." *The Fortnightly Review* 15 (January 1871), 68–69.

Rudé, George. *Wilkes and Liberty*. Oxford: Oxford University Press, 1962.

Russell, Jeffrey Burton. *Mephistopheles, the Devil in the Modern World*. Ithaca, NY, and London: Cornell University Press, 1986.

Sales, Roger. *English Literature in History 1780–1830: Pastoral and Politics*. New York: St. Martin's Press, 1983.

Scrivener, Michael Henry. *Radical Shelley: The Philosophical Anarchism and Utopian Thought of Percy Bysshe Shelley*. Princeton: Princeton University Press, 1982.

Seidel, Michael. *Satiric Inheritance, Rabelais to Sterne.* Princeton: Princeton University Press, 1979.

Sewell, William H., Jr. "How Classes Are Made: Critical Reflections on E. P. Thompson's Theory of Working-Class Formation." In *E. P. Thompson: Critical Perspectives.* Ed. Harvey J. Kaye and Keity McClelland. Philadelphia: Temple University Press, 1990. Pp. 50–77.

Shakespeare, William. *The Riverside Shakespeare.* Ed. G. Blakemore Evans et al. Boston: Houghton Mifflin, 1974.

Shelley, Mary Wollstonecraft. *The Letters of Mary Wollstonecraft Shelley.* Ed. Betty T. Bennett. 3 vols. Baltimore and London: Johns Hopkins University Press, 1980.

Shelley, Percy Bysshe. Bodleian MS Shelley adds e. 17, 18. Oxford University.

———. *The Complete Works of Percy Bysshe Shelley.* Ed. Roger Ingpen and Walter E. Peck. 10 vols. New York: Charles Scribner's Sons, 1930.

———. *The Letters of Percy Bysshe Shelley.* Ed. Frederick L. Jones. 2 vols. Oxford: Clarendon Press, 1964.

———. *The Poems of Shelley.* Vol. I. Ed. Geoffrey Matthews and Kelvin Everest. London and New York: Longman, 1989.

———. *Shelley: Poetical Works.* Ed. Thomas Hutchinson. Corr. G. M. Matthews. London: Oxford University Press, 1970.

———. *Shelley: Selected Poems.* Ed. Timothy Webb. London: Everyman's Library, 1977.

———. *Shelley's Poetry and Prose.* Ed. Donald H. Reiman and Sharon B. Powers. New York and London: W. W. Norton, 1977.

Siebers, Tobin. *The Ethics of Criticism.* Ithaca, NY: Cornell University Press, 1988.

———. *The Mirror of Medusa.* Berkeley: University of California Press, 1983.

Southey, Robert. *Poems of Robert Southey.* Ed. Maurice H. Fitzgerald. London, New York, Toronto, Melbourne: Oxford University Press, 1909.

Speaight, George. *Punch and Judy: A History.* London: Studio Vista, 1970.

Stafford, Barbara Maria. *Body Criticism: Imaging the Unseen in Enlightenment Art and Medicine.* Cambridge, MA, and London: MIT Press, 1991.

Stallybrass, Peter, and Allon White, *The Politics and Poetics of Transgression.* Ithaca, NY: Cornell University Press, 1986.

Stanton, Samuel. *The Principles of Duelling: With Rules to Be Observed in Every Particular Respecting It.* London: T. Hookham, 1790.

Strong, Roy. *Splendour at Court: Renaissance Spectacle and Illusion.* London: Weidenfeld & Nicolson, 1973.

Stryker, Lloyd Paul. *For the Defense: Thomas Erskine.* Garden City, NY: Doubleday, 1947.

Swetnam, Ford T. "The Satiric Voices of *The Prelude.*" In *Bicentenary Wordsworth Studies.* Ed. Jonathan Wordsworth. Ithaca, NY, and London: Cornell University Press, 1970. Pp. 92–110.

Taylor, Donald S. *Thomas Chatterton's Art: Experiments in Imagined History.* Princeton: Princeton University Press, 1978.

Thompson, Ann. "Shelley and 'Satire's Scourge.' " In *Literature of the Romantic Period 1750–1850.* Ed. R. T. Davies and B. G. Beatty. Liverpool: Liverpool University Press, 1976. Pp. 135–50.

Thompson, E. P. *Customs in Common: Studies in Traditional Popular Culture.* New York: New Press, 1991.

———. *The Making of the English Working Class.* New York: Vintage Books, 1966.

Todhunter, John. *A Study of Shelley.* London: C. Kegan Paul, 1880.

Veeser, H. Aram, ed. *The New Historicism.* New York and London: Routledge, 1989.

Walmsley, Robert. *Peterloo: The Case Reopened.* Manchester: Manchester University Press, 1969.

Webb, Timothy. *The Violet in the Crucible: Shelley and Translation.* Oxford: Clarendon Press, 1976.

White, Newman Ivey. "Literature and the Law of Libel: Shelley and the Radicals of 1840–42." *Studies in Philology* 22 (January 1925), 34–47.

———. *Shelley.* 2 vols. London: Secker & Warburg, 1947.

———. "Shelley's Swell-Foot the Tyrant in Relation to Contemporary Political Satires." *PMLA* 36 (1921), 332–46.

Whitford, R. C. "Juvenal in England, 1750–1802." *Philological Quarterly* 7 (1928), 9–16.

Wilberforce, Robert Isaac, and Samuel Wilberforce. *The Life of William Wilberforce.* 5 vols. London: J. Murray, 1838.

Wills, Gary. *Inventing America: Jefferson's Declaration of Independence.* New York: Vintage Books, 1979.

Woodring, Carl W. *Politics in English Romantic Poetry.* Cambridge, MA: Harvard University Press, 1970.

———. "Shaping Life in *The Prelude.*" In *Nineteenth-Century Lives.* Ed. Laurence S. Lockridge, John Maynard, and Donald D. Stone. Cambridge: Cambridge University Press, 1989. Pp. 9–25.

————. *Wordsworth*. Boston: Houghton Mifflin, 1965.

Worcester, David. *The Art of Satire*. New York: Russell & Russell, 1960.

Wordsworth, William. *The Letters of William and Dorothy Wordsworth*. Ed. Ernest de Selincourt. Rev. Alan G. Hill. 6 vols. Oxford: Clarendon Press, 1935–39; rev. 1982.

————. *The Poetical Works of William Wordsworth*. Ed. Ernest de Selincourt and Helen Darbishire. 5 vols. Oxford: Clarendon Press, 1940–49.

————. *The Prelude: 1799, 1805, 1850*. Ed. Jonathan Wordsworth, M. H. Abrams, and Stephen Gill. New York and London: W. W. Norton, 1979.

Index